the Craft Heritage Trails of Western North Carolina

Third Edition

Project Coordinator/Writer
Betty Hurst

Chief Author
Jay Fields

Designer
Scott Smith
1250 Design, Asheville, NC

Published by HandMade in America, Inc.
111 Central Avenue, Asheville, North Carolina 28801 • (828) 252-0121
For book orders, call 1-800-331-4154
www.handmadeinamerica.org
©2003

Acknowledgments

This guidebook was developed under the auspices of HandMade in America, an organization dedicated to the nurturance of craft culture and community in Western North Carolina. Research, creative development and the third printing of the guidebook has been supported by the NC Community Development Initiative and funded through sales of the second edition of the guidebook and administrative fees from the trail participants.

In addition to the working committees and board of HandMade in America, other Western North Carolina associations aided in the composition of both the loop tours and the guidebook itself. Those groups include the arts councils in each county, the chambers of commerce and visitors' centers, and the three regional tourism organizations: Blue Ridge Mountain Host, High Country Host, and Smoky Mountain Host. The editors also gratefully acknowledge the assistance and generosity of craftspeople and galleries in identifying prospective new participants in the loop system.

HANDMADE
in
AMERICA

3rd edition © 2003 by HandMade in America, Inc. All rights reserved.
Library of Congress Catalog Card Number 96-76-105. ISBN 0-9651905-4-4

HandMade in America

Executive Director
Rebecca Anderson

Board of Directors
David Newell, Chairman

Ms. Marilyn Cole, Ms. Sue Counts, Mr. Rick Eckerd, Mr. Jon Ellenbogen,
Ms. Catharine Ellis, Mr. David Erickson, Ms. Carla Filippelli, Mr. Joseph Fox,
Ms. Mary Jaeger-Gale, Mr. John Gernandt, Ms. Suzanne Gernandt,
Mr. Michael Hughey, Mr. Christopher Just, Ms. Mary Jane Letts,
Ms. Susan Leveille, Ms. Dian Magie, Mr. Kenneth Michalove,
Mr. C. Leon Murphy, Ms. Darcy Orr, Mr. Ray Rapp, Ms. Kathy Tripplett,
Mr. Greg Walker-Wilson, Ms Linda Wilkerson, Mr. Oak Winters

Table of Contents

Thisismorethanasimpleguide-book to craft. It is the story of people. People whose lives are colored by their art and whose art colors the lives of anyone who comes to know their work. And where are these people? They're "down the road a piece" or "round the bend" or "within shoutin' distance." And they're in this book. Consider, for example, the following: *Under the roof of a 100-year-old chestnut barn somewhere outside Sylva, a young woman patiently coaxes a human form out of a block of marble in the method of a Renaissance master.*  *In the shadow of the Smokies, a Cherokee woman weaves river cane into a basket using movements that belong not only to her, but to an ancestry that predates our country.*  *At the edge of the Penland campus, a former rocket scientist experiments with new dinner-ware glazes in his basement studio.* ✋ *On looms that have shuttled for decades, women of the Crossnore community make woven goods prized by presidents and favorite uncles.* ✋ *Not far from Brevard, hundreds of summer campers get up to their elbows in wet clay under the joyous guidance of a kindred spirit.* ✋ *And near John C. Campbell Folk School in Brasstown, a slender, friendly gentlemen shows guests his work— gouged-out bowls and platters made from trees he planted as seedlings.* ✋ This book is an invitation. It invites you to discover a world you may have no idea existed. Because here in the mountains and hill country of Western North Carolina, where you can see only as far as the next bend, something of timeless grace unfolds.

FYI
Helpful Stuff To Know

CELEBRATING THE ROAD LESS TRAVELED.

Throughout North Carolina, 44 scenic byways are designated and maintained by the Department of Transportation. The byways offer something more than a simple route from one point to another. They lead you past shifting landscapes of natural beauty and wonder. Panoramic vistas give way to intimate drives under evergreen canopies and quickly open up again to the sight of distant mountains. Whitewater rivers and quiet streams sidle up for a stretch then wander off. Patchwork fields and hillsides stretch to the horizon, sown with colors of the season.

HOW TO USE THIS GUIDEBOOK

We've detailed eight driving loops of varying lengths, with almost 500 stops listed. There is no set time for discovering the crafts and attractions on a single trail. Depending on the time you have to invest, you can bite off all or part of any loop.

For each trail a map shows the location and category of the stops. Listings are numbered sequentially based on a starting point and routing that seemed most natural to the editors. However, feel free to pick up the loop at any point and go in any direction you please. You may even wish to combine parts of two adjoining loops. A map of North Carolina, which is available by calling the N.C. Division of Travel and Tourism at 800-847-4862, is a nice item to have handy for jumping from one trail to the next and complements the maps provided.

In addition to the specific trails, which in most cases are often actual loops, there are "spurs" indicated that strike out from the loop to capture a destination or scenic highway of high interest. We encourage you to include these excursions as part of your overall tour.

PLANNING YOUR TRIP

To enrich your experience, we suggest that you:

Come ready to enjoy yourself

According to your interest, sample some of the books listed on pages 14 and 15 under "Recommended Reading".

Go with the flow

The mountains have a rhythm and a pace of their own. The more slowly you go, the richer the experience. Here's a rule to go by: Determine how long it normally takes you to do something. Then double it.

Learn about the maker

The real treasure is often the story behind the piece. Ask questions. Crafts work is close to the heart; people like to talk about it. On the other hand, it's good to remember that craftspeople's time is precious. Please respect posted hours for all sites listed in this book.

Strike out on your own

If you see an interesting road that's off the map, take it. Getting lost (and found again) is half the fun.

Wherever practical, our trails overlay the N.C. Scenic Byways routes.

A RED, WHITE AND BLUE RIDGE PARKWAY

The North Carolina section of the Blue Ridge Parkway, the connecting ribbon of our Craft Heritage Trails system has been recognized as an "All American Road" by the Federal Highway Administration To find out more visit www.blueridgepark-way.org on the web.

For more information about HandMade in America, check out www.handmade inamerica.org

NC Division of Travel and Tourism www.visitnc.com

NC Arts Council www.ncarts.org

FYI

Helpful Stuff To Know

STUFF THE KNAPSACK (OR TRUNK)

How about: binoculars; *Peterson Field Guides* to birds, trees, and wildflowers; extra sweater; shoes to wade in; copy of *War and Peace* (unabridged) for pressing dried flowers, four leaf clovers and other treasures; compass; a tin of Altoids (or other mints); flashlight; pocket-knife for slicing apples or spreading peanut butter for sandwiches on the run; a blanket for naps on hillsides or for stargazing on mountain tops; reading glasses; sunscreen; floppy hat, and walking-stick.

And, be sure to bring your checkbook since some studios are not set up for credit cards.

Record your good times

Whether you choose a notebook, sketch pad, camera or watercolors, recording your journey will allow you to revisit your experiences.

Call ahead about special needs

If you or someone in your party has physical restrictions and needs special assistance, we strongly suggest you call ahead. Many studios are in private homes so handicap access varies considerably.

Pick up the phone

Some of the sites featured are open for business on a limited basis. If their schedules and yours don't mesh, give them a call. Often you can arrange special meeting times.

LISTING CRITERIA

Individual committees and host groups within the 21-county region submitted sites for consideration. The editors used the following criteria:

- *Studios that offer dependable times for guests to visit.*

- *Galleries that primarily carry objects made in the U.S.A., with a focus on North Carolina.*

• *Restaurants with a reputation for fine food and featuring dishes indigenous to the region.*

• *Inns and bed and breakfasts with a historical underpinning and an architecture that, in and of itself, bespeaks craft.*

We double-checked each site against these criteria and, in most cases, visited personally to capture a sense of each place. We know that sites on these trails will continue to evolve. This is the 3rd edition of a volume HandMade hopes to publish, with updates, over many years. Telephone numbers, addresses, and other information contained within are accurate, to the best of our knowledge, as of the date of publication. We know there are other studios, galleries, restaurants, and inns in the region that qualify for a listing in this directory. For those we missed in this volume, we apologize and urge you to ask for a listing in subsequent editions.

TO FIND EVEN MORE ARTISTS, CRAFTS AND STUDIOS.

We encourage you to inquire further at galleries and information centers about those craft demonstration sites and studios that are open on a "by appointment" basis and, for that reason, not included in this book. You can also find them by searching on-line at www.handmadein americacraft registry.org

Another good starting place for finding more sites to visit is the directory of local chambers of commerce and host group organizations on the following pages.

And, if you enjoy this guidebook, make sure you get a copy of HandMade In America's *Farms, Gardens & Countryside Trails of WNC* as well.

FYI
Helpful Stuff To Know

There's a great tradition of music in these mountains. Here is just a sampling of places where you can catch our talented local artists live on stage:

Asheville
Asheville Music Zone
(828) 255-8811
Barley's Tap Room
(828) 255-0504
Bean Streets
(828) 255-8180
The Bier Garden
(828) 285-0002
Broadway's
(828) 285-0400
Grey Eagle
(828) 232-5800
Hannah Flannagan's
(828) 252-1922
Jack of the Wood
(828) 252-5445
KarmaSonics
(828) 259-9949
Malaprops
(828) 254-6734
Stella Blue
(828) 236-2424
Stoney Knob Cafe & Patio
(828) 645-3309
Tressa's
(828) 254-7072
Black Mountain
Monte Vista
(828) 669-2119

HELPFUL CONTACTS

North Carolina Travel & Tourism..(800) 847-4862
www.visitnc.com

Blue Ridge Mountain Host..............(800) 807-3391
www.ncblueridge.com
High Country Host ....(800) 438-7500
www.mountainsofnc.com

Smoky Mountain Host....................(800) 432-4678
www.smokymtnhost.com

Great Smoky Mtn. Nat. Park...........(423) 436-1200
Pisgah National Forest.....................(828) 877-3265
Blue Ridge Parkway........................(828) 298-0398

Chambers of Commerce & Visitors Centers

Andrews .... (828) 321-3584
Asheville/Buncombe County......... (800) 257-5583
Banner Elk/Avery County...............(800) 972-2183
Black Mountain/Swannanoa...........(800) 669-2301
Blowing Rock...................................(800) 295-7851
Boone... (800) 852-9506
Brevard/Transylvania County..........(800) 648-4523
Bryson City/Swain County ....(800) 867-9246
Burnsville/Yancey County...............(800) 948-1632
Cashiers/Jackson County.................(828) 743-5191
Cherokee Reservation Info..............(800) 438-1601

Franklin/Macon County.............(866) 372-5546

Hayesville/Clay County...............(828) 389-3704

Hendersonville/

Henderson County ....(800) 828-4244

Hickory Nut Gorge.....................(828) 625-2725

Highlands.....................................(828) 526-2112

Maggie Valley...............................(800) 624-4431

Marion/McDowell County ....(888) 233-6111

Mars Hill/Madison County.........(828) 680-9031

Morganton/Burke County ....(828) 437-3021

Murphy/Cherokee County ....(828) 837-2242

Robbinsville/Graham County ...(800) 470-3790

Rutherfordton/

Rutherford County ....(800) 849-5998

Sparta/Alleghany County ....(800) 372-5473

Spruce Pine/Mitchell County ...(800) 227-3912

Sylva/Jackson County..................(800) 962-1911

Tryon/Polk County.....................(800) 440-7848

Waynesville/Haywood County ...(800) 334-9036

West Jefferson/Ashe County .....(336) 246-9550

Emergency Numbers

N.C. Highway Patrol...................(800) 445-1772

Cellular phones............................*47 (Toll free)

Town Pump
(828) 669-9151
Blowing Rock
Canyon's
(828) 295-7661
Twigs
(828) 295-5050
Boone
Caribbean Cafe
(828) 265-2233
Brevard
Falls Landing
(828) 884-2835
Celo
Celo Inn
(828) 675-5132
Flat Rock
Highland Lake Inn
(828) 693-6812
Franklin
Sweet Carolina Nights
(828) 349-1961
Hot Springs
Bridge Street Cafe
(828) 622-0002
Saluda
The Purple Onion
(828) 749-1179
Sylva
Soul Infusion Tea House
(828) 586-1717
Spring Street Cafe
(828) 586-1600
Morganton
Comma
(828) 433-SHOW
  or (828) 433-7409
Rutherfordton
The Vineyard
(828) 288-0240
Valdese
Old Rock School
(828) 879-2129

FYI
Helpful Stuff To Know

CONTEMPORARY FOLK MUSIC
The mountains of Western North Carolina have become home to a number of contemporary folk singers/songwriters who travel all over the world as ambassadors of the area. Here is a list of the current titles from some area musicians:
"Here We Are" by **An Asheville Area Acoustic Songwriters' Sampler**
"Letters in the Dirt", "Radio" and "Last of the Old Time" by **Chuck Brodsky**
"Casting Shadows" by **Leigh Hilger**
"A Hundred Lies" by **Malcolm Holcombe**
"Life So Far" by **Billy Jonas**
"A Thousand Girls" and "This Time Last Year" by **Christine Kane**
"Promise" by **Annie Lalley**
"Good Again" by **Josh Lamkin**

RECOMMENDED READING

Garry G. Barker, *The Handcraft Revival in Southern Appalachia,* 1930-1990. Knoxville: The University of Tennessee Press, 1991.

Blue Ridge Mountains Guidebooks, *Inns of the Blue Ridge, Mountain Hospitality in the Best Southern Tradition from Virginia to Georgia.* McLean Virginia: EMP Publication, Inc. 1993.

LeGuette Blythe, ed., *Gift Of The Hills: Miss Lucy Morgan's Story Of Her Unique Penland School.* Chapel Hill: University of North Carolina Press, 1958, 1971.

Robert S. Brunk, ed., *May We All Remember Well, Vol. 1 and Vol. II A Journal of the History and Culture of Western North Carolina.* Published by Robert S. Brunk Auction Services, Inc. 1997.

Fred Chappell, *I Am One Of You Forever.* Baton Rouge: Louisiana State University Press, 1985.

Wilma Dykeman, *The French Broad.* Newport, Tennessee: Wakestone Books, 1992.

Allen H. Eaton, *Handicrafts of the Southern Highlands.* New York: Dover Publications, Inc., 1937, 1973. (Supported and originally published by Russell Sage Foundation, 1946)

John Ehle, *The Journey of August King.*
Hyperion Paperback, 1995.

Frances Louisa Goodrich, with a new
introduction by Jan Davidson. *Mountain
Homespun.* Knoxville: The University of
Tennessee Press, 1989. A facsimile of the
original published in 1931.

Suzanne W. Jones, *Growing Up in the South,
An Anthology of Modern Southern Literature,*
Mentor Book, 1991.

Sara Pacher and Linda Davis March,
*The Insiders Guide To North Carolina's
Mountains.* Charlotte: Knight Publishing
Company, 1995.

Carolyn Sakowski, *Touring the Western North
Carolina Backroads.* Winston-Salem: John F.
Blair Publisher, 1990.

Tova Martin, *Tasha Tudor's Heirloom Crafts.*
Boston, New York: Houghton Mifflin, 1995

Thomas Wolfe, *Look Homeward, Angel.* New
York: Chas. Scribner's, 1957.

Also check out Lark Books, the Asheville-based
publisher of over 300 books on crafts and
craft-related subjects, several written by crafts
people featured in this guidebook.
(800) 284-3388. www.larkbooks.com

"Hard Earned Smile"
and "Flying" by
David LaMotte
"Life is Good" and "Let
Go" by **Jimmy Landry**
"Archaeology" and
"The Holy Fool" by
Chris Rosser
"Late Night Radio" and
"New Blood" by
Beth Wood

**Also, John Ludovico
of KarmaSonics
recommends these
local artists:
Jazz:**
"Hold Back the Rain"
and "Bittersweet" by
Evans & Coppola
"Anthem" and "Chelsea
Bridge" by **Frank
Southecorvo Jazz
Band**
Bluegrass:
"Real Live Music" by
Greasy Beans
"Grab a Root and
Growl" by
Sons of Ralph
"Old Dreams and New
Dreams" by **Steep
Canyon Rangers**
Old Time Bluegrass:
"Neighbor Girl" by
Cary Fridley
Instrumental:
"Kadotume" and
"Dancing with
Shadows" by
Bonfield & Ebel

High Country Ramble

The treasures of the High Country utterly refuse to confine themselves to one simple route or one tidy description. Rare finds, discoveries and must-sees branch off the main trail like the offshoots of a young evergreen. ☼ The ground over which you travel is just as varied as the discoveries you will make. Heading into Ashe and Alleghany counties from Boone, you watch the mountains flatten out to a loose shrug. Or maybe it's just a trick of the eye; for here you are not dodging through hollows and coves but skirting above them on the crest of the Blue Ridge. It feels like you are traveling along the very rim of the earth. Swinging back for the remainder of the loop, the mountains deepen and you find yourself once again in their folds. ☼ Whether on top of the mountains or amongst them, prepare for surprises. In Glendale Springs and West Jefferson, beautiful frescoes remind you of those created centuries ago for European cathedrals. At the Dr. Grabow plant in Sparta, woodworkers transform Mediterranean heather into drugstore pipes that become personal treasures. In Todd and

Sometimes we wonder if it's the air up here that makes people so creative.

Along the Rim of the Earth

Valle Crucis, turn-of-the-century general stores look and feel as though they've been frozen in time. And in Linville, homes and churches designed by one of the great architects of this century, Francis Bacon, are clad in chestnut bark. ☼ Boone, Foscoe, and Blowing Rock offer up an unrivaled collection of galleries featuring traditional and contemporary work from the hands of craftspeople who are scattered throughout the high country. Although some of these crafters are newcomers, others have been here their whole lives. And, all of them have found in these high places the right mixture of solitude and community that fuels inspiration. ☼ Finally, in Crossnore, a tiny community carries on a weaving tradition that has created an artful way of life for generations of mountain women. ☼ All of this and much more are out there waiting for you on the High Country Ramble. To uncover all the journey has to offer, bring along your sense of adventure. Follow the trail. Take the side trips. Then strike out on your own. And remember: on a ramble, there are no rules and no wrong turns.

High Country Ramble

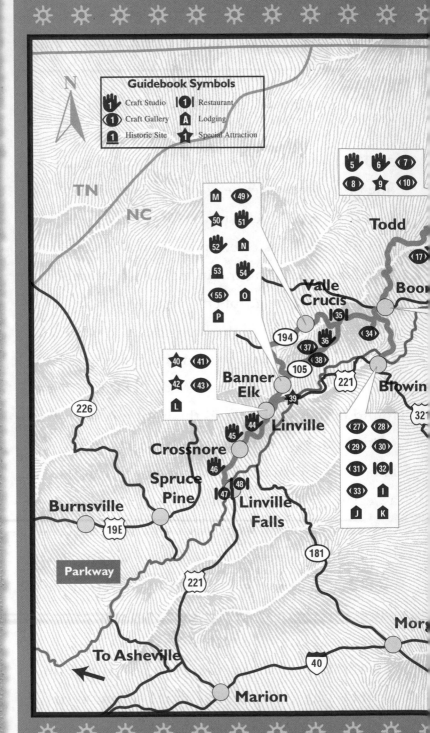

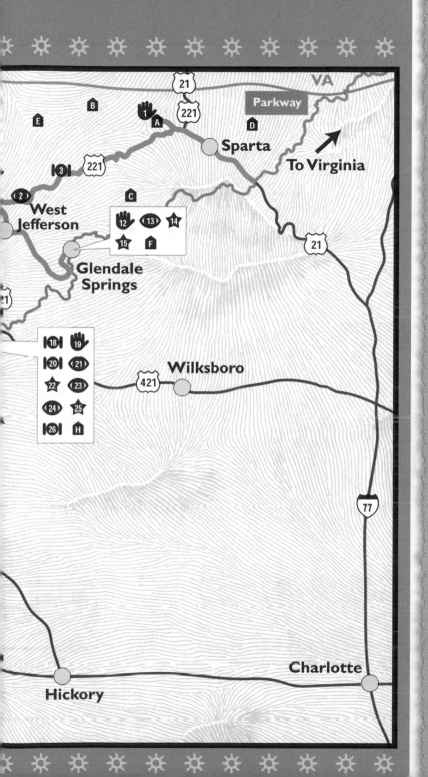

If you're traveling from the east or from the north, it's easy to make a case for plunging into High Country Ramble as your first loop experience. First, it's convenient to the metropolitan centers of Raleigh, Durham, Greensboro, and Winston-Salem and to parts north. Second, its crafts are as elevated as the ribbons of roads that lead you from one discovery to the next.

In places like Boone, Blowing Rock, and West Jefferson, the ribbon turns into a sidewalk. Park your car, put plenty of time on the meter, and plan to stay awhile, maybe overnight or longer. Craft pioneers who have blazed this trail heartily recommend an itinerary of at least four days. Adventurers on a tighter schedule can still cinch together a joyous set of memories.

230

Exit Blue Ridge Parkway (BRP) near Mile Post 230 on Hwy 21 and travel N 5 mi to Sparta. Alternative routes to Sparta Loop include: Hwy 421 from Greensboro, I-77 from VA or Charlotte, Hwy 58 and Hwy 21S from VA and Hwys 88 and 221 from Boone.

SPARTA LOOP

Welcome to the whimsy of Mangum Pottery.

From intersection of Hwy 18 and Hwy 21 in Sparta, travel N on Hwy 21 (away from BRP) for 3 mi. At Hwy 21/221 junction, take Hwy 221S (actually keeping straight at this junction.) Travel .9 mi and turn R on Hwy 93. Travel 3 mi on Hwy 93 and turn L on Halsey Knob Rd. Travel .5 mi and turn R on Turkey Knob. Studio is at very end of road.

1 **Mangum Pottery of Turkey Knob** 280 TURKEY HOLLOW LANE – Since 1974, Rob and Bet Mangum have been enjoying a clay collaboration at the home and studio they built on Turkey Knob. They do it all: porcelain, terra cotta, raku, sculptural pieces, majolica, and more, each in their own style. "My stuff looks like something," says Bet. "His is very abstract." In any case, the creative spark generated by these two has enough candlepower to light Alleghany County for a month of Sundays. Open May–Dec Sat 10am–4pm. Call for other hours. (336)372-5291.

Leaving studio, return to Hwy 93 and turn R. Travel 3 mi back to intersection with Hwy 221. Turn R on Hwy 221 and travel 24 mi to Jefferson.

The Road Goes On Forever
Side trips, tidbits, adventures, and treasure hunts

The psychic powers of certain small mountain creatures are held in such esteem that they are honored with important social functions like the Boone Firefly Festival in July and the Banner Elk Wooly Worm Festival in October.

Sparta Area B&B's

A **Harmony Hill B&B** 1740 HALSEY KNOB RD – A carved, solid wood staircase, original to the house, provides a warm welcome to the elegantly restored Victorian-era home. The parlor is simply grand. (336)372-6868.

B **Allen Farm House** 1479 ALLEN RD – Built in 1883, the home was originally owned by Elizabeth Allen Templeton, who opened her home to guests on an ongoing basis. Beth, her granddaughter, has kept up the tradition. The B&B is furnished with antiques original to the home. (336)359-8358.

C **Doughton-Hall B&B** 12668 HWY 18, LAUREL SPRINGS – Doughton Hall is steeped in North Carolina history. It was once the homeplace of the father of the Blue Ridge Parkway, Congressman Bob Doughton. (336)359-2341.

D **Bald Knob Farm House** 50 BALD KNOB RD – Constructed in 1918 and still owned by the Crouse family, this historic B&B is decorated with antiques and local crafts. (336)372-4191. www.sparta-nc.com/aur

JEFFERSON

Follow Hwy 221S into Jefferson as it merges with Hwy 16 and Hwy 88. Bear R on Hwy 88W as it splits off from Hwy 221. Summit Emporium is .5 mi on R from the split.

2 **Summit Emporium** 406 COURT ST – The colorful patchwork quilt painted on the front face of the Summit Emporium is a clue to what's in store. Coffee, fresh-baked goodies, hearty sandwiches, zany handcrafted cards, and gifts from nature's bounty–all of it brought to you by folks with more challenges than most. Open Mon–Fri 9am–4pm. (336) 246-3456.

Turn R back on Hwy 88W and travel N for 5.8 mi to Warrensville.

SPARTA INDUSTRIES
1731 US 21 S
The folks at Sparta Industries have been making Dr. Grabow Pipes for the past three generations. They start by selecting the best root balls from one of the densest, most fire-resistant woods available, imported Mediterranean heather. Then they carve, drill, cut, machine, stain, polish, lacquer, inspect and pre-smoke eight-hundred-thousand pipes a year. And, the work isn't all done by machine; some 45 pairs of hands contribute to each pipe. Call in advance and arrange for a tour. Mon–Fri 7am–11am and 12noon–3pm. (336) 372-5521.

Guidebook Symbols

✋	Craft Studio	🍴	Restaurant
①	Craft Gallery	A	Lodging
1	Historic Site	⭐	Special Attraction

Jefferson Area B&B's and Restaurants

3 **Shatley Springs Inn Restaurant** SHATLEY SPRINGS RD *(Off Hwy 16 North as you come into Jefferson)* – People once came from far-and-wide to bathe in the healing waters of the nearby spring. Today they flock here for the yummy, belt-loosening meals created and served up the old-fashioned way. Bring your grandmother. She'll approve. Open daily May–Oct 7am–9pm. (336)982-2236.

E **River House** 1896 OLD FIELD CREEK RD – An historic inn and a five-star restaurant in a pristine riverside setting. Perfect for just about any kind of getaway. A mile of riverfront, walking trails through 170 acres, two tennis courts, rocking chairs on the porch, armchairs by the fire, coffee outside your door in the morning...heaven. Meal reservations suggested. (336)982-2109. www.riverhousenc.com

Loosen your belt: it's dinner at Shatley Springs.

WARRENSVILLE

Heading N on Hwy 88W/194N, turn R on North West School Rd. Continue around bend and turn R on Warrensville Dr. Turn L in .2 mi on Warrensville School Rd. Showroom is on R.

4 **Buffalo Creek Weavers** 154 WARRENSVILLE SCHOOL RD – Mike Harmon is a sixth generation weaver. His family–the Goodwins–have been weaving in this country since one of them arrived from England in 1812! A visit to Buffalo Creek Weavers will cause you to consider the etymology of the word "heirloom." One

Buffalo Creek Weavers– 188 years and counting.

look at the authentic colonial coverlets and 18th century looms Mike has so lovingly coaxed into action and you'll never hear the word "heirloom" again without thinking of these treasures. Open daily 8am–5pm. Call for other hours. (336)384-3632. www.doubleweave.com

The Road Goes On Forever
Side trips, tidbits, adventures, and treasure hunts

Return to Hwy 88W/194S and turn L (south.) Travel 6 mi S on Hwy 194 into West Jefferson.

WEST JEFFERSON

Park on N Jefferson Ave (Hwy 194) for the following sites which are within walking distance of each other.

 R.T. Morgan Art Gallery and Glass by Camille 120 N. JEFFERSON AVE – R.T. and Camille have created a high octane gallery charged with his sculptures, her glass art and some of their fine talented

friends' ceramic vessels and imaginative paintings. You'll be scheduling a return visit before you leave! Open Wed–Sat 10am–5pm or by appointment anytime. (336)246-3328.

 De Pree Studio and Gallery 109 N JEFFERSON AVE – Lenore De Pree translates her lifetime of rich experiences from living in the Appalachians, Hong Kong, and Saudi Arabia into paintings heavily influenced by the Persian Art of the 1400-1600's. She paints Blue Ridge mountain scenes which celebrate the joy and color of purposeful work and play – a Christmas tree harvest, canoeing on the New River, a fiddlers convention. You'll enjoy browsing in her lively gallery and noting work in progress. Open Mon–Fri 9am–5pm & Sat 9am–4pm. (336) 246-7399. www.depreestudio.com

7 River Rock Gallery 1 N. JEFFERSON AVE – Another stunning example of West Jefferson's thriving arts scene. All the artisans represented by this gallery live within a 25-mile radius. Paintings, pottery, wearable art, jewelry, fiber and photography. Open Apr–Dec Mon–Sun 10am–6pm. Jan–Mar Fri–Sun 10am–6pm. (336)219-0089. www.riverrockgallery.com

A West Jefferson mural by Robert Johnson. See other murals in town by local artist Stephen Shoemaker.

The stylish art of Lenore De Pree.

The murals of West Jefferson: How many can you count?

Guidebook Symbols

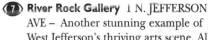

Craft Studio	Restaurant
Craft Gallery	Lodging
Historic Site	Special Attraction

The purple trim signals all are welcome at the Acorn Gallery.

⑧ Ashe Custom Framing and Gallery
105 S JEFFERSON AVE – A charming shop with a beautifully displayed collection of local pottery, handcrafted wormy chestnut vases and clocks, and other fine crafts. Open Tues–Fri 10am–5pm & Sat 10am–2pm. (336) 246-2218.

⑨ Ashe Arts Center 303 SCHOOL AVE – A renovated 1930's WPA building is home to the local arts council and serves as the hub for the burgeoning arts community in Ashe County. The Center features on-going art exhibits and sponsors a semi-annual studio and gallery crawl. Don't forget to ask about the murals you'll see all over town. Open year-round Mon–Fri 9am–4pm & Apr–Christmas Sat 10am–4pm. (336) 246-ARTS. www.ashecountyarts.org

Return to your car and continue S on Jefferson Ave. Long St. is 3 blocks down on R. Gallery is on L side of Long St.

⑩ Acorn Gallery 103 LONG ST – As an artist, Raney Rogers has a genuine interest in animals and natural places. In addition to her own water colors and mixed media, part of her gallery is given over to pottery, small wood pieces, quilts, and other items. Open year-round Tue–Fri 11am–5pm & Sat 11am–2pm. (336) 246-3388. www.raneyrogers.com

Return to Jefferson Ave(Hwy 194) and turn R. Travel 1.2 mi to Beaver Creek Rd. Turn R and church is .5 mi on R.

⑪ Church of the Fresco - St. Mary's Episcopal Church 400 BEAVER CREEK RD – In the 1970's, Rev. J. Faulton Hodge had painter Ben Long adorn the church with "Mary Great with Child," "John the Baptist," and "The Mystery of Faith" to inspire parishioners and guests. Open year-round Mon–Sun 9am–6pm. Parish (336) 246-3552.

Inside treasures: The murals at St. Mary's Episcopal Church.

Return to Hwy 194 and Business 221 and turn R.

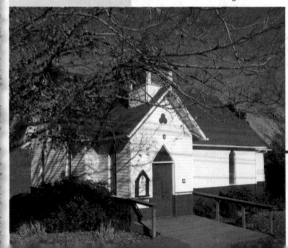

To travel to Glendale Springs Loop, continue
through intersection. (Hwy 194 turns R; Hwy 163
continues straight ahead. Take Hwy 163. Travel 9.5 mi
on Hwy 163 to Hwy 16. Turn L on Hwy 16 and travel
2.6 mi to Glendale Springs.)

To travel on to Todd from intersection of Hwy 194/221/163,
turn R on Hwy 221/194 and travel S for 3.5 mi. Turn R as
Hwy 194 splits off Hwy 221 and travel 7.5 mi to Todd.

GLENDALE SPRINGS LOOP

Turn L off Hwy 16 at Glendale Springs Inn and Restaurant.
Make immediate R on John Luke Rd. Next three sites are within
walking distance of each other on this road.

12 **Silver Designs** 275 JOHN LUKE RD – A
gallery and studio of silver jewelry with an owner
whose hospitality is the genuine article. Open
Apr–Dec Mon–Tue & Thu–Sat 10am–5pm &
Sun 12am–5pm. Open Jan–Mar Thu–Sun at
11am, but call to verify. (336)982-4102.

13 **Greenhouse Crafts** 248 J W LUKE RD –
Across from Holy Trinity, a fine collection
of local musicians' music on tapes and CDs
along with a mix of handmade instruments,
gifts and other curiosities. Open Apr–Dec
Mon–Sun 10am–5pm. Jan–Mar call before
visiting. (336)982-2618.

14 **Church of the Fresco - Holy Trinity
Episcopal Church** HWY 16 AT GLENDALE
SPRINGS – Four ecclesiastical frescoes. The
largest work, "The Last Supper," is by Ben Long.
The others were painted by his students. The
technique, sensitivity, and beauty in these works
is astonishing. Open year-round Mon–Sun
9am–6pm. Parish (828)246-3552.

Return to Hwy 16 and cross it onto Trading Post Rd (directly
across from Glendale Springs Inn and Restaurant). Travel .3 mi
to Trading Post on R.

15 **Northwestern Trading Post** 414 TRADING
POST RD – A non-profit emporium featuring
crafts, antiques, souvenirs, and food. Open
Apr 15–Oct 31 Mon–Sun 9am–5:30pm.
(336)982-2543.

*A working lunch at
Silver Designs.*

*See Ben Long's fresco work in
West Jefferson, Glendale Springs,
Montreat, Wilkesboro, Statesville,
Morganton, and Charlotte.*

Guidebook Symbols

Craft Studio   Restaurant

Craft Gallery   Lodging

Historic Site   Special Attraction

How many musicians can fit in a Todd jam session?

A convening of the regulars at Todd General Store.

The Todd Mercantile: Old building, new art.

Return to Hwy 16, turn L and travel back to West Jefferson.

Glendale Springs B&B

F **Glendale Springs Inn and Restaurant** 7414 HWY 16 – Amanda and Larry Smith have given a thoughtful restoration to the inn, which is listed on the National Register of Historic Places. The inn's wrap-around porch is a fine place to wile away an afternoon or enjoy a Sunday brunch. Open year-round Mon–Tue & Thu–Sun 8am–10pm. (336)982-2103 or (800)287-1206. www.glendalespringsinn.com

TODD

To travel on to Todd from intersection off Hwy 194/221/163 in West Jefferson, turn R from West Jefferson on Hwy 221/194 and travel S for 3.5 mi. Turn R as Hwy 194 splits of Hwy 221 and travel 7.5 mi to Todd. Turn L on Three Top Rd., travel .3 mi and next two sites are across from each other.

16 **Todd General Store** 9636 HWY 194 N – A rumpled, but proud survivor of days gone by. Load up on dry goods, groceries, penny candy, and garden seeds. Local news, wisdom, and a few outright whoppers are also plentiful as neighbors congregate on the front porch or around the pot-bellied stove. It opened in 1914, and the only thing that's changed is the trains don't run by anymore. If you happen to be around on a Friday night, treat yourself to the weekly in-house Todd Jam Session. Open Apr–Oct Mon–Thu & Sat 8am–7pm. Fri 8am–?. Sun 12noon–5pm. Nov–Mar Mon–Thu & Sat 8am–6pm. Fri 8am–?. Sun 12noon–5pm. (336)877-1067.

17 **Todd Mercantile** 3899 TODD RAILROAD GRADE RD – A new enterprise in a very old building. Emilie Enzmann has put together a collection of Ashe County handcrafted arts and crafts items, which she offers for sale here. Featured work includes that of Martha Enzmann and Tom Sternal of Elkland Handwerke across the way. Open May–Dec Tue–Sat 10am–5pm & Sun 12noon–5pm. (336)877-5401.

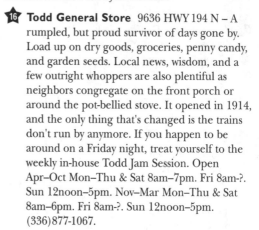

The Road Goes On Forever

Side trips, tidbits, adventures, and treasure hunts

A tip of the hat to the Todd General Store and Joe Morgan, proprietor.

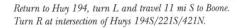

**ELKLAND SCHOOL ART CENTER
10279 THREE TOP RD IN TODD –**
*Tom Sternal and Martha Enzmann's
restored school house now functions as
a center for learning wood and stone
carving, puppet-making, drawing,
painting, and basic photography.
Regardless of the season, you'll find it
to be a hothouse of creativity. "I'm a scrounger," says
Tom, who often uses objects he finds for sculptural
material. His hewn wooden tables and chairs look and feel like
they're rooted in the earth. Martha paints and creates whimsical
wearable sculpture. A store offers pieces by teachers, students, and
craftspeople of the area. During the summer, courses are taught by
Tom, Martha, and Joe Potter, a silversmith, and others. Call for
schedule of summer classes. (336)877-5016.*

*Return to Hwy 194, turn L and travel 11 mi S to Boone.
Turn R at intersection of Hwys 194S/221S/421N.*

Todd Area B&B

🏠 **Buffalo Tavern B&B** 958 WEST BUFFALO RD
– Circa 1872, the Buffalo Tavern (turned B&B)
weaves its own stories, beginning with
guestrooms named "The Madam's Room,"
"Flapper's Room," and "The Governor's Room."
It'll be hard to refrain from creating your own
tales. (336)877-2873. www.buffalotavern.com

BOONE

*From intersection of Hwy 194S/221S/421N, travel N on Hwy 421
which becomes King St. Next five sites are on King St.*

18 Daniel Boone Inn AT THE JUNCTION OF
HWY 321 AND HWY 421 – Traditional mountain
foods served in abundance, one platter after
another. Popular with families
across the street and across the
country. Open for lunch and
dinner. (828)264-8657.

19 Doe Ridge Pottery 149 W.
KING ST. After a meal at Daniel
Boone Inn, it's a pleasant stroll
around the block to Bob Meier's

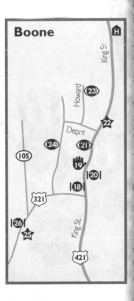

Boone

Guidebook Symbols

🔨 1	Craft Studio	🍴 1	Restaurant
👐 1	Craft Gallery	🏠	Lodging
🏛 1	Historic Site	⭐	Special Attraction

The delicious side of vegetarianism, currently at Angelica's.

distinctive studio and gallery. Even from the street, Bob's colorful, decorative, and quite functional pottery will catch your eye. Open year-round Mon–Sat 10am–6pm. (828)264-1127. www.doeridgepottery.com

20 Angelica's Vegetarian Restaurant and Juice Bar 506 W. KING RD – Nora and Mike Nelson's restaurant is known far and wide for its organic ethnic cuisine. The couple grows their own produce, uses eggs from their farm and supports local growers. Open year-round Mon–Fri 11am–9pm & Sat–Sun 11am–9:30pm. (828)265-0809. www.angelicasboone.com

21 Hands Gallery 543 W. KING ST – The High Country's oldest fine crafts co-op with many of the area's best craftspeople represented. One of the artists will likely be staffing the place when you drop in. Pottery, woodwork, aluminum sculpture, handmade clothing, silk screen original prints, and other original work at a dizzying level of artistry. Open year-round Mon–Sun 10am–6pm. (828)262-1970.

22 Mast General Store 630 W. KING ST – An Appalachian tradition since 1883, Mast Store's historic downtown emporiums are wonderful reminders of by-gone times just too good to leave behind. The Boone store, like the others, is a restored old-time mercantile building. It features traditional housewares and candies, casual clothing and outdoor gear well-suited to the High Country. Open year-round Mon–Sat 10am–6pm & Sun 1pm–6pm. During the winter, the store closes at 5pm. (828)262-0000. www.mastgeneralstore.com

Turn L on Depot St and then R on Howard St. Emporium is on R.

23 Wilcox Emporium 161 HOWARD ST – Located in a sprawling turn-of-the-century ware-house that's supported by beams recycled from old suspension bridges. Inside, honeycombed chambers are abuzz with merchants, and some quiet corners are filled with fine crafts. Open Jan–Apr Mon–Sat 10am–6pm & Sun 1pm–6pm.

The Road Goes On Forever

Side trips, tidbits, adventures, and treasure hunts

May–Dec Mon–Sat 10am–9pm & Sun 1pm–6pm. (828)262-1221.

Return to Depot St, turn R and then take L on Rivers St and travel .7 mi to Hwy 321. Sculpture gardens are on R on Rivers St.

24 Sculpture Gardens at ASU

733 RIVERS ST – Begun in 1987 as The Rosen Outdoor Sculpture Competition and Exhibition, ASU's sculpture garden now impresses students and visitors throughout the year.

Turn R on Hwy 321/Blowing Rock Rd. Travel 1 mi and turn L on University Hall Dr. Travel .3 mi. Museum is at end of drive.

25 Appalachian Cultural Museum
UNIVERSITY HALL DR – Reflecting Appalachian life in both permanent and temporary exhibits, this Appalachian State University museum features a variety of shows from fiber to fine arts. Open year-round Tue–Sat 10am–5pm & Sun 1pm–5pm. (828)262-3117.

Return to Hwy 321/Blowing Rock Rd. The Ham Shoppe is across from University Hall Dr on R.

26 The Ham Shoppe's Corner Deli
128 MEADOWVIEW DR – Fill up here before heading out again. Open year-round Mon–Fri 8am–5pm & Sat 9am–4pm. (828)268-1550.

To travel to Blowing Rock Loop, travel 11 mi to Blowing Rock on Hwy 321.

To travel to Hwy 105 South (to Linville section of trail) return to intersection with Hwy 105 and turn L, going south on Hwy 105.

Boone B&B's

H Lovill House Inn
404 OLD BRISTOL RD – A beautifully restored 1875 farmhouse that's cut off from the madcap traffic of Boone by a fortification of hemlock shrubs. It has a large country kitchen and woodburning fireplace with enough gravitational pull to draw guests from every corner of the house. (800)847-9466. www.lovillhouseinn.com

One of the permanent pieces in ASU's Sculpture Garden.

Fly-in accommodations at Lovill House.

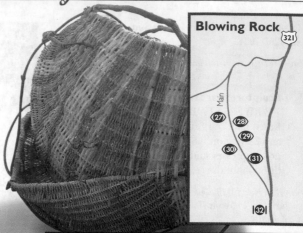

Blowing Rock

Barbara Cox basketry at Main Street Gallery.

BLOWING ROCK LOOP

Turn off Hwy 321 into downtown Blowing Rock (R if coming from Boone.) Travel 1 mi into downtown and park on Main St. Next 5 sites are within walking distance of each other.

(27) Main Street Gallery 960 MAIN ST – Significant cooperative gallery. A serious collection of pottery, handwoven garments, baskets, and other fine crafts. Most members live and work in the area. Open Apr–Dec Mon–Sun 10am–6pm. July–Aug Fri–Sat open til 9pm. (828) 295-7839.

(28) Morning Star Gallery 915 MAIN ST – Distinctive crafts dramatize this artfully arrayed and beautifully chosen collection. Open daily May–Oct 10am–5pm. Winter hours may vary. (828) 295-6991.

(29) Starwood Gallery 1505 MAIN ST – A collection that's bold, whimsical and fun. Featuring dozens of regional crafts people who have no problem with this collection's theme. Open June–Oct Mon–Thu 10am–6pm, Fri–Sat 10am–9pm & Sun 10am–5pm. Nov–May Mon–Sat 10am–5pm & Sun 11am–5pm. (828)295-9229.

(30) Gems by Gemini 1098 S MAIN ST – Custom-designed 14-carat gold jewelry, lovely gems, and gifts. Open year-round Mon–Sun 10:30am–5pm. (828)295-7700.

It's forever at Gems by Gemini.

The Road Goes On Forever
Side trips, tidbits, adventures, and treasure hunts

The oldest river in America is... you guessed it, The New River! Its north and south forks run through Watauga, Ashe and Alleghany counties.

(31) IAGO 1165 MAIN ST – A unique collection of glass, jewelry, and home accessories handcrafted by both regional and national artists. Open year-round Mon–Sat 10am–6pm & Sun 11am–6pm. (828)295-0033.

Drive down Main St/Hwy 321. It will merge with Bypass Hwy321. Continue on Hwy 321 and Canyon's is .7 mi on R.

|32| Canyon's 8960 VALLEY BLVD/HWY 321 – Just the place to refuel after a gallery crawl. Eclectic cuisine, live music nightly and jazz at Sunday brunch. The views are spectacular from Canyon's perch on the rim of the Blue Ridge. Open year round Mon–Thu 11am–9:30pm. Fri–Sat 11am–10pm. Sun 11am–9:30pm. (828)295-7661. www.canyonsbr.com

Turn L back on Hwy 321 and continue through Blowing Rock. Turn R onto Blue Ridge Parkway traveling S. Moses Cone Manor is about 2 mi with signs directing you to parking area.

(33) Southern Highland Craft Guild and Parkway Craft Center INSIDE MOSES CONE MANOR, MILE POST 294, BLUE RIDGE PARKWAY – The stately, former residence of textile manufacturer Moses Cone is today home to the Parkway Craft Center, and the Southern Highland Craft Guild retail center. On-site craft demonstrations. Open Mar 15-Nov Mon–Sun 9am–5pm. (828)295-7938. www.southernhighlandguild.org

Return to Hwy 321 and travel back to Boone, approximately 8 mi, or continue on Parkway to other connector roads to trail.

Blowing Rock Inns and B&B's

▮ Green Park Inn 9239 VALLEY BLVD – A wonderful survivor of the rambling, frame hotels of the 1880's. Pearl Buck and Calvin Coolidge stayed here, as did John D. Rockefeller who, consistent with his style, tipped with dimes and searched for golf tees after striking blows on "links as green as Emerald Isle." (828)295-3141. www.greenparkinn.com

▮ Maple Lodge B&B 152 SUNSET DR – Historic B&B located in the heart of the village.

Any dining experience at Canyon's includes a view that's unforgettable.

Not only does the Moses Cone Manor offer crafts of all kinds, it also serves as trail-head for miles and miles of easy walking paths. Ask for a map inside and head out for some fresh mountain air.

Guidebook Symbols

 Craft Studio |▮| Restaurant

 Craft Gallery   Ⓐ Lodging

 Historic Site   ★ Special Attraction

The warmth of crafted hard woods at Wildwoods Gallery.

It has eleven rooms and guests are served a full breakfast with all the fixin's'. (828) 295-3331. www.maplelodge.net

K **The Inn at Ragged Garden** 203 SUNSET DR – A handsome and stalwart inn with bark siding and a flagstone drive. (828) 295-9703. www.ragged-gardens.com

HWY105 SOUTH TO LINVILLE

Hwy 105 S of Boone to Linville. From intersection of Hwy 105 and Hwy 321 (Blowing Rock Rd) in Boone, travel S 2.1 mi on Hwy 105 and turn L on Poplar Grove Rd (just before the Hwy 105 Bypass traffic light). Poplar Grove Rd curves behind fruit stand. Travel 1.3 mi to Gallery on L.

34 **Wildwoods Gallery** 1345 POPLAR GROVE RD – Behind its hand-built front door, a beautiful collection of handcrafted furniture and fine art. Open year-round Mon–Sat 10am–5pm. (828) 963-8190. www.mountainconstruction.com

Return to Hwy 105, turn L and continue S for 3 mi. Ham Shoppe is on R at intersection with Broadstone Rd.

35 **The Ham Shoppe** 124 BROADSTONE RD – Famous for its ham biscuits, this oasis offers plenty of sandwiches, soups, salads, and shelves stocked with locally-made foods you can take home with you as a reminder of your visit. Open year-round Mon–Fri 8am–5pm. Sat 8am–6pm. Sun 9am–5pm. (828) 963-6310.

Return to Hwy 105, turn R. Continue S 1.1 mi. Miters is on R.

36 **Miters Touch Woodworking** 6858 HWY 105S – What more perfect structure to hold heirloom quality wood furniture and cabinetry than a rustic log cabin? Here you'll find pieces you could literally build a room around, along with quite affordable keepsake boxes to hold wishes in. Open Mon–Thu 8:30am–5pm & Fri 8:30am–3pm. May 15–Sep Sat 11am–3pm. (828) 963-4445. www.miterstouchinc.com

Continue traveling S on Hwy 105 3.6 mi. Gallery 9 is on R.

The Miters Touch... turning wood into gold.

The Road Goes On Forever
Side trips, tidbits, adventures, and treasure hunts

Avery County is the Christmas Tree Capitol of the world. More Fraser firs are grown in Avery than any other county in America.

(37) Gallery 9 10244 HWY 105S – Hard-to-categorize work in a contemporary space. Is it art? Is it craft? Is it "other?" Before you leave, your own definitions will certainly be reshaped in some way. And that's the fun of it. Open year-round Mon–Sat 11am–5pm & Sun 12noon–5pm. (828)963-6068. www.gallery9.com

Continue S on Hwy 105. Carlton Gallery is .5 mi on L.

(38) Carlton Gallery at Creekside Galleries HWY 105S – From the parking lot, follow the winding footpath, cross over the bridge, pass the leaping sculpture of a fish and a wading bird, and climb the stairs to a wonderland of crafts and art. Toni Carlton has created a magical atmosphere with a selection of spirited work from over 200 local, regional, and national artists. Open May–Jan 10 Mon–Sat 10am–5pm & Sun 11am–5pm. Jan 10–Apr Wed–Sat 11am–5pm & Sun 1pm–5pm. (828)963-4288.

Continue traveling S on Hwy 105 into Linville 7.4 mi.

Gallery 9, can you say "contemporary"?

LINVILLE

At intersection of Hwy 221/181 and Hwy 105, take Hwy 221 (L if traveling from Boone). Travel 2 mi to Grandfather Mountain on L.

(39) Grandfather Mountain HWY 221 – It's the only privately-owned International Biosphere Reserve, a place where man and nature exist in harmony. Along with the highest swinging footbridge in America, native animals and wondrous views, you can also enjoy watching carver-extraordinaire Tom Wolfe at work. Open daily except Thanksgiving & Christmas days. Winter 8am–5pm. Spring & Fall 8am–6pm. Summer 8am–7pm. Tickets sold up to one hour before closing. (828)733-2013. www.grandfather.com

Return to intersection of Hwy 105 and 221 in Linville and turn L. Travel .5 mi. Turn L on Roseboro Rd. Make immediate L on Carolina Ave. Church is .2 mi on R.

Carlton Gallery. The treasure at the end of the path.

The nature of discovery at Grandfather Mountain.

Guidebook Symbols

 Craft Studio    Restaurant

Craft Gallery   **A** Lodging

Historic Site   Special Attraction

A bark-enclosed sacred space at All Saints Episcopal Church.

40 All Saints Episcopal Church CAROLINA AVE – Commissioned in 1910 by Agnes MacRae Parsley. Twigs, logs and bark elevated by a master architect to inspirational levels. Architect Henry Bacon also designed the Lincoln Memorial. Open daily year-round.

Return to intersection of Hwy 105 and 221/181 and turn L on Hwy 181. Travel .3 mi on Hwy 221/181 and turn R on Ruffin St. Next four sites are within walking distance of each other.

41 Linville River Studio and Frame Shop 61 RUFFIN ST – Located in Linville's original post office, this frame shop does double duty as a gallery for local artists and craftspeople. Don't miss the photographs. Open year-round Mon–Sat 10am–5pm. (828)733-2427.

42 Old Hampton Store and Grist Mill 77 RUFFIN ST – Don't you know this old store bears witness to some great events? Browse the eclectic array of merchandise while waiting for delivery of your tasty sandwich. Open Oct–Apr Mon–Sat 9am–5pm. May–Sep Mon–Sat 9am–7pm. (828)733-5213.

43 87 Ruffin St 87 RUFFIN ST – Abigail Sheets has searched the mountains for inspired folk artists and their work. What she found includes art dolls, masks, inventive lamps and shades, carved folk art animals in many incarnations, pottery, and last, but certainly not least, a collection of folk art paintings. Open Apr 15–Nov 15 Mon–Sat 10am–5pm & call ahead on Sun. Nov 16– Dec Thu–Sat 10am–5pm & call ahead on Sun–Wed. (828)737-0420.

L Linville Cottage Inn RUFFIN ST – Built three generations ago and still held by a member of the family. If you like antiques and garden herbs with your breakfast, this is your place. (828)733-6551.

Return to Hwy 221/181 and turn R. Travel .3 mi and turn L as Hwy 221S turns L off of Hwy 181. Travel about 2.5 mi and turn R at Land Harbor. Travel 1.4 mi to Oak Hill Section and turn R on Oak Hills Dr. Turn R on second Hemlock Loop. Studio is 3rd house on L.

A bunch of carved friends at 87 Ruffin.

The Road Goes On Forever
Side trips, tidbits, adventures, and treasure hunts

When the original Crossnore Weaving house burned in 1935, 120 school kids formed a human chain to bring river rock from the stream for a new house.

Roberta Nosti 470 HEMLOCK LOOP –
Painting on silk is akin to capturing moonbeams
in a jar. As challenging as this ancient Oriental
technique is, Roberta Nosti has most certainly
become a master. Her mountain landscapes and
indigenous wildflowers are the result of
"something I have a really strong feeling about."
Her beautiful abstract scarves come from the
same deep reservoir. Open year-round Mon–Fri
11am–3pm. (828) 737-0820.

*A delicate artistry:
the silk paintings of
Roberta Nosti.*

Return to Hwy 221S, turn R and travel 3.5 mi to Crossnore.

CROSSNORE & LINVILLE FALLS

*From intersection of Crossnore Dr and Hwy 221, turn R on
Crossnore Dr (if you are traveling S) and travel .5 mi and turn R
on Johnson Lane. Weaving Room is .1 mi on L.*

 Crossnore Weavers and Gallery
205 JOHNSON LANE – On the looms in this
rock cottage, now a National Historic Site,
community women have woven pieces that have
warmed mountain folks and comforted states-
men. The folks of Crossnore Weavers continue
to weave heirloom garments with contemporary
colors and styles. Open year-round Mon–Fri
8:30am–5pm & Sat 9am–4pm. (828) 733-4660.
www.crossnore.com

*The
art of
Crossnore
Weavers: best
experienced when
curled up on
your couch.*

*Return to Hwy 221 and turn R, traveling S for 4.7 mi.
Anvil Art Studio is on R.*

 Anvil Arts Studio 9600 LINVILLE FALLS
HWY/HWY 221 – Bill Brown hammers, heats
and braises and does all manner of things to
steel, copper, bronze and other material to
produce award winning sculpture. From
massive outdoor sculpture to artful lamp forms,
you are in for a treat at the Anvil Arts Studio.
Speaking of which, his gardens are a wonderful
place to indulge the picnic lunch you brought
along. Open year-round Mon–Fri 9am–5pm &
Sat–Sun by appointment. (828) 765-6226.
www.studiosculpture.com

**SCULPTURE
Garden
&
Gallery**

*At Anvil Art,
encounter a
combination
of sculpture
and gardens.*

*Continue S on Hwy 221 for 1.3 mi. Next two sites are across the
road from each other.*

Guidebook Symbols

	Craft Studio		Restaurant
	Craft Gallery		Lodging
	Historic Site		Special Attraction

Louise's Famous Rock House, serving famous food daily.

|47| Spears B-B-Q and Grill INTERSECTION OF HWY 221 & HWY 183 – A place of divided loyalties. Some swear by the pork, ribs and chicken from the smokehouse out back and simmered in Betty and David Huskins' famous barbecue sauce. Others remain loyal to the mountain trout, country ham, and vegetables served southern style. You'll be in one camp or the other before you leave. Open daily mid-May–Oct 11am–9pm. Nov–mid-May Fri 5pm–9pm, Sat 11pm–9pm & Sun 11am–7pm. (828)765-2658.

|48| Louise's Famous Rock House HWY 221 & HWY 183 – Outlaws steer clear. Louise's is a popular stop for state troopers. Daily specials keep the troopers, and the law-abiding citizens well satisfied. But on Fridays and Saturdays, when they start throwing ribeyes on the outside grill, even the bad guys can't stay away. Open for breakfast, lunch and dinner. Mon–Thu 6am––7:30pm. Fri–Sat 6am–8pm. Sun 6am–7pm. (828)765-2702.

Parkway is .7 mi N on Hwy 221.

VALLE CRUCIS/BANNER ELK

From intersection of Hwy 105S and Broadstone Rd (approximately 5 miles S of Boone), travel 2.5 mi on Broadstone Rd. Inn is on L.

If you don't have enough time to explore everything in this gallery, just spend the night.

M The Mast Farm Inn 2543 BROADSTONE RD – Time passes most agreeably on the expansive wrap-around porch of this 18th century inn. The site's two-story, loghouse was the loom house for Aunt Josie and Aunt Leona Mast, who wove linens for President Woodrow Wilson's White House. Reservations are suggested for bountiful lunches and dinners. Open year-round Tue–Sat 5:30am–8:30pm & Sun 12:30pm–2:30pm. (828)963-5857. www.mastfarminn.com

Continue on Broadstone Rd. and Gallery is .4 mi on L.

49 Alta Vista Gallery and B&B 2839 BROAD-STONE RD – In just the sort of hillside historic farmhouse that makes Valle Crucis everything it

The Road Goes On Forever
Side trips, tidbits, adventures, and treasure hunts

The Mountain Times *will Keep you abreast of current goings-on.*

is–rural, warm, welcoming–Lee and Maria Hyde run a cheerful gallery and B&B that would be delightful in any century. Pottery, prints, and paintings by local artists–notably B Jean Baird, William Mangum, Louise Pinto,and Will Moses, the great-grandson of Grandma Moses. Open May–Oct Mon–Sat 10am–5pm. Nov–Apr Fri–Sat 11am–5pm. (828)963-5247. www.altavistagallery.com.

In this wonderful icon of a store, you may run into your own childhood.

Continue on Broadstone (which becomes Hwy 194) for .3 mi. Mast General Store is on R, and the Pottery is in a building back of the store.

 Mast General Store (the original)
HWY 194 – The tradition of the country store, gussied up. Purveyors of quality goods since 1882. Folks have been known to get lost in here, so beware. Open Mon–Sat 7am–6:30pm & Sun 1pm–6pm. Mid-Jan–Easter Mon–Fri 7am–6pm, Sat 7am–6:30pm & Sun 1pm–5pm. (828)963-6511. www.mastgeneralstore.com

 J and S Beaumont Pottery 3597 HWY 194 S – (Behind the Mast General Store) This man loves to throw pots. Roland Hamner continues to hand-throw classic, functional dinnerware as timeless as the 1907 school house his studio and showroom occupy. Mon–Sat 10am–6pm. Sun 1pm–6pm. (828) 963-6999. www.jsbeaumontpottery.com

Turn L back on Hwy 194 and make immediate R as Hwy 194 turns R. Travel .8 mi and Gallery is on R.

 Kevin Beck Artist Studio SCENIC BYWAY 194 – Located in a cove surrounded by mountains, Kevin Beck's pastel paintings of the natural world are at one with their place. His work has been described by collectors as "paintings with heart." You'll also find Judi Beck's functional pottery on display as well. Open year-round Fri 12noon–5pm, Sat 10am–6pm & Sun 12noon–4pm. June–Oct Mon & Thu 12noon–5pm. (828)295-6868 or (828)963-2582. www.kevinbeck.com

Essence of Halloween at J and S Beaumont Pottery.

Guidebook Symbols

 Craft Studio   Restaurant

Craft Gallery   **A** Lodging

Historic Site   Special Attraction

Once at the Taylor House, you'll want to stay longer.

A contemplative destination: The Valle Crucis Conference Center.

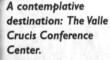

One of the peaceful valleys of the High Country.

Next two sites are immediately on R as you continue on Hwy 194.

Taylor House B&B HWY 194 – This stately 86-year-old farmhouse has had hospitality running across its floorboards for as far back as anyone can recall. Miss Lou, the Inn's first hostess, took borders for $7 a day. Although the tariff is higher now, it's no less a bargain. A morning or afternoon wiled away in a rocker on the wraparound front porch is an experience you just can't put a price on. (828)963-5581.

53 The Valle Crucis Conference Center 146 SKILES WAY – A quiet place high on a mountain, this center is a year-round retreat for non-profit groups. The stone church was established in 1842 by the Right Reverend Levi Ives. Among the many gardens are two outdoor labyrinths guests are invited to enjoy as well as miles of hiking trails. Open year-round Mon–Fri 8am–4pm. (828)963-4453. www.highsouth.com/vallecrucis

The Road Goes On Forever

Side trips, tidbits, adventures, and treasure hunts

Are the Brown Mountain Lights really out there? Somewhere north of Morganton people have reported seeing "lights" in the mountains. Theories abound as to their source, but to this day they still haven't been explained.

Continue traveling on Hwy 194 for 2.4 mi. Turn R on Rominger Rd. Sheer Bliss is .3 mi on R.

54 Sheer Bliss/Little Bear Rock Shop 410 ROMINGER RD – A shop full of gold and silver jewelry, as well as gems which local students sometimes use to research class assignments. But the real gem here is the owner, Doris Bliss, who has penned the delightful books, "Dobie'n Me in Hoot Owl Holler" and "Echoes from Hoot Owl Holler." Open Jun–Dec Mon–Sat 10am–5pm. Jan–May by appointment. (828) 963-8898.

Return to Hwy 194, turn R. Travel 4.3 mi into Banner Elk. Turn L on Hwy 184S. Continue traveling on Hwy 184 for .7 mi. Gallery is on R.

For Doris Bliss, all gems are precious.

55 Art Cellar Gallery 920 SHAWHEEHAW AVE – Original fine art by renowned regional artists. The Art Cellar prides itself on its reputation as one of the South's leading galleries for folk, visionary and outsider art. Pamela McKay's enthusiasm for the richness of North Carolina's art and natural beauty combines beautifully with her passion for creating compelling and artful exhibit spaces. Open year-round Mon–Sat 10am–5pm. (828)898-5175. www.artcellaronline.com

North Carolina artists, well-displayed at the Art Cellar Gallery.

Continue traveling on Hwy 184 for 3.5 mi into Invershiel and intersection with Hwy 105. Turn L to Hwy 105 Trail and Boone or R to Linville (2.1 mi).

Banner Elk B&Bs

O Tufts House Inn EDGAR TUFTS RD – Estate of the Tuft's family, revered for development in Banner Elk including the establishment of Lee's McRae College. (828)898-7944.

P Banner Elk B&B Hwy 194 – Once a church, now a raspberry-colored guesthouse. (828)898-6223.

Guidebook Symbols

✋	Craft Studio	🍴	Restaurant
①	Craft Gallery	A	Lodging
1	Historic Site	★	Special Attraction

Blue Ridge Parkway

The first rural parkway
in the United States

A common thread cinches together the pearl-like trails of the craft heritage system. It drifts across ridge tops, tumbles into fertile river valleys, and zips back up to panoramic heights with natural grace. It brushes against waterfalls, rhododendron hells, and ancient mountainsides. And its very name—the Blue Ridge Parkway—conjures up a certain Jack Kerouac-Charles Kuralt all-American romance with the open-road sort of thing.

Wildcat Rocks overlook, 1947.

The Blue Ridge Parkway is truly a fitting entrance to the treasures of craft in the mountains of Western North Carolina.

Traveling south from Virginia, the Parkway follows the Blue Ridge, eastern rampart of the Appalachian mountains. It passes Mt. Mitchell, highest peak east of the Mississsippi (6,684 feet), where you will skirt the southern end of the brooding Black Mountains, named for their dark green cloak of spruce and fir. The road goes on to dodge through the Craggies, the Pisgahs, the Balsams and the Great Smokies.

As you travel along this engineering masterpiece,

*Pedestrian overlook at Fox Hunter's
Paradise, 1940.*

keep in mind that
the designers not only
wished to create a
road, but an illusion —
the sense that each
and every panorama
along its entire length
is part of one
magnificent park.

The road is also part
of the physical evidence
of one of the greatest
public works projects of
the twentieth century.
It was built by the Civil

Top: Elk Mountain parking overlook, 1953.
Bottom: Mahogany Rock, 1953.

Conservation Corp, which President Franklin D. Roosevelt
established in the early 1930's to help put Americans back to work
during the Great Depression.

And, finally, don't forget to ease off the accelerator. This is one
road that's a destination in and of itself.

Tunnel Construction, 1955.

PHOTOS COURTESY OF BLUE RIDGE PARKWAY MUSEUM COLLECTION

Circle The Mountains

The "Circle The Mountain" driving tour is rich in diversity, crossing a century of rural life as easily as it runs beside tobacco farms or plunges down hillsides of mountain laurel and rhododendron. ⊚ You will drive through hamlets wedged between hills and streams where craft developed as a pure necessity of life. Some of these farm communities and villages evoke a time when the mountains were largely cut off from the outside world. ⊚ Quilts, hooked rugs, hankerchief dolls, whittled pieces, iron tools, vine baskets and musical instruments. These became the art forged of the hard life in the mountains. ⊚ Along your way, watch for places where tobacco is harvested and cured in barns. Where a rock schoolhouse, now abandoned, stubbornly holds a piece of history that refuses to yield to modern contrivance. Where footbridges are the only way to the far side of the stream, and home. ⊚ Just past the relaxed, front porch town of Burnsville, you'll soon find yourself in the gravitational pull of the Penland School, one

Ideas on top of inspiration on top of insights in the studio at Sedberry's Pottery.

With Each Hand Different

of the great shapers of the American craft movement. In a certain way, Penland represents both hallowed ground and new frontier. In textiles. In glass. In ironwork. In photography as craft. In the traditional zen of throwing and glazing pottery. ⊚ The school radiates energy. And so does the work that comes out of it. In its shops and classrooms, and in studios and fine galleries that dot the surrounding region, you will be drawn toward pieces of amazing beauty, whimsy, and charm. ⊚ Up the Toe River, in and around Bakersville and Spruce Pine, throughout the surprising and wonderful nooks and crannies of the Celo Community, at Little Switzerland where the world unfurls beneath you, this driving trail offers hundreds of opportunities to appreciate the influence of Miss Lucy's Penland. And the influence of the craftspeople who came by their craft in the most natural and cherished of ways. Handed down, one generation to the next, with each hand different.

Circle The Mountains

Burnsville

19E

To Asheville

197

Guidebook Symbols

Craft Studio   Restaurant

Craft Gallery   Lodging

Historic Site   Special Attraction

N

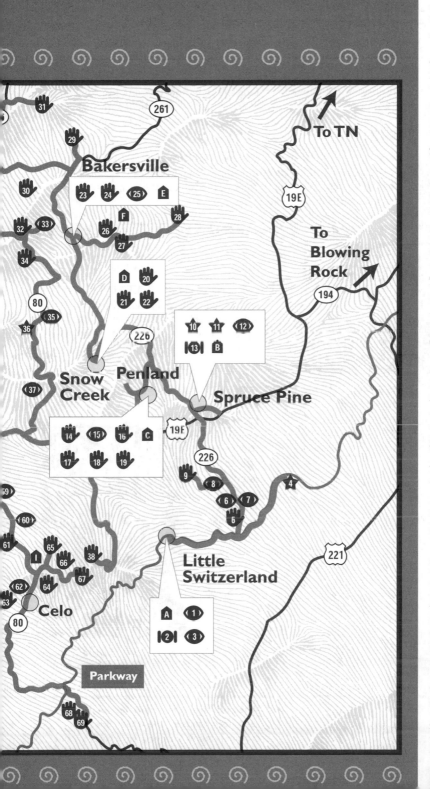

Circle to your left. Circle to your right. Swing your partner any which way that strikes your fancy. If you're looking to ease into this great gathering of craft, we suggest you travel in a counter-clockwise direction (circling left) and slow dance your way from stop to stop before the tempo picks up.

But if you want to do some fancy footwork right from the start, by all means circle right (working back from the end of the listings). You'll immediately meet up with one charmer after another: Little Switzerland, Celo, Burnsville, Bakersville, Penland, and Spruce Pine.

Whichever direction you choose, give yourself plenty of time. To travel the loop in its entirety–making every stop–can take up to a week depending on your individual pace. But even in a day or two you can still manage to have yourself a real wing-ding of a good time.

LITTLE SWITZERLAND

At Milepost 334 on the Blue Ridge Parkway, exit heading S on Hwy 226A. The Switzerland Inn is immediately to your L.

A **Switzerland Inn** CHALET RD – A sprawling, fanciful hotel plucked straight from the Alps with wonderful meals and a view to match. On a clear day, you can practically see Europe. Open Apr–Nov. (828) 765-2153.

Gallery is directly across drive from Switzerland Inn.

1 **Trillium Gallery** CHALET RD – A high altitude collection of exquisite regional work. Distinctive pottery and glass pieces *(don't sneeze)* along with jewelry and paintings. Open mid-Apr–Sep Mon–Sun 9am–5pm. Oct Mon–Sun 8:30am–6pm. (828) 765-0024.

Return to Hwy 226A continue S. Next two sites are .5 mi on L.

At the Little Switzerland Inn you might just forget you are still in North Carolina.

At the Trillium Gallery.

The Road Goes On Forever

Side trips, tidbits, adventures, and treasure hunts

When driving in the mountains you want to keep both hands on the wheel. But local custom requires that you wave to every one you pass. The solution? The One Finger Wave. Neighborly. And easy to master.

|2| Switzerland Café and General Store

HWY 226A – Gourmet sandwiches, soups to clear the fog, cheeses to toss in the car and desserts to kill for (including a notorious cola cake.) The General Store features the work of several local craftspeople. Open Apr & May Sun–Thu 10am–5pm & Fri–Sat 10am–8pm. June–Aug Mon–Sat 10am–8pm & Sun 10am–5pm. Sep–Oct Mon–Thu 10am–5pm & Fri–Sun 10am–8pm. (828)765-5289. www.switzerlandcafe.com

(3) Blue Ridge Soap Shed

HWY 226A – Indulge your senses in the delights of over 100 recipes of handmade soap. Native plants provide many of the scents in the shop: mint, lavender, magnolia, apple. Open daily year-round 10am–5pm. (828)765-6001. www.soapshed.com

Baskets of utter cleanliness at Blue Ridge Soap Shed.

Return to the Blue Ridge Parkway heading N. Travel 6 mi and Orchard is on R just off the Blue Ridge Parkway at Milepost 328.3.

The Orchard at Altapass

1025 ORCHARD RD – This classic packing house sits just under the Parkway in the midst of a 280-acre orchard started by the railroad over 100 years ago. Let's see, there's apple butter, apple cider, apple fudge, apple orchard tours, and apples of six-teen varieties. Look for Darrell Rhudy's turned bowls gouged out of applewood. Many NC crafts people represented. And, up the gorge, thirty-three trains a day. Open late May–Oct Mon–Sat 10am–6pm & Sun 12noon–6pm. (828)765-9531. www.altapassorchard.com

Leaf looking at Trillium Gallery in Little Switzerland.

Return to the Blue Ridge Parkway and head S. Exit the Blue Ridge Parkway at Hwy 226 and travel toward Spruce Pine. From the Blue Ridge Parkway, Bea Hensley's Forge is .5 mi on L.

 Bea Hensley and Son Hand Forge

HWY 226 AT DULA RD – Bea and Mike create 15th and 16th century-style, masterful iron works. From small hooks to 20-foot-high gates gracing a California avocado ranch, they do it all with skill and humor. Bea also knows every good trout stream in the area along with stories to match. Open year-round Mon–Sat 8am–5pm.

Step 1   Step 2

Guidebook Symbols

Craft Studio		Restaurant	
Craft Gallery		Lodging	
Historic Site		Special Attraction	

Primitive as well as traditional craft make Pine Crossings a history lesson as well as a craft gallery.

Return to Hwy 226, turn L and travel .2 mi. Gallery is on L.

6 Pine Crossings 14842 HWY 226 – A goodly while back, Al and Linda Vesely bought Bea Hensley's place, (yep, Bea, the blacksmith) and opened a gallery that marries the primitives from the 1800's and the traditional crafts of select North Carolina artists. Its new and old pots and other things that'll make you consider where we come from and what we're made of. Open Apr–Nov Mon–Sat 10am–5pm & Sun 1pm–5pm. (828) 765-8400.

Directly across Hwy 226, you'll find the next site.

7 Gems for You – Jewelry by Anita HWY 226 – "Jewelry that touches the spirit as well as the body." That's Anita Lawson's guiding principle as she creates elegant gold and silver wire-art jewelry with gemstones and other arresting objects. Open May–Oct Mon–Sat 10am–5pm & Sun 1pm–5pm. Nov–Apr Mon–Sat 11am–4pm & Sun 1pm–4pm, weather permitting. (828) 766-7624 or (888) 390-GEMS. www.jewelrybyanita.com

Continue on Hwy 226 toward Spruce Pine for 2.2 mi. Woody's Chair Shop is on L.

8 Woody's Chair Shop 34 DALE RD OFF HWY 226 – Third-generation chairmaker operating in the same location as his grandfather. First-generation quality. Chairs are primary focus, but you'll also find walking sticks, boxes and more. Open year-round Mon–Fri 8am–4:30pm & Sat 9am–4:30pm. (828) 765-9277.

Colors of the earth at Boyd Pottery.

Continue down Dale Rd for .3 mi and turn R on Rockhouse Creek Rd. Travel 1 mi and turn L on Pond Rd. The Pottery is 1.1 mi at the end of a very steep gravel road.

9 Boyd Pottery 865 POND RD – Pots, jugs and cocky teapots, scribbled over and joyful to the touch; plates and bowls, earthy and sensual as the hills surrounding the studio. Brought to you by Katherine and Mark

The Road Goes On Forever

Side trips, tidbits, adventures, and treasure hunts

Boyd. Open daily year-round 10am–6pm.
(828)766-6024. www.boydpottery.com

*Return to Hwy 226, turn L and travel 2 mi to intersection of Hwy
19E. Turn R on Hwy 19E and travel .5 mi. Turn L on Altapass
Hwy and travel .3 mi to stoplight. Turn L on Oak St, travel .2 mi
and find a place to park.*

SPRUCE PINE

In downtown Spruce Pine, park on Oak St. Next two sites are on R.

10 **Blue Moon Books** 211 OAK AVE – In an old
storefront building, you can take a load off, suck
down some joe, and become a more brilliant
person with hardly anyone noticing. You'll find
area crafters well-represented here. Open year-
round Mon–Sat 10am–6pm. (828)766-5000.

11 **Toe River Arts Council Center** 269 OAK
AVE – It's Grand Central Station for exhibits
featuring Toe River area artists and for
information and maps detailing the seasonal
studio tours that wind throughout the
Penland-Celo-Bakersville area featuring upwards
of a hundred artists. All the energy of an
enthusiastic cooperative from the floor up -
which happens to be wonderfully hand-painted!
Open year-round Tue–Sat 10am–5pm.
(828)765-0520.

Next two sites are on Locust Ave, one street down from Oak Ave.

12 **Twisted Laurel Gallery** 221 LOCUST AVE –
An inspirational place with a singular collection
of glass from many gifted folks, including John
Littleton, Kate Vogel, Gary Beecham–most glass
and other fine crafts are from within a 25-mile
radius. Clockmaker Luther Stroup, an owner,
often drops by with a story or two that would
charm a smile out of a dead dog. Open Apr–Dec
Tue–Sat 10am–5pm. Jan–Mar Fri–Sat
10am–5pm. (828)765-1532.

*TRAC: A "must stop"
for information about
studio tours and area
exhibits.*

*John Littleton and
Kate Vogel as seen at
Twisted Laurel.*

Guidebook Symbols

🖐**1** Craft Studio		🍴**1** Restaurant	
🔵**1** Craft Gallery		**A** Lodging	
1 Historic Site		**1** Special Attraction	

A textile weaving class at Penland.

Hand-wrought iron railing at Penland.

In hushed tones craftspeople tell the tales of time spent at Penland discovering passions and perfecting skills. Each piece created is born on hallowed ground.

|◧| Cedar Crest Restaurant 243 LOCUST AVE – Save room for the homemade desserts. Open year-round Tue–Sat 6am–9pm. (828) 765-6124.

Follow Oak St for 2.3 mi to Hwy 226. Turn R and travel 1.7 mi. Turn L on Penland Rd.

Spruce Pine Area B&B's

🅑 Richmond Inn 51 PINE AVE – A stone and wood-frame building dating from 1939 and a full southern breakfast. (828) 765-6993. www.richmond-inn.com

PENLAND AREA

At junction of Hwy 226 and Penland Rd, turn L (traveling from Spruce Pine) on Penland Rd. Pottery is .1 mi on R.

🖐 Shawn Ireland Pottery 134 PENLAND RD – Shawn, a past resident potter at Penland, hangs his work on a long tradition. You dig the clay, use local glaze materials, throw a kick wheel and fire with wood. The result is the world around you and under your feet. And just as beautiful. Open daily year-round 10am–5pm. (828) 765-5737.

Continue on Penland Rd for approximately 1 mi. Turn R on Conley Ridge Rd and travel .8 mi. Penland Gallery is on R.

⑮ Penland Gallery CONLEY RIDGE RD – Totally out of the ordinary crafts. Most are products of mentors, teachers, and artisans of Penland, recognized as one of the finest schools for craft-making in America. (See Heritage Piece: Penland School pgs 70-71) Ask at the Gallery for details and directions to the school's resident artist studios. Tours of the Penland School are by reservation during Mar–Dec Tue & Thu. Work shown in the gallery is nothing short of stunning. Gallery open Mar–Dec Tue–Sat 10am–5pm & Sun 12noon–5pm. Jan–Feb Fri–Sat 10am–5pm. (828) 765-6211 and (828) 765-2359. www.penland.org

Across from Penland Gallery on Conley Ridge Rd, drive down Lucy Morgan Lane. Studio at end of lane on R.

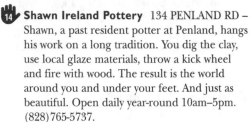

The Road Goes On Forever
Side trips, tidbits, adventures, and treasure hunts

16 Bringle Gallery and Studio 160 LUCY MORGAN LANE – One-of-a-kind functional pieces and large vessels you can see being born out of the imagination and by the hand of Cynthia Bringle, a teacher and mentor at Penland, under whose tutelage many master potters have entered the world. Her works display a straightforward beauty and integrity of form. Under the same roof, sister Edwina's colorful woven blankets and free-motion machine embroidery share wall space with Cynthia's colorful paintings. Open daily year-round 10am–5pm but always good to call first. (828) 765-0240.

Return to Conley Ridge Rd, turn L and travel about 1 mi. Inn is on R.

C Chinquapin Inn at Penland CONLEY RIDGE RD – A 1937 mountain house with a stone fireplace, sun porches, and garden paths. Just the place to base your Penland adventure from. (828) 765-0064.

Cynthia Bringle's masterful work.

From Inn, bear R as Conley Ridge Rd turns to R. Travel .75 mi and Barking Spider is on L.

The color of bells at Barking Spider Studio.

17 Barking Spider Studio 1446 CONLEY RIDGE RD– Rebecca Plummer and Jon Ellenbogen continue conjuring up sparkling ornaments and highly-useful earth-toned pottery in the airy, sun-filled space beneath their home. Enjoy the view from their studio – a quiet, meadowy mountainscape to the south – while you browse a gallery of artful stoneware. Open daily year-round 9am–5pm. (828) 765-2670. www.penlandpottery.com

Turn R back on Conley Ridge Rd and travel .75 mi back to top of ridge, cross the intersection and drive .1 mi down Beacon Church Rd. You can park in parking area and walk down drive to R or drive down to studio.

The enthusiasm of Jane Peiser's imagination.

18 Jane Peiser Pottery 68 BEACON CHURCH RD – Vases, glasses, figurines, and lamps of great illuminated personality created in a garden environment. Distinctive, inspiring, nationally-recognized work – often involving figures that fly and float over imaginary mountain land-

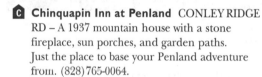

Guidebook Symbols	
Craft Studio	Restaurant
Craft Gallery	Lodging
Historic Site	Special Attraction

Fish scale glazing at The Pottery.

JABOBS, a one-woman epicenter of classically proportioned basketry.

scapes. Check out her local potters' line-up! Open year-round Mon–Sat 10am–5pm. (828)765-7123. www.janepeiser.com

Turn R back on Conley Ridge Rd and travel back to Penland Rd. Turn R, travel 1.5 mi. The Pottery is on R.

19 The Pottery 3050 PENLAND RD – Catherine and Tracy Dotson's artistic, functional pottery. Fish scale glazing is a lovely specialty of the house. So is just standing in this studio's peaceful setting surrounded by rhododendron thickets and favored by the invigorating winds of Penland. Open daily year-round 9am–5pm. (828)765-8222.

Turn L back on Penland Rd. Travel 3.1 mi to return to Hwy 226.

SNOW CREEK RD AREA

Turn L on Hwy 226 (from Penland Rd) and travel 2.2 mi. Turn L on Wing Rd. Cabin is .3 mi on L and Pottery is another .4 mi on R.

D Cabin in the Laurel 163 CABIN IN THE LAUREL – The original logwork in the main cabin is so old no one knows the truth about it. Even so, these woodsy digs are comfortable and fun. Open year-round. (888)701-4083. www.cabininthelaurel.com

20 Terry Gess Pottery 770 WING RD – About his salt-glazed stoneware Terry Gess says, "I love the element of surprise and unpredictability." His square plates, teapots, vases, jars and jugs come across as everyday and unpretentious, earthy and casually thumbed. But in this land of the familiar, there also emerges a subtle beauty that reveals itself, slowly, soulfully, over time. Open daily year-round 10am–6pm. (828)688-3863. www.terrygesspottery.com

Continue on Wing Rd for .7 mi. JABOBS on L.

21 JABOBS – Just a Bunch of Baskets 1535 WING RD – Billie Ruth Sudduth creates classical shaker and Appalachian-style baskets worthy of the Smithsonian collection where some reside.

The Road Goes On Forever
Side trips, tidbits, adventures, and treasure hunts

Near White Rock, in the early 1800s, "Duck" Shelton was publicly whipped for making coins from a secret silver mine. Duck, whose mine has never been rediscovered, hunted squirrels with silver bullets.

She attributes her wonderful red color to the "magic of the well water" where she lives and her shapes to Fibonacci Numbers, a 13th century math formula based on the geometries of nature. Open year-round Mon–Sat 10am–5pm & Sun 1pm–5pm but smart to call. (828)688-2399. www.brsbasket.com

Continue on Wing Rd until it joins Snow Creek Rd in .2 mi. Turn R on Snow Creek Rd and travel 1.7 mi, taking care to bear L as Snow Creek Rd does. Snow Creek Pottery is on R.

"Flower bricks" at Terry Gess' place.

 Snow Creek Pottery 353 SNOW CREEK RD – Deeply hued stoneware from David Ross (aka "Platterman"), practical enough for kitchen use, elegant enough for the next time the King and Queen of Prussia drop by for hors d'oeurves or whatever. His brushstroke imagery of animals adds spontaneous delight. Open year-round Mon–Sat 9am–5pm & Sun 12noon–4pm. (828)688-3196.

Continue traveling on Snow Creek Rd for .3 mi until it intersects Hwy 226. Turn L and travel north on Hwy 226 to Bakersville, approximately 3.4 mi.

BAKERSVILLE

At intersection of Hwy 226 and Mitchell Ave, turn R on Mitchell Ave. Next four sites are within walking distance of each other.

 Local Color Weaving 7 MITCHELL AVE – "You think of something and just want to get it going," says former-Rutgers-professor-turned-weaver Fred Swift. Fred and co-owner Deborah Wheeler make silk, rayon chenille and mixed-fiber scarves and shibori hand-dyed pieces in colors that warp the imagination. Open year-round Thu–Sat 11am–5pm. (828)688-3186.

The awesomeness of colors juxtaposed at Local Color Weaving.

 Two Trees Pottery 20 N. MITCHELL AVE – Joe Comeau's functional and expressive forms, influenced by the Orient, include tableware, containers and boxes, faceted and elegantly nested. His art, given to whispers of color, can be cheerfully enjoyed in Bakersville's orginal main street bank, now Joe's studio and show-room. Open year-round Mon–Sat 10am–5pm. (828)688-9139. www.twotreespottery.com

Joe Comeau's work: Hints of the Orient.

The Road Goes
On Forever

Side trips, tidbits,
adventures, and
treasure hunts

25 Picket Fence Pottery & Fine Art 59 N
MITCHELL AVE – Jann Welch teaches at
Penland. But that's okay, there's still time to
restore a historic home, turn it into a B&B, and
convert an old medical building into a studio
and gallery full of her functional pottery,
sculpture and watercolors. She paints some of
her pottery with a cobalt oxide to mesmerizing
effect. Open daily year-round 8am–8pm except
major holidays. (828)688-9192.

E Bakersville B&B 71 N MITCHELL AVE – A
charming and quiet spot for relaxing along the
trail. Open year round. (877) 688-6012.
www.bakersvillebedandbreakfast.com

(Far Left)
DELLINGER'S MILL
Beautiful scenes are
often just around a
bend in the road or
standing, lost in
time, next to a
winding river.

CANE CREEK RD

Continue traveling on Mitchell Ave. for approximately 1.5 mi.
Mitchell Ave. turns into Cane Creek Rd. Look for mailbox # 1529
on L. GG Smith Pottery is on L at end of drive.

26 Gertrude Graham Smith Pottery 1529
CANE CREEK RD – There's just a bit of
hobnobbery about Gay's ruffled jars,
ovaled bowls and petticoat vases.
Her freckly, salt-brined pieces
have the stage presence of
long-time character
actors. You can
admire them
in the kiln
shed next
to the barn.
Open daily
year-round
10am–5pm. (828)688-
3686. www.gertrude-
grahamsmith.com

The salt-brined art of
Gertrude Graham
Smith Pottery.

Return to Cane Creek Rd and
turn L. Travel .5 mi and
turn L on Green Young
Rd.. Travel .5 mi and
turn R on Dallas
Young Rd. Travel .3 mi
and Bicycle Inn is at
end of road.

Guidebook Symbols

Craft Studio		Restaurant	
Craft Gallery		Lodging	
Historic Site		Special Attraction	

Bicycle Inn 319 DALLAS YOUNG RD – The name has it right. What a place to find at the end of a day's bike ride! Great food for lodgers as well as a soothing place for body and soul. (828)688-9333. www.bicycleinn.com

Return to Cane Creek Rd and turn L. Travel .4 mi to gallery on R. Drive up to studio in woods.

27 Cane Creek Pottery 2366 CANE CREEK RD – Dianne Borde-Sutherland derives inspiration from her setting above Cane Creek to create majolica glazed earthenware pottery of great note. Open Apr–Dec Mon–Sat 10am–5pm. (828)688-9051. www.tinglaze.com

Continue traveling on Cane Creek Rd for approximately 3 mi. Turn L in paved drive (watch for mailbox # 5271) and pottery is last house on R.

28 Shane Mickey Pottery 5271 CANE CREEK RD – In their bucolic, mountain cove studio, Shane and Lisa Mickey stoke a wood-fired kiln to produce extraordinarily functional and fun pottery. Open daily year-round 9am–6pm. (828)688-6982.

Return to Cane Creek Rd, turn R and travel approximately 7.6 mi back to Bakersville.

NORTH OF BAKERSVILLE

At intersection of Hwy 226 and Mitchell Ave, turn R on Hwy 226 and then stay straight on Hwy 261 as Hwy 226 makes sharp L. Travel 3.9 mi. on Hwy 261 and turn L on Hobson Rd. Travel .7 mi and turn L into drive flanked by iron baskets.

29 Southwood Atelier 767 HOBSON RD – In a studio built over the cascades of Cook Creek, the pit-fired clay vessels of Yvonne Hegney and Thom Kittredge blissfully marry up with found objects of metal, wood and stone. There's surprise in their work, playfulness, and an architectural nobility that's totally inventive. Open year-round Wed–Sun 10am–6pm. Other hours by appointment. (828)688-4308.

Return to Hwy 261 and turn R. Travel .2 mi and turn R on Fork Mountain Rd. Travel 2.4 mi and turn L into drive. Gallery is on R of drive.

The bright work of Cane Creek Pottery.

Evocative pieces from Southwood Atelier.

The Road Goes On Forever

Side trips, tidbits, adventures, and treasure hunts

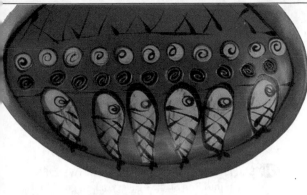

A bit of fun and whimsy in the useful art of Fork Mountain Pottery.

 Fork Mountain Pottery 1782 FORK MOUNTAIN RD – Here we have two potters creating worlds of useful pottery: Suze Lindsey's salt-fired animal-natured pots and bowls, full of fun and clamoring for attention, some with four legs and Kent McLaughlin's reduction fired pots and pitchers and cups, exuding a ruffled grace, in earthen oranges and coppers. Open year-round Mon–Sat 10am–5pm. (828)688-9297. www.forkmountainpottery.com

Turn L on Fork Mountain Rd and travel 1.8 mi to junction with Hwy 226. Turn R on Hwy 226 and travel 2.5 mi. Turn R on Pine Root Branch Rd and travel 1.2 mi. Studio is on R at end of paved road.

Pine Root Pottery 1108 PINE ROOT BRANCH RD – Mark and Erin Peters fell in love with the chestnut farmhouse, its apple orchard and mountain views and the old barn. Now, out of the kiln comes wonderfully organic pitchers, cups and teapots, nothing plum, just flowing and wavy and soil colored and close of heart. Open daily year-round 10am–5pm. (828) 688-1332. www.pinerootpottery.com

Return to Hwy 226, turn back L and travel 8.5 mi. back toward Bakersville. Studio is on R.

Cadell Studio 2702 HWY 226 N – Melissa Cadell's figurative work, in low-fire earthenware,

Melissa Cadell's heartfelt figures.

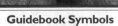

Guidebook Symbols

Craft Studio   Restaurant
Craft Gallery   Lodging
Historic Site   Special Attraction

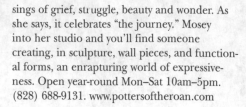

A gleeful assemblage at Ron Slagle's.

sings of grief, struggle, beauty and wonder. As she says, it celebrates "the journey." Mosey into her studio and you'll find someone creating, in sculpture, wall pieces, and functional forms, an enrapturing world of expressiveness. Open year-round Mon–Sat 10am–5pm. (828) 688-9131. www.pottersoftheroan.com

Continue traveling on Hwy 226 toward Bakersville for about a mile and Slagle's Gallery is on L.

33 Slagle Studio and Gallery 2052 HWY 226N – Step into Ron Slagle's gallery, take a good look around (there is plenty to see) and experience a mixture of woodfired sculptural pieces and utilitarian work guaranteed to tickle your fancy. (And what are those characters outside?) Open daily year-round 10am–5pm. (828) 688-4204. www.slaglestudio.com

Turn R back on Hwy 226. Travel .5 mi and turn L on Hwy 80/226A.

HWY 80 N. BACK TO HWY 19E

From intersection of Hwy 80/226A and Hwy 226, travel .3 mi on Hwy 80/226A. Sedberry's Clay Studio is on R at end of drive.

In Ken Sedberry's wonderous world.

34 Sedberry Pottery 344 NC 80 – Woodfired stoneware and handbuilt terra cotta, swimming with rich and colorful imagery of seas and forests. From trips to Central America, Ken has gathered in a palette of greens and teals, crimson and citrus, and brings it to his own distinctive version of flora and fauna. Be respectful of the seahorses who insist on having their own space. Open daily year-round 10am–6pm. (828) 688-3386. www.sedberrypottery.com

Turn R out of Sedberry's drive on Hwy 80. After 1.7 mi, Hwy 80 splits to R. Take Hwy 80 for 5.3 mi and Gallery is on L.

The serene view at Laurel Oaks.

35 Mountain Hill Country Gallery 7159 HWY 80 – With a view like this, it would be hard not to be inspired to pick up a brush. Nice folks.

The Road Goes On Forever

Side trips, tidbits, adventures, and treasure hunts

Open year-round Wed–Sun 12noon–sunset.
(828)688-1030.

Turn L on Hwy 80. Laurel Oaks Farm is .3 mi on R.

36 Laurel Oaks Farm 7334 HWY 80 – On this
picturesque working sheep farm, you can stay in
a cozy chalet or large log cabin. With advance
notice, Yvonne Bessin will gladly demonstrate
wool-spinning for you or you can purchase wool
blankets woven by the Pendleton Wool Company
from the Bessin's wool. Open year-round
Mon–Sat 10am–3pm & Sun 1pm–3pm weather
permitting. (828)688-2652.

*Turn R on Hwy 80 and travel 3 mi to Yancey Mitchell Solid
Waste Transfer Station Rd. Turn R and travel .4 mi to end of
road. EnergyXchange Gallery and Studios are at end of road on L.*

37 EnergyXchange YANCEY MITCHELL SOLID
WASTE TRANSFER STATION RD – One of the
craft industry's most innovative energy-recovery
projects in which gases from decomposing trash
are drawn from a six-acre landfill to power ovens
for glass blowers and kilns for pottery makers,
saving about a million dollars in energy costs
over the 12 to 20 years the gas is expected to
last. Just the idea of it is worth the visit, not to
mention the opportunity to witness resident
artists working their craft. You're welcome to
roam about and to enjoy the lovely result of all
this ingenuity at an on-site gallery. (See sidebar.)
(828)675-5541. www.energyxchange.org

*EnergyXchange:
Successful experiments
In recycled energy and
fresh craft.*

Return to Hwy 80 and turn R. Travel 2.2 mi to intersection with Hwy 19E. To continue on main trail, turn R and travel 6.7 mi into Burnsville.

Sharpless Pottery Side Trip

To take side trip, turn L and travel about 2 mi. Turn R on Crabtree Creek Rd. Travel 5 mi and turn R on Chestnut Mountain Rd. Pottery is 1 mi on R.

 Sharpless Pottery and Shepherd's Ridge Guest House 1280 CHESTNUT MOUNTAIN RD – An idyllic spot to peruse Linda Sharpless' enthusiastic outpouring of functional stoneware. Whites, blues, browns – they all abound in her mugs and dinnerware. You can also treat yourself to a night at her guest house. Open year-round Mon–Sat 10am–5pm & Sun 12noon–5pm. (828)765-7809.

Return to Hwy 19E and turn L, heading W toward Burnsville, approximately 8 mi.

BURNSVILLE

Follow your imagination at The Design Gallery.

At intersection of Hwy 19E and S. Main, turn R (traveling from Penland area) on S. Main. The Design Gallery is on R and the next 9 sites are on the town square or on W. Main, just off the square.

(39) **The Design Gallery** 7 S MAIN ST – A place of enthusiasms that will have you drifting around from one thing to another in no time – paintings, pottery, hand-carved furniture, Arts and Crafts light fixtures, photography – a collection of high energy and good taste. Open year-round Mon–Sat 10am–5pm. (828)678-9869.

The Garden Deli, under a weeping willow.

|40| **The Garden Deli** 107 TOWN SQUARE – An enormous willow tree offers shade and atmosphere while you enjoy a salad, sandwich or bowl of freshly-made soup. Indoor seating provides a birds-eye view of local landscapes painted by Burnsville area artists. Open year-round Mon–Sat 11am–2pm. (828)682-3946.

(41) **The Country Peddler** 3 TOWN SQUARE – Custom-made quilts and supplies with a few

The Road Goes On Forever

Side trips, tidbits, adventures, and treasure hunts

quilted characters hanging about. Open year-round Mon–Fri 9am–5pm & Sat 9am–3pm. (828)682-7810.

Intricate designs at Archer Glass.

|🖐| Halo's Gallery and Café
8 W MAIN ST – A great café and gallery setting for enjoying the wealth of craft found in this town. (828) 682-9559.

43 Museum of Yancey County History 11 ACADEMY ST – Look up behind the Yancey County Visitors Center and you'll see the Museum and the path you'll take to get there. Open Apr Fri & Sat 10am–4pm. May–Sep Wed–Sat 10am–4pm. Oct Fri & Sat 10am–4pm. (828)682-3671.

44 Needle-Me-This 112 W MAIN ST – A nice selection of quilting fabrics and supplies. Carol makes good use of some of them in her wearable art. Open year-round Mon–Fri 9:30am–5pm & Sat 9:30am–3pm. (828)682-9462.

You'll have to listen well.

45 Archer Glass 116 WALNUT ST – Look up from Needle-Me-This and take the stairs from street level. Stained glass creations of ethereal beauty await you. Sylvia Archer is the muse here. Open year-round Mon–Sat 10am–5pm. (828)682-3403.

120 West Main Street
Silent Poetry
Art Expressions of the Mountains

46 Silent Poetry Gallery 120 W MAIN ST – Joe Peek has created a stimulating environment of contemporary work, drawing the support of local artisans and the patronage of regional collectors. Worthy of at least 10 "ah-hah's." Open Jan–Mar Fri & Sat 10am–5pm. Apr–Dec Mon–Thur 10am–5pm. Fri 10am–6pm. Sat 10am–5pm. (828)682-7998.

Making hand-made papers at DK Puttyroot.

47 DK Puttyroot 132 W MAIN ST – Sisters Dana and Karen have named their place after an Appalachian orchid and, indeed, it has all the delicate charms. They make their own hand-

Guidebook Symbols

🖐 **1** Craft Studio	**|1|** Restaurant		
(1) Craft Gallery	**A** Lodging		
1 Historic Site	**★** Special Attraction		

made papers, using corn and tobacco and teas for shadings. They carry all kinds of papers, handmade books and writing materials in a shop chambered with rooms for sippin' tea, munchin' dainties, and just relaxin'. Open Mar–Dec Mon–Sat 10am–5pm. Jan–Feb Wed–Sat 10am–5pm. (828)678-9588.

(48) UpStart Art 115 W MAIN ST – Tucked back in a side alley, this small gallery lives up to its name. Glass, pottery, paintings, jewelry—all representative of local emerging artists known for their fresh approaches to craft. Open Jan–Apr Thu–Sat 10am–5pm. May–Dec 24 Mon Tue & Thu–Sat 10am–5pm. (828)678-9663.

Travel down W Main St. one block from DK Puttyroot and turn R on Swiss Way. Turn L at next street, Shepherd's Way. Lace Toadstool Pottery is on L as Shepherd's Way makes immediate sharp turn to R.

Mary Whitesides' UpStart Art.

 The Lace Toadstool Studio 101 SHEPHERD'S WAY – Joy Bennett handbuilds her pottery and then imprints designs on it using antique doilies, dresser scarves and bits of lace handed down from her grandmother and mother as well as leaves, ferns and such from mother nature. Open year-round Mon–Sat 10am–5pm, but do call ahead. (828) 682-2919. www.thelacetoadstool.com

Namesakes at the Lace Toad Stool Studio.

Continue on Shepherd's Way. Julia Mann's Studio is up the hill on R.

 Julia Mann Studio 126 SHEPHERD'S WAY – Another talented graduate of the WCU and Haywood Community College craft programs. Julia has created her dream studio here in

The Road Goes On Forever

Side trips, tidbits, adventures, and treasure hunts

Burnsville where she creates her own glazes and a full-line of functional pottery. Open Tues–Wed 10am–5pm (828)682-6459.

Return to Hwy 19E.

Burnsville B&B's

 Wray House B&B 2 S MAIN ST – This 1902 Federal-style B&B features a Charleston-style, cloistered courtyard garden, complete with vintage fruit trees, grape arbors and roses. Full southern breakfasts. gourmet dinners and afternoon tea in the garden by reservations only. (828)682-0445. www.wrayhouse.com

 Terrell House B&B 109 ROBERTSON ST – A colonial-style inn which was once a dormitory for school girls but is now a luxurious garden sanctuary. Breakfast with crystal and china. (828)682-4505.

Waiting to be fired at Julia Mann's Studio.

Squash to showpiece at Dyan's.

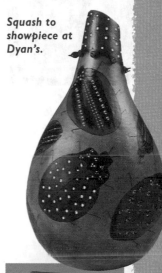

WEST OF BURNSVILLE

From intersection of S. Main St and Hwy 19E, travel W (toward Asheville) on Hwy 19E for 4.7 mi. Turn L on Prices Creek Rd, travel .4 mi and take first R (Horton Creek Rd but there is no sign.) Travel 2.9 mi and turn R on Penland Branch Rd (first R after old general store building.) Take first driveway on R. Log home and studio can be seen from road. Next two sites are at this location.

 Gourds by Dyan 1125 PENLAND BRANCH RD – In the hands of Dyan Mai Peterson, the gourd, a demure relative of the squash, becomes a three-dimensional canvas of timeless beauty. Her deep colorations and stylized markings somehow tie us to life on earth before time was measured in nanoseconds and sound bites. Open year-round Tue–Sat 10am–5pm. (828)678-3451.

 Gary Peterson Woodworking 1125 PENLAND BRANCH RD – Gary Peterson crafts classic mission furniture with a contemporary flair. All his work is solid wood with a decided preference for quarter sawn white oak. You'll want to start your collection here. Open year-round Tue–Sat 10am–5pm. (828)678-3451.

Dressing stand by Gary Peterson.

Two forms of expression: Alice and David Wiley.

Return to Hwy 19E and turn R, travel 1.7 mi and turn L on Jacks Creek Rd. Travel 3 mi and turn L on Coxes Creek Rd. Travel 3.5 mi and turn L into drive for next two sites.

 Alice Wiley Textile Arts Studio 3829 COXES CREEK RD – An intriguing studio. You'll wonder if you fell through Alice's magic hole as you witness the transformation here. Alice paints fabrics to replicate missing vintage quilt pieces. You will also enjoy her own quilted masterpieces. Open year-round Tue–Fri 9am–5pm & Sat 8am–12noon. (828)682-6854.

 Wiley's Ornamental Metals 3829 COXES CREEK RD – David Wiley creates ornamental metalwork. He cuts, forges and assembles his designs in the studio he built for himself on Coxes Creek. The results speak for themselves. Open Tue–Fri 9am–5pm & Sat 8am–12noon. (828)682-9494.

Return to Hwy 19E, turn L and travel 3.5 mi back to Burnsville.

PENSACOLA LOOP

In Burnsville, at intersection of Hwy 19E and Hwy 197S (Pensacola Rd), turn R. Travel .7 mi and turn L on Bolen Creek Rd. Travel about 1 mi. and turn L into drive. Follow sign to gallery at end of drive.

 McFarling Pottery 39 PISGAH MINE RD – In a picturesque cove a little outside Burnsville, Linda McFarling sits at her wheel producing startlingly beautiful pots. Her new gallery beside the studio is a welcome spot to spend time admiring her latest work. Open daily year-round Mon–Sun 10am–5pm. (828)682-7565.

Return to Pensacola Rd and turn L. Travel about 13 mi and turn L into Elk Fork Studios' drive at sign. Drive up to parking area.

 Elk Fork Studios 12447 NC 197S – How many Zen elements can you find here? Waterfalls on the Elk Fork Creek, forests cascading down the mountainside, antique log cabins converted into the home and studio space of Tim Clark and Linda MacMichael— that's just for starters! Linda and Tim work

The Road Goes On Forever
Side trips, tidbits, adventures, and treasure hunts

together to craft Bagettes, small decorative purses, artfully designed and painstakingly executed, complete with custom braided straps using the Japanese technique, Kumihimo. Open year-round daily 10am–4pm. Good idea to call ahead. (828)678-9364.

Return to Hwy 19E in Burnsville.

OFF HWY 19E AND HWY 80

Micaville/Celo/Toe River Area

From intersection of Hwy 197S and Hwy 19E in Burnsville, turn R going E on Hwy 19E and travel 4.5 mi. Turn R on Cane Branch Rd and travel 1.5 mi. Studio is on L.

 Pond Branch Pottery CANE BRANCH RD – Michael Rutkowsky's spiraled bowls and platters evoke the mountains and the hues of forest floors. Trails of clay slip, like seeps of streams, embellish high-fired stoneware. You know you are at the right place when you see the graceful marks of a potter as details on the exterior of his new studio. Open daily year-round 10am–5pm or by appointment. (800)818-6004. www.pondbranch.com

Michael Rutkowsky graceful works at Pond Branch Pottery.

Return to Hwy 19E and turn R. Travel .1 mi to junction with Hwy 80 and bear R. Travel 2.5 mi, bearing R as Hwy 80 turns R, and turn R on Hickory Springs Rd. Travel about .5 mi and turn L after the factory. Studio is first building on L past factory.

 Okra Pottery 25 BLUE BONNET LANE – An old mushroom factory now houses Michael Kline's pottery. Wood-fired, salt-glazed pottery, especially pitchers and tureens, wonderfully-batik-looking with the impress of plant and forest forms. All of which is to say it is a blessing Michael decided to stay in these mountains after coming to Penland as a resident artist. Daily 11am–5pm. (828) 675-4097.

A well handled piece at McFarling Pottery.

Return to Hwy 80 and turn R. Travel 2.5 mi and The Candlelight is on L.

(59) **The Candlelight** 3155 HWY 80 – Especially nice stained glass, from sun-catchers to custom windows. Open daily June–Oct 9am–5pm. (828)675-4189.

An Elk Fork Studios "Bagette".

Guidebook Symbols

 Craft Studio   Restaurant

 Craft Gallery   Lodging

 Historic Site   Special Attraction

Jeffery Lynn Standen at her Rosebay Studio.

On the shelves at McWhirter Pottery.

Faces of Bernstein Glass.

Continue traveling S on Hwy 80 for .8 mi. Rosebay Studio and Gallery is on L.

⟨60⟩ Rosebay Studio and Gallery 51 ROSEBAY LANE – Tucked in the rhododendrons, Jefferie Lynn Standen works in her studio producing functional pots as she has since coming to these mountains. She also offers a select collection of glass, wearable art, wood, candles and other local potters' work. Open May–Nov Sat 12noon–5pm & Sun 1pm–5pm. (828) 675-0505.

Turn L on Hwy 80 and travel .5 mi. McWhirter Pottery is on R

✋61 McWhirter Pottery 4088 HWY 80S – In a family-operated studio centered on simple, decorative, cherished designs, Pete McWhirter focuses on his art and life's good things. Open year-round Mon–Sat 10am–5pm. (828) 675-4559.

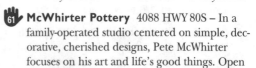

Continue traveling S on Hwy 80 for another .9 mi and turn R into Gallery parking area.

⟨62⟩ Toe River Crafts 4590 HWY 80S – Crafts of the renowned Toe River artisans' community. From the fresh and whimsical to the traditional and contemporary, the sheer number of items will amaze you. A cooperative venture managed by its members in a very personal way. A restorative stop. Open May, Sep & Dec Fri–Sat 10am–5pm & Sun 12noon–5pm. June–Aug & Oct Mon–Sat 10am–5pm & Sun 12noon–5pm. (828) 675-4998.

Continue S on Hwy 80 for .1 mi. Turn R on White Oak Creek Rd and Studio is on R.

The Road Goes On Forever
Side trips, tidbits, adventures, and treasure hunts

If you want to get rich quick then start digging. A mother lode of gems have been found in Mitchell Co., among them emeralds, rubies, gold and diamonds. See them all at the Museum of North Carolina Minerals, B.R.P. milepost 331 (828) 765-2761

Bernstein Glass WHITE OAK CREEK RD –
Colorful, urbane, and vibrant face sketches and
swashy figures on goblets, vessels, and bowls in a
small free-standing studio stoked with energy. A
talented trio of glass blowers work here—Billy,
Katie and Alex Bernstein. Open year-round
Tue–Fri 9:30am–1:30pm. (828)675-9748.

*Return to Hwy 80 and turn L. Travel .2 mi to Seven Mile Ridge
Rd. Turn R. Inn is immediately to L.*

 Celo Inn 45 SEVEN MILE RIDGE RD
– Within walking distance of several
studios. A charming timber-frame
inn in harmony with its surroundings.
Bountiful gardens and the
boulder-strewn Toe River add to the
delight. Open mid-Mar–Dec.
Reservations are required. (828)675-5132.

*Continue on Seven Mile Ridge Rd and immediately after crossing
river bridge, bear L and then make immediate R up drive past Celo
Health Center. Follow signs to Pot Hole Studio.*

**At the Pot Hole, brush-
stroked pottery, plus a
trail valet.**

 The Pot Hole 390 SEVEN MILE RIDGE RD –
Pottery for the kitchen, table and bath, graced
with Danielle LeHardy's swirling brushstrokes,
spare and lovely–flowered saucers, platters and
teapots with puckered snouts. A freestanding
studio in the laurel. Should you decide to hike
a nearby trail, Danielle will watch over your
animals while you're out there. Open daily year-
round 10am–5pm. (828)675-5217.

*Return to Seven Mile Ridge Rd and turn R. Travel .3 mi and bear
L on Halls Chapel Rd. Travel about 1.5 mi and turn L into
Pieper's drive. Studio is in green building at bottom of drive.*

**Ken Pieper's
glass work
as seen at
Twisted
Laurel.**

 Pieper Glass 1449 HALLS CHAPEL RD – Red
and gold can be temperamental in glass. You
wouldn't know that, however, when you look at
what Ken Pieper's doing in collections like
"Autumn Primavera." His work in goblets, vessels
and ornaments—exuberant, informed by
Venetian glass techniques–is nothing short of a
visual party. Open year-round Mon–Fri
9am–5pm, but best to call ahead. (828)675-1113.

Guidebook Symbols

	Craft Studio		Restaurant
	Craft Gallery		Lodging
	Historic Site		Special Attraction

Turn R back on Halls Chapel Rd and return to Seven Mile Ridge Rd and turn L. Travel .3 mi and turn L on Hickory Hill Rd. Travel .4 mi to studio on L (blue house.)

Some of the colorful examples of Tzadi Tiles.

 Tzadi Tiles 305 HICKORY HILL RD – Tzadi Turrou's handmade tiles are spellbinding. Her designs and glazes come to life with timeless appeal. She specializes in the Arts and Crafts style, both for home and gifts. Open year-round Wed–Fri 10am–4pm. Other days by appointment only. (828)675-5592.

Return to Seven Mile Ridge Rd and turn L. Travel .2 mi and turn R on gravel road. Gallery is .4 mi at end of road.

 Grover's Pots & Rocks 3640 SEVEN MILE RIDGE RD – Up on the crest of this ridge, discover Mary Foley's raku pottery and Bill Grover's minerals. Rustic gallery on a crest with views to the east and west. Open May–Oct Mon–Sat 10am–7pm. (828)675-9633.

Return to Seven Mile Ridge, turn L, and return to Hwy 80S. Turn L to head S on Hwy 80 and travel 6 mi to the Blue Ridge Parkway. Next two sites are about 4 mi past the Blue Ridge Parkway on Hwy 80S toward Marion.

 Buck Creek Bowls 8117 BUCK CREEK RD – Wood vessels, deftly made from native trees by Darrell Rhudy. Demonstrations and instruction. Open daily June–Sep 9am–5pm. (828)724-9048 (day) and (828)724-9047 (evening).

Just Wood Custom Millwork 7825 BUCK CREEK RD – Barry Tribble's working shop and gallery where you can see samples of his work from sleek and contemporary to faux-finished traditional. Open year round Mon–Fri 10am–4pm & Sat 10am–3pm. (828)724-9873. http://mcdowell.main.nc.us/btribble

Now your choice is to head on down Hwy 80 into Marion and the Farm to Maket Trail or return to Parkway and enjoy the view!

The Road Goes On Forever

Side trips, tidbits, adventures, and treasure hunts

Recovered methane turns into fuel for glass blowing at EnergyXchange.

Penland School

Hallowed Ground and New Frontier

Penland fulfills three criteria for being a wonderful place to learn. First, it is isolated, cloistered from the distractions of the everyday world. Secondly, personal needs, like food and lodging, are provided. And, finally, it is a place that encourages the deepest and most intimate expressions of the heart.

It might not be the way Miss Lucy Morgan would have described the school she founded in 1929. But there is little doubt she would approve of what has transpired since she first brought together mountain women to rekindle the art of hand-weaving in a modest cabin, a gathering place constructed by mountain neighbors with logs signed and donated as individual gifts.

The Penland of today is a place where you can immerse yourself so deeply in craft that time becomes practically immaterial. The studio doors stay open day and night. Professionals and beginners, teenagers and octa-generians, sit side-by-side in classrooms. Secrets are freely shared. Perhaps the only competition you'll encounter is over the last dish of cobbler at dinner.

Top: Basketmaking at Penland in the late 1920s. Bottom: Working on the Craft House – a large log structure still in use today built by neighbors with donated logs.

Miss Lucy Morgan and Howard C. Ford with the cabin that was taken to the 1932 Words Fair in Chicago.

The credit for this celebratory, open, affirming atmosphere circles back to Bill Brown, who was Miss Lucy's hand-picked choice for director when she retired in 1962. Brown expanded the curriculum and broadened its scope, turning the school into an international destination. Among students from Bolivia, Japan, and Germany, the most likely common language is craft.

Bill Brown also made Penland a destination for instructors. He used a very simple formula – teach what you like, bring your families, and take advantage of instruction for yourself, inside or outside your own discipline.

These days, offerings span a diverse range of classes, from neon to functional teapots.

A potter loading a kiln in the 30s.

There are eight different core areas: textiles, ceramics, glass, metals, wood, photography, printmaking, and books, with many classes making connections between media. In glass, for example, the works of Penland graduates appear in galleries in London, Zurich, Tokyo, and Milan. But in all these media, the name Penland gives off its own special aura—the kinship of a place and a time where the imaginings of the heart are transformed into something you can touch.

farm To Market

The craft of this loop trail is the craft of southern towns, courthouse squares, and the circular seasons of the farm. 🌷 You won't find heavy concentrations of craftspeople–potters or glassmakers, for example–but you will find a merging and mingling of many works of hand across a rumpled landscape of orchards and cotton fields. 🌷 It's a handwork of straw wreaths and paper angels, bird houses and apple butter. Kudzu jelly and fig preserves. Apples, pumpkins, and walnuts. And things you take home, but never buy. Like the pitch of a Victorian farmhouse roof. Or a mainstreet overhung with magnolias. Orchards that crowd against the back of country stores. Farmer's markets, and courthouses with silvery domes. 🌷 Motoring along the base of this trail, you'll drift into a belt of warmer air–a zone where warm air tends to pool up, tempering the seasons, making them more reminiscent of the Deep South than the high mountains. This delightful phenomenon makes it possible to grow cotton and peaches and

What do you call a family of pumpkins?
(We think it's a "grin".)

A Slow Dance Up Main

to encounter courthouse lawns full of blooms when you wouldn't expect to see them.  Valdese is a short hop from the art-conscious, beautifully restored town of Morganton, and both places are well worth a visit. There is enough history between Valdese's bocci courts and stone schoolhouse to fill a travel journal. Small towns are the way of this loop tour: the mountain gateways of Old Fort and Marion; the traditional farm-to-market hubs of Shelby, Forest City and Rutherfordton. In Forest City, you'll drive down a main street divided by a kind of linear park. Small shops, eateries and mercantiles open their doors to the street along both sides, reminiscent of, well, pick a decade. Between towns, the highway skims along by farms and homesteads and through wide places and crossroads that might attract a store or two or, in season, a fruit-stand ripe with color. We advise you to adjust to the proper rhythm: you'll need to slow dance your way along this trail.

farm To Market

Parkway

80

Guidebook Symbols

- Craft Studio
- Craft Gallery
- Historic Site
- Restaurant
- Lodging
- Special Attraction

N

Black Mountain

40

27

A
B

D

30

28

Marion

29

Old Fort

221

To Asheville

74A

221

Hendersonville

Chimney Rock

74A

Rutherfordton

26

22 C

24 25

26

Tryon

Linville
Falls

Lenoir

Valdese

70

40

Morganton

64

18

indale

21

74B

Shelby

Forest
City

221

15

20

19

16

18

17

The Farm-To-Market tour sorts itself out from the others simply on the merits of its shape, terrain and climate. The route dips well into low country topography on its bottom side while climbing into mountains at its northern edge; and it straddles two distinct climate zones–one which is friendly to cotton, the other to northern hemlock.

Farm-To-Market is easily accessble from east or west via I-40, which bisects the upper half of the loop. The two distinct halves each constitute a comfortable weekend excursion of 75 miles or so. The upper tour is characterized by the hill towns of Old Fort, Marion, Morganton and Valdese. The lower tour evokes memories of the Deep South, expressed by Shelby, Forest City and Rutherfordton.

MARION

From I-40 or Hwy 70, follow Hwy 221 into downtown Marion. Both sites in Marion are just off Main St/Hwy 221 in downtown Marion.

It's a Matter of Taste.

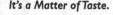

|❶| A Matter of Taste Café 64 HILLCREST DR – A beautifully restored, turn-of-the-century mansion with expansive porches and well-presented lunches. The building is listed on the National Register. Open year-round for lunch Mon–Fri 11am–3pm and dinner by reservation only. (828)659-1157.

Ⓐ Shamrock Inn 28 W HENDERSON ST – Oversized rooms and a downtown location add to the Irish-style hospitality which characterizes this comfortable place. (828)652-5773. www.home.wnclink.com/shamrock

If you're lucky, you'll stay at the Shamrock Inn.

Ⓑ The Cottages at Spring House Farm 219 HAYNES RD – The restored 1826 historic house of Albertus Ledbetter, a Scottish immigrant, sits amidst 92 pristine acres of woodlands, walking trails, creeks and streams. Arthur and Zee Campbell added four unique and private cabins on the property where you can rediscover nature and reconnect with yourself by way of hot tub or trail walk. Listed on the National Register of Historic Places, this eco-retreat is open year–round to guests of the B&B. For tour only call ahead for appointment. (828)738-9798. www.springhousefarm.com

The Road Goes On Forever

Side trips, tidbits, adventures, and treasure hunts

From intersection of Hwy 221/Main St and Hwy 70/126 at McDowell County Courthouse on Main St in Marion, turn E on Hwy 70 and travel 20.5 mi to Morganton.

MORGANTON

Traveling from Marion on Hwy 70 into Morganton, turn L at 1st traffic light on Greenlee Ford Rd. Restaurant is at end of road by river.

|2| **Judge's Riverside Restaurant** GREENLEE FORD RD – A rambling smokehouse barbeque place where you can sit inside and enjoy the view or outside under spreading walnut trees on a deck above the river. In either case, you can basically pig out. Open daily year-round 11am–10pm. (828)433-5798.

In Morganton, art over-hanging a city alleyway.

Return to Hwy 70 (W. Union St.). Union St and turn L toward downtown Morganton. Turn R on Burkemont Ave/Bus 64 (3rd traffic light traveling in to Morganton) and travel .6 mi to Greenbriar Ln. Turn R on Greenbriar and R again on Forest Hill. Fouth Creek Folk Art Studio is 1st drive on L.

AN AMERICAN TREASURE
The Carson House, just west of Marion on US Highway 70, embodies a sweep of American history beginning as a log cabin in 1790. An Irish immigrant, Colonel John Carson, first lived at the house, shortly after he joined other North Carolina delegates in ratifying the Constitution. His son Samuel, a U.S. congressman, shot and killed a political adversary, then he headed off to a frontier called Texas with friends Davy Crockett and Sam Houston. Andrew Jackson once lost money at Carson House when he gambled on a horse race. Later on, Union soldiers tried to torch the place. It now stands as a museum, and invites wonderment, if for no other reason, because of its incredible staying power. Open year-round Tue–Sat 10am–5pm & Sun 2pm–5pm. (828)724-4948.

Guidebook Symbols

Craft Studio		2	Restaurant
(1) Craft Gallery	A Lodging
1 Historic Site	Special Attraction

3 Fourth Creek Folk Art Studio 308 FOREST HILL – Yes, Don Stevenson wanted to build bird houses. But why do something, well, usual? Why not hand build bird houses that are replicas of historical wooden buildings in Western North Carolina? For example, a Carolina Wren nesting house under Mr. Stevenson's hand becomes a scale model of a Mordecai Plantation herb garden tool house. One of his birdfeeder roofs requires 3,500 shingles individually snuggled into place. Open Aug–June Tue–Thu 9am–5pm. (828) 433-6118.

Return to Hwy 70/W Union St and turn R. Travel 1 mi and W Union St becomes Meeting St in downtown Morganton. Park near the corner of Meeting and Sterling Sts to walk to next 3 sites.

4 Jailhouse Gallery 115 E. MEETING ST – Once a home for criminals, now the home of the Burke County Arts Council. Each month the staff hangs art shows, not to be confused with people. And, in a small gift shop, visitors can shoplift pottery, blown-glass ornaments, shawls, and other fine things as long as they pay before leaving. Otherwise, it's jail. Open year-round Tue–Fri 9am–4pm. (828) 433-7282. www.burkearts.org

Don Stevenson preserves history via birdfeeder.

5 Old Burke County Courthouse TOWN SQUARE – Handsomely restored building finished in 1837. The Supreme Court of North Carolina met here from 1847 to 1852. Revolving historical exhibits take place in the Heritage Museum on the ground floor. Open year-round Tue–Fri 10am–4pm. (828) 437-4104.

Discovered wonder at Signature/Studio XI.

6 Signature/Studio XI 117 W UNION ST – The paintings and compositions of this group of developmentally disabled artists are so energetic and spirit-filled, they can make your heart jump. The work flows out of a program in which these gifted artists' grow in self-esteem through self-expression—not to mention

The Road Goes On Forever
Side trips, tidbits, adventures, and treasure hunts

what they bring into the world, an outpouring of spontaneous wonder. The work of the group's visual artists could just as easily be exhibited in galleries in Manhattan—and sometimes is. This small universe built on love and encouragement is a miracle that keeps unfolding. Open year-round Mon–Fri 9am–4pm. (828)433-0056.

Return to your car. Turn R on Sterling St off of Meeting St and follow Sterling St to Enola Rd. Turn R on Enola Rd and the Western Carolina Center is on R just after crossing over I-40. South Mountain Crafts is on campus of WCC.

7 South Mountain Crafts 300 ENOLA RD – A collection of cottages where handicapped residents of Western Carolina Center make frontier furniture and craft pieces. The only NC teaching facility of its kind where handcrafted objects are clearly the focus. Your purchase will help ensure the program's future. Open year-round Mon–Fri 10am–4pm. (828)438-6464.

If you want to see more of Mangum's pottery, stop by Jacob's Fork Gallery, just off the trail at 4912 Hwy 127 S in Hickory. (704) 462-1877.

Return to Sterling St. To travel to Valdese, see directions under Valdese Side Trip. To travel on to Shelby, turn R on Sterling St/Hwy 18 and travel approximately 30 mi.

8 Apple Hill Orchard and Cider Mill 5205 APPLETREE LANE – Here on the edge of the high mountains, apple picking is the harbinger of cool weather and sweet cider. But there is a definite picking order according to variety. The schedule, which runs from early-August to October, is: Gala, Golden Delicious, Jonagold, Stayman, Winesap, Red Rome, Red Fuji, Braeburn, Granny Smith. To enjoy the fruits of the labor, including the yummy jams, jellies, apple butters, and ciders, stop on by. Open Sep–Oct Mon–Sat 9:30am–6pm. Nov–Dec 25 Mon–Fri 10am–4pm & Sat 9am–5pm. (828)437-1224.

Guidebook Symbols

Craft Studio | Restaurant
Craft Gallery | Lodging
Historic Site | Special Attraction

VALDESE

To travel to Valdese from Morganton, travel east on Hwy 70 for 7 mi. Follow the signs to Main St for all the Valdese sites.

9 Waldensian Church 109 E MAIN ST – The church was originally built of fieldstone and true grit. Each year, the Waldensians celebrate the end of three centuries of persecution with a service honoring the 1848 Edict of Emancipation issued by King Alberto of Italy. Visitors are welcome. Open year-round Mon–Fri 9am–5pm. (828)874-2531.

10 Waldensian Heritage Museum RODORET ST – A museum that's really a journey of the families and each generation that is a part of the historical mosaic of Valdese. Memorabilia from both the Italian and the American experiences: Waldensian dress and linens, references to the trip over—from the steamships to the carried traditions—and the story of this community since 1893. Open Apr–Oct Sun 3pm–5pm. Or ask at the church office any day of the week and a docent will open the door for you.

11 Valdese Public Library JUST OFF MAIN ST – Inside this building, large stained glass works depict the traditional dress of the Waldensians and the fruits of their New World labor.

12 Old Rock School MAIN ST – Classic turn-of-the-century rock schoolhouse built of fieldstone cleared from farmland. The building boasts a renovated auditorium, art exhibits and a surprisingly large, and detailed miniature train system that depicts the trip to Asheville and west. The Community Affairs Office is located in the building. (828)879-2129.

13 Villar Vintners of Valdese ON VILLAR LANE, JUST OFF N LAUREL ST – It's the only place in North Carolina where the production of wine was legal during prohibition. Open year-round for tours and tasting Thu–Sat 10am–6pm & Sun 1pm–6pm. (828)879-3202.

A Waldensian place of worship.

Join Joe Dalmas for a taste of wines made in the hills of WNC.

The Road Goes On Forever

Side trips, tidbits, adventures, and treasure hunts

In 1893, a group of 29 Northern Italians arrived in western North Carolina in search of a home in America. The town of Valdese, with its streets named for early families—Praly, Rodoret, Colombo, Ribet— is a testament to their enterprise and faith.

Old Colony Players Amphitheater
CHURCH ST – Site of the historical Waldensian
Drama "From This Day Forward." First and
second weekends in August. For ticket
information, (828)874-0176.

*To return to Morganton, retrace your route on Hwy 70 back W. To
continue on to Shelby, after returning to Morganton on Hwy 70W,
travel about 1 mi into Morganton and turn L going S on Hwy 18.
Travel about 30 mi into Shelby.*

SHELBY

*Traveling about 30 mi S from Morganton into Shelby on Hwy 18,
turn R on Wallace Grove Rd (next to livestock restaurant.) Travel
.4 mi and turn R into drive. Studio at end of drive on R.*

 **Philbecks' Studios: Ron
Philbeck Pottery and
Jewelry for the Journey**
757 WALLACE GROVE RD –
Two artists working in two
separate studios, both
creating work of charm and
great character. Ron's pots,
plates and bowls, in the colors
of river clays and sands, are
pieces you'll want to leave out in clear view.
Sarah's pendants and necklaces and rings,
simple in arrangement, elegant in design,
are journeys of delight in and of themselves.
Open daily year-round by appointment.
(704)480-6046. www.philbeckstudios.com

*Elegantly crafted work
from Philbecks' Studios.*

*Return to Hwy 18 and turn R. Travel about 4.5 mi into Shelby.
Turn L on Lafayette and travel .3 mi. Gallery is on R.*

 B.J. Silver Gallery/Twisted Iron Forge
511 N LAFAYETTE ST – Jean and
Robert Silver's gallery spans a broad spectrum
of work in a small space. From fine jewelry
to ornamental iron tables to watercolors to
imaginative lamps—and you haven't gotten
past half the energetic outpouring of this
talented couple. Open year-round Tue–Fri
10am–5pm. Mon & Sat by appointment
only. (704)484-2620 or (704)487-5345.

Guidebook Symbols

Craft Studio | Restaurant
Craft Gallery | Lodging
Historic Site | Special Attraction

Continue S on LaFollete for .2 mi and park near the town square. Next 2 sites are across street from each other.

HORSES OF DIFFERENT COLORS
The City of Shelby continues to restore a 1919 Herschell-Spillman Carousel that operated in City Park for three decades. You can see one of the carousels' fully restored horses at the Clevland County Historical Museum.

17 Cleveland County Historical Museum THE FORMER COUNTY COURTHOUSE BUILDING AT MARION AND LAFAYETTE STREETS – Classical revival courthouse with a lawn of arching trees. Listed on the National Register with exhibits that position Shelby in world history. Open year-round Tue–Fri 9am–4pm. (704)482-8186.

18 Cleveland County Arts Council 111 S WASHINGTON ST – A former post office turned gallery and shop features the work of local artists—visual arts, sculpture, crafts. The colonial revival building dates from 1916. Open year-round Mon–Fri 9am–5pm. (704)484-2787. www.ccartscouncil.org

Turn R on Hwy 74 heading W. Travel about 10 mi and veer R on Hwy 74 Bus. Travel 2.5 mi and turn R on Campfield Church Rd. Travel .4 mi and turn R into studio's drive. Studio is through arbor path.

ELLENSBORO

19 Custom Stained Glass and Interiors 318 CAMPFIELD CHURCH RD – Behind the arbor entrance to his studio, John Fisher melds fractures, flipits, foundlings, and other such whatchamacallits of stained glass into decorative figures of a joyous nature. His hummingbirds alone will make you stop and hover in mid-space. And he also creates stained glass for church windows. Quite a change from his previous life in the textile world. Open year- round Mon, Wed & Fri 10am–5pm. Tue 10am–4pm. Thu 10am–12noon. Sat 10am–2pm. Sun and evenings by appointment. (828)453-0490. www.fishmanstainedglass.com

An illuminated path at Custom Stained Glass and Interiors.

Return to Hwy 74 Bus and turn R. Travel 4.3 mi to Old Hwy 74 and make sharp veer R as it does. Travel 1.5 mi to Church Rd. Turn R and travel 1.5 mi. Turn R on Main St in Bostic and R again on small street across from Town Hall. Travel .2 mi, bearing R at top of hill. Studio is on L.

The Road Goes On Forever
Side trips, tidbits, adventures, and treasure hunts

If you have an idea of what this is...let them know at the Rutherford County Farm Museum. They have no idea.

BOSTIC

 Rose Tripoli Mueller 149 OLD SUNSHINE RD – In a restored parsonage on the brow of a hill, Rose Mueller expresses her "joys and sorrows, loves and losses" in the artful wood-fired pottery you can see in her gallery. "The clay is my connection," she says, and she's been connecting with lots of folks for a good while in galleries and festivals from Shelby to New York City. Open year-round Thu—Fri 10am–4pm. (828)248-1566.

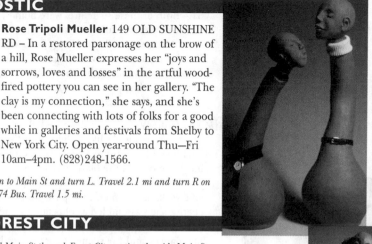

Return to Main St and turn L. Travel 2.1 mi and turn R on Hwy 74 Bus. Travel 1.5 mi.

FOREST CITY

Travel Main St through Forest City, noting the wide Main St. Turn L and then R to get to Museum on Depot St, one block S of Main St.

The pottery of Rose Mueller.

 Rutherford County Farm Museum 240 DEPOT ST – Left-handed plows and livermush paddles. Hair straighteners and wooden refrigerators. Rope beds, homemade radios and molasses skimmers. If you've ever heard a story about a farm, this place will decorate it with implements of a lost time. Open year-round Wed–Sat 9am–4pm. (828)248-1248.

Return to Main St/Hwy 74 Bus, turn L and continue traveling W for 5 mi into Spindale and then another 1.4 mi into Rutherfordton, bearing R as Hwy 221Bus splits off downtown.

You can see Clive's work all over Rutherfordton. Just don't walk into it.

RUTHERFORDTON

Main St in Rutherfordton is also Hwy 221Bus. Park on Main St for the following four sites.

 Main Street Murals MAIN ST – This is the work of Clive Haynes, an artist brought up in England who continues to turn Rutherfordton into something else. You can't miss these wall-sized scenes if you stroll the downtown. Main Street Rutherfordton is listed in the National Register of Historic Places.

Guidebook Symbols

 Craft Studio   Restaurant

 Craft Gallery   Lodging

 Historic Site   Special Attraction

The owners of Legal Grounds Coffee only brew upstanding java.

"It's a Wonderful Life" at The Gallery.

Make sure to stop by MaimyEtta Black Fine Arts Museum and Historical Society at 404 Hardin Road. A collection of Global Black Art and African American artifacts, including those of local families from the Forest City area. The exhibits in the Connected Passages document the vital contributions the African American community made in the development of this region. (704) 248-1525

C **The Carrier Houses** 249 AND 255 N MAIN ST – Both of these structures were built by tinner-carpenter Garland Carrier in the 1800's. Hosts Barbara and Boyce Hodge have lovingly refurbished both National Register homes in the likeness of the original houses: country Victorian with southern charm. (828) 287-4222. www.carrierhouses.com

23 **The Gallery** 181 N MAIN ST – Behind a storefront that looks like a still from "It's a Wonderful Life," there actually is a wonderful life going on—of the blazing, rich, contemporary variety. Judith Padgett makes glass jewelry and works as a framer. In a space crowded with energy, she's assembled a collection of fine pottery, mirrors, other jewelry, photography, fine papers, and the stained glass work of John Fisher. Open Jan–Nov Mon–Fri 9am–5pm. Dec Mon–Thu 9am–5pm. Fri 9am–8pm. Sat 10am–3pm. (828) 287-5647.

24 **Legal Grounds Cafe and Coffee Shop** 217 MAIN ST – Just the place to refresh yourself after hard squinting on the trails. Fresh-brewed coffee, sandwiches, dinner specials, and live entertainment on weekend nights. Open year-round Mon–Wed 7am–11pm. Thu 7am–1am. Fri 7am–12midnight. Sat 8am–12midnight. Sun 12noon–8pm. (828) 286-9955.

Continue up Main St/Hwy 221Bus and turn R on Hwy 64. Turn L on Rock Rd and Airport is about 3 mi.

25 **57 Alpha Café** AT THE RUTHERFORDTON AIRPORT – It's the local pilot's favorite and worth the drive even if you're grounded. Known high and low for its homemade chili, banana pudding, lemonade (made with both limes and lemons), and country ham. Serving lunch only. Open year-round Tue–Sat 10am–3pm. (828) 286-1677.

Return to Hwy 221. Turn R to go N and continue on to Marion and Old Fort. Green River Plantation is L turn on Hwy 221 to Coxe Rd S of Rutherfordton. Turn R on Coxe Rd and travel about 2.7 mi to Plantation.

The Road Goes On Forever

Side trips, tidbits, adventures, and treasure hunts

26 Green River Plantation
6333 COXE RD – Built in
1804 with hand-carved
mantles and bricks brought
from Charleston. Hoofprints
of Union Army horses are
still visible in the heart-pine
floors. Genteel belles tested
the integrity of their
diamonds by scratching
them on a now-200-year-old
glass pane in the front lobby.
The Cantrell family serves
up Southern hospitality and
originality in their tours,
weddings, receptions, meals,
gift shop and B&B service.
The 366-acre plantation
features gardens and trails.
Included in the National Register. Admission fee
for tours. (828) 286-1461. www.green-river.net

*Green River Plantation:
A genteel history
well-maintained.*

*Return to Hwy 221, turn L and travel about 20 mi N to Marion.
In Marion, follow Hwy 221 to intersection with Hwy 70W or turn
W onto I-40W.*

WEST OF MARION

*Traveling from Marion toward Old Fort on Hwy 70, Woody's
Chair Shop is on L in Pleasant Gardens community, about mid way
between Marion and Old Fort.*

27 Max Woody's Chair Shop HWY 70 – Behind
those dusty windows are rows of handcrafted
rocking chairs of the finest quality. Hours irregu-
lar, but with good intentions. (828) 724-4158.

Note on the door.

*Continue traveling W on Hwy 70 for 2.9 mi. Turn L on Greenlee
Rd. Travel 1.2 mi and turn L into drive. Studio is .2 mi up drive.*

28 A Warp in Time 4366 GREENLEE RD – Anne
and David Allison have demonstrated 18th
century-style weaving for 12 years. Watch
them create a variety of period linens on a 19th
century loom. Custom orders welcome. Open
year-round Mon–Fri after 5pm & Sat–Sun
10am–7pm. (828) 668-4885.

Guidebook Symbols

Craft Studio   Restaurant
Craft Gallery   Lodging
Historic Site   Special Attraction

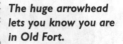

The huge arrowhead lets you know you are in Old Fort.

Continue to travel down Greenlee Rd for 3.1 mi. Turn L on Padgett Rd. Travel about 1 mi, crossing I-40. Pottery is to your R.

OLD FORT

If you are traveling on I-40, take exit 75 and travel S on Padgett Rd for about .5 mi. Pottery is on R.

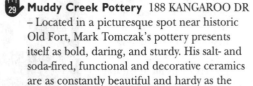

29 Muddy Creek Pottery 188 KANGAROO DR – Located in a picturesque spot near historic Old Fort, Mark Tomczak's pottery presents itself as bold, daring, and sturdy. His salt- and soda-fired, functional and decorative ceramics are as constantly beautiful and hardy as the

At Muddy Creek Pottery.

For a surprising bit of history see the Mountain Gateway Museum.

place he calls home. Open year-round Thu–Sat 10am–5pm. Sun 12noon–5pm. Mon–Wed by appointment only. (828) 668-8084.

Return to Padgett Rd and travel back across I-40. Turn L on Curtis Creek Rd and travel about .6 mi to Hwy 70. Turn L to go W on Hwy 70 and travel into Old Fort. Turn L at Arrowhead Monument. Museum is about one block on the L.

 30 Mountain Gateway Museum 24 WATER ST – This charming historic building houses the life of the early pioneer. With two log cabins from the 1800's on the site of

---

The Road Goes On Forever
Side trips, tidbits, adventures, and treasure hunts

historic Davidson's Fort, the Museum
houses exhibits, programs, living history
demonstrations, picnic area and amphitheater.
Ask about Pioneer Day events. Open year-round
Tue–Sat 9am–5pm. (828)668-9254.

*To travel to Inn on Mill Creek, return to Hwy 70, turn L and then
R on Old Hwy 70. Travel about 2.5 mi and turn R on Mill Creek
Rd at sign. Travel about .7 mi and turn L on gravel road where
Mill Creek continues at intersection with Graphite Rd. Travel 1.5
mi, going under 2nd railroad overpass. Inn is on L.*

**Time for reflections at
The Inn on Mill Creek.**

D **Inn on Mill Creek** 3895 MILL CREEK RD –
Not only is it a tranquil life at Jim and Aline
Carillon's luxurious seven-suite inn, it's the perfect place to rest your head after a day of trail-
riding. Bring along your walking shoes for an
amble in their pick-your-own five-variety apple
orchard. Grapes, peaches, apricots, blueberries,
and blackberries also await trail by taste. Try
your luck at trout-fishing in a one-acre lake,
headwaters of nearby Andrews Geyser.
(877)735-2964 or (828)668-1115.
www.inn-on-mill-creek.com

*Return to Hwy 70 and/or I-40. Asheville and the Mountain City
trail is just to your W. The Mountain City Trail starts in
Swannanoa. The String of Pearls Trail starts in Black Mountain.*

Guidebook Symbols

 Craft Studio	**1** Restaurant	
1 Craft Gallery	**A** Lodging	
1 Historic Site	**1** Special Attraction	

Southern Highland Craft Guild

Born on a Mountaintop

On a snowy winter's day in 1928, 11 members of the Conference of the Southern Mountain Workers gathered in the Weaver's Cabin atop Conley's Ridge at Penland School. Hosted by Miss Lucy Morgan, the group included President William J. Hutchins of Berea College, Dr. Mary Martin Sloop of the Crossnore School, Mrs. John C. Campbell from the John C. Campbell Folk School in Brasstown and "Miss Fuller," representing Francis Goodrich and the Allanstand Cottage Industries in Asheville.

PHOTO COURTESY OF UNC CHAPEL HILL

PHOTO COURTESY OF SOUTHERN HIGHLAND CRAFT GUILD

When they departed two days later, they had made a guild dedicated to the conservation and development of crafts. Of course, the ground work was laid many years earlier by these same trailblazers who, through their impassioned community work, sparked a crafts revival in the mountains of Southern Appalachia.

The Guild got an early, and significant, boost thanks to the contribution by Francis

Top: Allanstand, NC c. 1910, where Allanstand Cottage Industries began with the work of Frances Goodrich. Bottom: The "Weaving Cabin" showed the first exhibition by the "Allanstand Cottage Industries Guild" in 1899.

Goodrich of the Allanstand Shop. She had started Allanstand in a Madison County cabin 40 years earlier to breathe life into the craft of the mountains. By the time she made her gift, Allanstand represented the industry of many craftspeople, some of whom became Guild members.

Today, there are over 700 Guild members representing an astonishing spectrum of textures and techniques. You can get a glimpse of the eclectic outpouring at the Guild's own fairs held at the Asheville Civic Center in July and October or practically any day of the year at the Guild's Folk Art Center on the Blue Ridge Parkway.

Frances Goodrich in 1943 with the "Double Bowknot" coverlet that inspired the handicraft revival work.

The Allanstand Cottage Industries Salesroom at 55 Haywood Street in Asheville in the 1920s.

"Dream Basket" by Aunt Cord Richey, c. 1920.

Mountain Cities

You should know there is something in the air here. 回 How else would you explain such strange and wonderful behavior? 回 A railroad baron's grandson envisions a mountain villa and finds himself, a half-dozen years later, inviting New York friends down for a gathering at his 225-room French chateau. In the adjoining village called "Biltmore," an industry of handcraft flares to life under the care and nurturance of the lady of the chateau. 回 A successful tonic salesman builds a world class resort out of boulders on the side of a mountain. And fills its rooms with custom-made "Arts and Crafts" furnishings. 回 A Spanish master of the arch, using Moorish building techniques, constructs a Catholic church on a knoll. The church's self-supporting elliptical dome—the largest in America—consists solely of tile and concrete. 回 A Paris-inspired architect, commissioned to design Asheville's city building,

Tale written in fabric, geometry, and heart
by Bernie Rowell.

An Irrepressible Spirit

brings forth the red and green tones of the mountains in a cake-like, art deco masterpiece. ▣ You are about to follow in the footsteps of some truly audacious people who have shaped the implausible landscape of this Mountain City loop. George and Edith Vanderbilt, E.W. Grove, Raphael Guastavino, and Douglas Ellington, among many others. The spirit of these visionary individuals, so brilliantly evident in the architecture of this loop trail, gives rise to the whole of the creative environment here. ▣ For what you will find throughout Asheville and its neighboring towns and communities is that same beguiling attitude that makes these landmarks so stunning. It's an artistic license, handed down by irrepressible people–handed down into the very hands of the artists you are about to meet, in the studios, shops and galleries along the way, where the passions of invention are a matter of physical record.

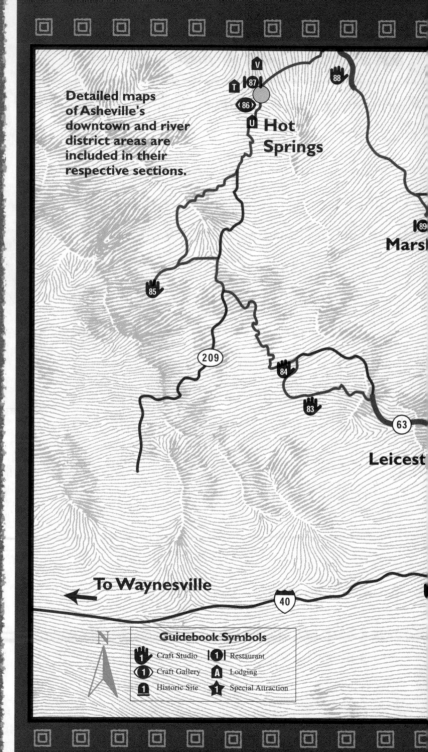

Mountain Cities

Detailed maps of Asheville's downtown and river district areas are included in their respective sections.

Hot Springs

Marsh

Leicest

To Waynesville

Guidebook Symbols

Craft Studio | Restaurant
Craft Gallery | Lodging
Historic Site | Special Attraction

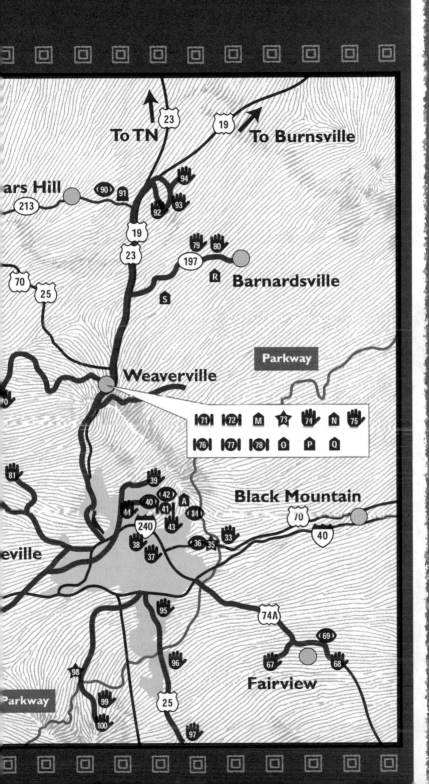

Mountain Cities

With all its pathways to craft in the city and outstretched trails to surrounding mountain communities, you could easily spend two weeks exploring the riches of Mountain Cities. Intrepid explorers will want to spend that much time; for others who don't have the luxury, there are several ways to shape a shorter, but no less dramatic, experience.

Several destinations make ideal half-day and one-day mini-tours. Biltmore Village, the River District, the Grove Park area, the road out to Hot Springs, for example, all represent a great way to romance a morning, afternoon or leisurely full day.

If you do have more than a day to spend, certainly invest one of them getting rapturously lost in Asheville. Other days can be spent cherry picking along the way according to taste. No matter how much of it you get to savor, you'll want to come back for more.

Point to point along the Urban Trail.

YMI Cultural Center

DOWNTOWN ASHEVILLE

For anyone relishing to see the city by foot, it is very possible to park anywhere downtown and walk to all the addresses shown below. For those desiring easier access, public parking is available near all the sites.

Pack Place Neighborhood *To park near these locations, you can pull into the public parking garage on Biltmore Ave.*

1 Urban Trail STARTING AT PACK PLACE – A great way to see Asheville, its achievements, and the personalities that shaped its colorful past. Walk point to point and visit times gone by. You'll generally find yourself in the pleasant company of outdoor sculpture that commemorates a celebrated moment.
(See Heritage Profile. on pages 136–137.)

2 Asheville Art Museum 2 S PACK SQUARE – One of the country's great small city museums, focused on American art beginning with the 20th century and especially art significant to the Southeast. Admission fee is charged. Open year-round Tue–Sat 10am–5pm & Sun 1pm–5pm. (828) 253-3227. www.ashevilleart.org
(See Sidebar on page 95)

3 YMI Cultural Center 39 S MARKET ST– JUST BEHIND PACK PLACE ON EAGLE ST – A notable institution in the history of Asheville, a long-time center of Asheville's African-American community, and a continuing

The Road Goes On Forever

Side trips, tidbits, adventures, and treasure hunts

THE ASHEVILLE AREA ART MUSEUM

Brought together as it is within the walls of a 1926 Italian Renaissance building next door to the entrance of Pack Place, the Asheville Art Museum could easily be taken for a staid and motionless citizen of Asheville's scrambling, eclectic downtown. Nothing could be further from the truth. Behind the facade is an ever-changing, ever-flowing theater of art, exhibition, learning opportunities and preservation.

The Museum annually presents 10-12 exhibitions of grace and energy, along with a delightful permanent collection. Wander in most any day (except Mondays) and you will come face-to-face with a canvas by Rauschenberg or Philip Noland, both of whom studied at nearby Black Mountain College, or you'll encounter an exhibit as touchingly close as a documentary of life in Madison County or as worldly as an early twentieth century show of the gathered work of women photographers held in Paris.

In recent years, the Museum has curated exhibitions from collections of the Whitney Museum of American Art, the Isamu Noguchi Museum, the Jewish Museum, and the Milwaukee Art Museum. In eight galleries over five levels, there is, quite literally, never a dull moment. This same message of excitement and expression is delivered to school kids on a near constant basis through tours, workshops, and camps.

On the main floor level of Pack Place, of which the Museum is a part, you're welcome to stop in for a "what's happening?" conversation with a docent or a staff member, spin through the Holden Gallery (devoted to regional art and free of charge), or fall in love with one of the most wonderful small museum gift shops you'll ever find, anywhere. The Asheville Art Museum, is an exhilarating work, in and of itself.

Open year-round Tue–Sat 10am–5pm (Fri until 8pm) & Sun 1pm–5pm. A small entrance fee is charged for non-members.

Guidebook Symbols

Craft Studio	Restaurant		
Craft Gallery	**A** Lodging		
1 Historic Site	Special Attraction		

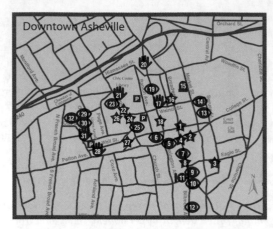

Downtown Asheville

Enjoy a day of discovery in Pack Place Education, Arts and Science Center.

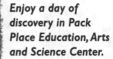

An art-filled corner: 16 Patton.

hothouse of cultural activity, exhibits and folks coming together. Permanent collection on display. Open year-round Tue–Sat 10am–5pm & Sun 1pm–5pm. (828)252-4614.

4 Pack Place Education, Arts & Science Center 2 S PACK SQUARE – A multi-faceted cultural center for the region that just keeps getting better. There's always plenty to see and do—exhibits at the Health Adventure and the Colburn Gem & Mineral Museum, a show in the lobby gallery, an addition at the Asheville Art Museum, a retrospective at the YMI, a first-rate stage performance at Diana Wortham Theater. It stretches the imagination, regardless of one's chronological age. Admission fee is charged. Open year-round Tue–Sat 10am–5pm & Sun 1pm–5pm. (828)257-4500. www.pack-place.org

5 16 Patton 16 PATTON AVE – Try to get by this corner without being drawn in. The gallery, a forerunner in Asheville's renaissance as an arts center, fills its windows with large, classically painted canvases–often landscapes–which whisper into the romantic heart of anyone who passes by. The sensibilities of its owners and staff continue to make 16 Patton a gift to the entire region. Glass and paintings are a particular focus. Open year-round Tue–Sat 11am–6pm. (828)236-2889. www.16patton.com

The Road Goes On Forever

Side trips, tidbits, adventures, and treasure hunts

6 Kress Emporium 19 PATTON AVE
– An arts and crafts retail experience awaits discovery in a newly-restored, 75-year-old, neoclassical building. Over 80 regional artists and craftspeople: milliners, jewelers, wood-carvers, potters and practitioners of the ageless art of collecting assorted old things. Open Jan–June Mon–Sat 11am–6pm. July–Dec Mon–Thu 11am–6pm, Fri–Sat 11am–7pm & Sun 12noon–5pm. (828)281-2252.

7 Asheville Area Arts Council
11 BILTMORE AVE – A front gallery, open to the street, exhibits the work of new artists in a kaleidoscope of shows throughout the year, usually one a month. Sometimes experimental and edgy, the work is always fresh. A welcoming space and a very welcoming organization for anyone who is or wants to be involved with the arts in the Asheville area. Open year-round Mon–Fri 10am–5pm. (828)258-0710. www.ashevillearts.com

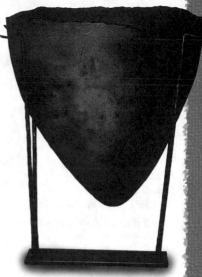

At the Asheville Area Arts Council Front Gallery.

8 Mast General Store 15
BILTMORE AVE – Asheville's own incarnation of the Valle Crucis original Mast General Store, an Appalachian tradition since 1883. The old-time mercantile features casual clothing and traditional housewares, old timey toys and candies, and outdoor gear and hiking apparel, as well as footwear for every season of discovery. Open year-round. Mid-Jan–Easter: Mon–Fri 10am–5pm, Sat 10am–6pm & Sun 1pm–5pm. Easter–Dec: Mon–Thu 10am–6pm, Fri–Sat 10am–8pm & Sun 12noon–6pm. (828)232-1883. www.mastgeneralstore.com

The sweets department at Mast General Store.

Guidebook Symbols

 Craft Studio   Restaurant

 Craft Gallery   **A** Lodging

1 Historic Site   Special Attraction

Blue Spiral.

SOUTHERN ART AND CRAFT

FIELD OF DREAMS
Fodor's Ballpark Vacations calls Asheville's McCormick Field, "one of the most beautiful little fields in all of baseball." Built in 1924 and reconstructed in 1992, McCormick has retained its singular distinctive feature: a backdrop of tall trees on a sloping hillside beyond the outfield fences. The history of the field is equally engaging. Ty Cobb hit a home run in the first exhibition at the field. In later years, the base paths were run by such legends as Lou Gehrig, Jackie Robinson and Babe Ruth, who considered McCormick one of his favorites. Today, McCormick Field is home to the Asheville Tourists, a Single-A farm club of the Colorado Rockies. For tickets and season schedule call (828)258-0428.

(9) Blue Spiral 1 38 BILTMORE AVE – Luminous regional work spread over three floors and 14,000 square feet, including 30 thematic and one-person exhibits throughout the year and a more permanent collection from regional artists of glass and ceramic pieces and paintings. A portion of this gallery is dedicated to Will Henry Stevens (1881-1949), an early 20th century modernist who painted landscapes in the mountains with a nostalgic and charmed brush. Open Nov–Apr Mon–Sat 10am–6pm. May–Oct Mon–Sat 10am–6pm & Sun 12noon–5pm. (828)251-0202. www.bluespiral1.com

(10) American Folk Art and Framing 64 BILTMORE AVE – A growing collection of contemporary N.C. folk art and wood-fired pottery with an assortment of whirly-gigs, face jugs, yard animals, and other-off-the-wall items proving our ancestors weren't playing with a full deck. Jimmy Lee Sudduth's folk art is just unforgettable. Open Apr–Dec Mon & Wed–Sat 10am–6pm & Tue 10am–5pm. Jan–Mar Mon–Wed 10am–5pm & Thu–Sat 10am–6pm. (828)281-2134. www.amerifolk.com

(11) Laurey's Catering, Inc. 67 BILTMORE AVE – Yes, this is a catering business and a great place to visit when you've committed to entertaining the Chinese delegation on your back patio. But wait, this is also a

Fuel for the tra

The Road Goes On Forever
Side trips, tidbits, adventures, and treasure hunts

READ ALL ABOUT IT *For the skinny on the local scene, check out the Friday edition of the Asheville Citizen-Times or pick up a copy of Mountain Express, a free weekly available in purple newsboxes all over town.*

fine address for an express lunch on the trail since most everything's ready to roll–perhaps a waldorf salad, an artichoke salad, or a fresh fruit salad–and then there's the omniscient, all-pervasive Kate Hepburn brownie sleeping at the register. Open year-round Mon–Fri 10am–6pm & Sat 10am–4pm. (828)252-1500. www.laureysyum.com

Glass encounter.

⑫ Biltmore Gallery Downtown 144 BILTMORE AVE – All the usual suspects are on display—pottery, glass, woodwork, jewelry—rounded up in an airy, browser-friendly place. The electric colors of glass bowls and sculptures in its front windows illuminate Biltmore Ave. Plan to drag your feet —there's much about our mountains to admire while here. Open Apr–Dec Mon–Sat 11am–6pm & Sun 1pm–6pm. Jan–Mar Mon–Sat 11am–5pm & Sun 1pm–5pm. (828)252-2979.

SPRUCE & MARKET STREETS

The next three sites can be easily accessed by parking on Spruce St. Biltmore Ave becomes Broadway on the N side of the Pack Square and Spruce St is two blocks E of Broadway.

⑬ The Rainbow Gallery 10 N SPRUCE ST – Len Whitaker has assembled a fine collection of art and craft from the region—photography, sculpture, paintings, music—all of which reflects the sprawling diversity of our mountains. Open year-round Mon–Thu 10am–5pm. Fri & Sat 10am–6pm. Sun 1pm–5pm. (828)285-0005.

⑭ Appalachian Craft Center 10 N SPRUCE ST – Traditional mountain crafts near the heart of downtown. Handcrafted brooms, quilts, face jugs, carvings, looper rugs, and other essential contraptions like a walnut boot puller. Open year-round Mon–Sat 10am–5pm. (828)253-8499. www.appalachiancraftcenter.com

⑮ Thomas Wolfe Memorial State Historic Site 25 N MARKET ST – Julia Wolfe's boarding house lives on forever in the pages of her son Thomas'

Keeping time at Rainbow Gallery.

Guidebook Symbols

 Craft Studio   Restaurant

 Craft Gallery   **A** Lodging

Historic Site   Special Attraction

novel *Look Homeward, Angel.* A new visitor center walks you through Wolfe's worlds. On the front porch of Julia's "Old Kentucky Home" you can practically still hear the clamor of the boarders coming and going over eighty years ago. Open Apr–Oct Mon–Sat 9am–5pm & Sun 1pm–5pm. Nov–Mar Tue–Sat 10am–4pm & Sun 1pm–4pm. (828) 253-8304. www.wolfememorial.com

LEXINGTON STREET AREA

A public parking garage is located on Rankin Ave just one block W of Lexington.

16 **Futon Designs** 39 BROADWAY – Two showrooms full of comfort and possibilities. Handcrafted, locally-made futon frames in pecan, maple, ash, oak and cherry. Mission slats are extra, but well worth the trip back in time. End tables, ottomans and more. Open year-round Mon–Fri 10am–6pm & Sat 10am–5pm. (828) 253-1138. www.futondesigns.com

17 **Mountain Lights** 1 WALNUT ST – In a shop so small you can meet yourself, Pamela Brown dips beeswax candles and directs your eye to candle holders, lamps, and lanterns that light up every wall, nook, and corner. Open Jan–Sep Mon & Wed–Sat 1pm–6pm. Oct–Dec Mon & Wed–Sat 11am–6pm. (828) 253-0080. www.brwm.org/mountainlights

18 **T. S. Morrison and Co.** 39 N LEXINGTON AVE – Asheville's oldest store and emporium. Handmade baskets and train whistles. Wooden toys from Berea College. And a cache of sweeter merchandise: licorice pulls, atomic fireballs, taffy, bonbons, peppermint puffs, pecan turtles, Wilbur buds, and rock candy. Open Jan–Mar Mon–Sat 10am–6pm. Apr–Dec Mon–Sat 10am–7pm & Sun 12noon–6pm. (828) 258-1891.

19 **Sky People Gallery & Design Studio and DIRT** 51 N LEXINGTON AVE – Two unique art and craft shops in one location. One features spiritual art, tools and home decor with a studio for the design of sacred spaces. The other features eclectic gifts for the home and garden with a constantly changing array of local fine art—photography, pottery and oils. Open year-round Mon–Sat 11am–6pm & in the summer Sun 12noon-4pm. (828)232-0076 or (828)281-3478.

20 **Crucible Glassworks** 106 N LEXINGTON AVE – Michael and Hilary Hatch will happily demonstrate their hot glass techniques if you happen by at the magical moment. Resplendent colors and fanciful shapes take form before your very eyes. Paperweights, vases, and wall pieces gracefully poised on the cusp of heirloomhood. Open year-round Tue–Sat 11am–5pm. (828)236-0920.

HAYWOOD/WALL ST. AREA

A public parking garage is located on Haywood St and another one is located around the corner from Wall St on O'Henry St.

21 **Jewels That Dance: Jewelry Design** 63 HAYWOOD ST – A galaxy of sparkling objects born of gold, silver, platinum and other gifts of the earth. Resident jewelers include owner and nationally recognized designer-goldsmith Paula Dawkins. You're welcome to gaze at this winsome, starry offering in a gallery setting. Open year-round Mon–Sat 10am–6pm. (828)254-5088, www.jewelsthatdance.com

22 **Malaprop's Bookstore and Cafe** 55 HAYWOOD ST – Hovering at the top of the list as one of the best independent bookstores in America, this gathering place exudes a kind of Left Bank charm that enraptures anyone with even the mildest of interest in books and the people behind them. Authors pop in on a frequent basis to talk about everything from how to survive the winter in Greenland to how dogs and cats see things differently. With its coffees and teas, its penchant toward the creative life in any form, Malaprop's is an institution of considerable tolerance and wisdom. Open year-round Mon–Thu 9am–9pm. Fri–Sat 9am–11pm. Sun 9am–6pm. (828)254-6734. www.malaprops.com

Michael Hatch's work.

At Malaprop's, an extensive collection of local writers work.

Guidebook Symbols

 Craft Studio  Restaurant

Craft Gallery Lodging

Historic Site Special Attraction

(23) Ariel Gallery 46 HAYWOOD ST – An artist cooperative in which the work is so great, you could quite easily have a conniption fit before you get back out to the street. There are about 20 artists involved in this endeavor. The work is juried in, and it spans clay, fiber, furniture, glass, iron and jewelry pieces. If the maker of a particular piece isn't minding the store that day, you can often get the skinny from the artist by phone. But whether it's the abstract fiber work of Suzanne Gernandt, the pendants and rings of Nancy Fleming, the clay work of Jane Peiser, the handmade books of Lynn McLure, or the whatever of whomever, this store can make you crazy from sheer joy. Open Apr–Dec Mon–Thu 10am–6pm & Fri–Sat 10am–7pm. Jan–Mar Mon–Sat 10am–6pm. (828) 236-2660.

Ariel Gallery: an artist cooperative.

Gourd art as seen at Woolworth Walk.

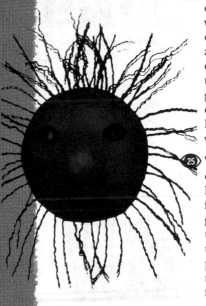

(24) Earth Guild 33 HAYWOOD ST – A long-established crafter's haven with an emphasis on weaving—looms for sale; baskets of yarn; skeins of wool, mohair, rayon, silk, cotton; ski shuttles and curved cards. And lots of how-to books on doing everything from knitting to chairmaking to throwing pots. You'll also find chisels, gouges, flats, mallets, pottery tools, and plenty of well-informed advice. Open year-round Mon–Sat 10am–6pm. (828) 255-7818. www.earthguild.com

(25) Woolworth Walk 25 HAYWOOD ST – An emporium of creative work representing over a hundred artists from the region who are, as front-desk hosts will explain, "close enough to get home and get back in one day." In addition to some very well-known and established artists, this is a fine place for emerging creative people to show their work and for patrons to make discoveries. Downstairs you'll typically find a handful of artists in the midst of doing

The Road Goes On Forever

Side trips, tidbits, adventures, and treasure hunts

things. You're welcome to ask questions and rummage for ideas. Open year-round Tue–Sat 11am–6pm & Sun 11am–4pm. (828) 254-9234. www.woolworthwalk.com

 True Blue Art
30 HAYWOOD ST – An art supply store for artists by artists. Supplies include everything from tools for etching to English watercolors to wares for papermaking. Open year-round Mon–Sat 10am–7pm. (828) 251-0028. www.cheapartsupply.com

Load up on supplies at True Blue Art.

 Beads and Beyond 19 WALL ST – One minute you're just an average Joe. Then the next, you're a gourd-painting, jewelry-designing, craft-making artist, and you have no idea how you got there. Hang out for a spell and enjoy owner Barry Olen's unpretentious view of craft. Open year-round Mon–Thu 10:30am–6pm. Fri–Sat 10:30am–8pm. Sun 12noon–5pm. (828) 254-7927. www.beads-and-beyond.com

 Craven Handbuilt Porcelain
58 WALL ST – Living on a mountaintop in Spain, Lydia Craven experimented with imprinting porcelain with heirloom lace she found in European markets. She's kept at the idea and now brings the concept to this intimate shop on Wall Street where she and her husband Ian continue innovating. Lately they're bringing to life pots for orchids, a joining of graceful proportions. Open year-round Mon–Sat 10am–5pm. (828) 232-1401. www.cravenstudio.com

Lace-impressed porcelain dinnerware at Craven Handbuilt Porcelain.

Guidebook Symbols

 Craft Studio   Restaurant

Craft Gallery   **A** Lodging

Historic Site   Special Attraction

*Crafts, strictly,
of our mountains.*

29 Mountain Made

THE GROVE ARCADE PUBLIC MARKET – As indicated by the name, the only imported item might be something coming out of a pine-shrouded cove on the other side of the river. About 80 artisans benefit from this outlet of the Micro Mountain Enterprise Fund, a supportive organization for artists and start-up entrepreneurs. You'll find blacksmithing works, jewelry, pottery, stained glass, handmade books and boxes, among other things, and CD's that feature local musicians and mountain music. Open year-round Mon–Sat 10am–6pm. Sun 12noon–5pm during the holiday season only. (828)350-0307.

30 The Warren Wilson Store

THE GROVE ARCADE PUBLIC MARKET – This space is all about the triad philosophy of study-work-service at Warren Wilson College as well as the indefatigable creative spirit that seems to underly everything at the school. You'll find imaginative pieces by alumni, faculty and students. And, if even for a second you think this work is just "college stuff," prepare yourself for a revelation. From the art of faculty members Dusty Benedict and Gwen Diehn through the student "work crew" offerings of herb teas and wrought iron, this store is a house of treasures. Open year-round Mon–Sat 10am–6pm. (828)225-3050. www.thewarrenwilsonstore.com

Student, teacher and alumni work at the Warren Wilson Store.

31 Larson Porcelain and Design

THE GROVE ARCADE PUBLIC MARKET – Heirloom-quality porcelain by artist-potters Julie and Tyrone Larson. Tyrone forms and shapes wheel-thrown pieces while Julie handpaints them on site. Extraordinarily handsome work in a beautiful new

The Road Goes On Forever

Side trips, tidbits, adventures, and treasure hunts

Hand-thrown work at Larson Porcelain and Design.

THE GROVE ARCADE

Completed in 1929, the Grove Arcade bustled with commerce until 1942 when 74 shops and 127 offices were given less than a month to relocate so the United State Government could move in to serve the war effort. In its heyday, the Grove Arcade was the center of commerce and civic life in the city and one of the only buildings in the country offering an indoor market on the first floor with offices above.

Now, more than a half century later, thanks to the combined efforts of the city, the Grove Arcade Foundation, and a host of granting agencies, E.W. Grove's vision of a public market is once again flourishing to life.

As a public market, the Grove Arcade's medley of shops and restaurants and stalls are individual expressions of the surrounding region of farms, schools, craft-makers, and cottage industries.

Walk into this deco masterpiece, (originally designed with a tower section that was never built) treat yourself to the sight of vegetable stalls and baked goods, hear the rustle of coffee cups, and peer into shop after glass-fronted shop, each one its own small symphony.

Come for coffee, stay for awhile.

Guidebook Symbols

Craft Studio	Restaurant
Craft Gallery	Lodging
Historic Site	Special Attraction

A store of cottage industry.

gallery location. Open year-round Mon–Sat 10am–6pm. Sun 12noon–6pm during summer and fall. (828) 350-7707.

(32) **Asheville N. C. Home Crafts** THE GROVE ARCADE PUBLIC MARKET – As partners Judy Quinn and Marie Hendrix are fond of saying, this shop of fiber-related products is actually an outgrowth of "4-H run amok." It all started when Marie bought two sheep for her children. She now has fifty, along with goats and llamas, all sources of yarn she spins for her works of art and comfort. Judy, a basket weaver, commissions baskets of honeysuckle and grapevine. The store has encouraged a cottage industry of quilts, handmade hats and topsy-turvey dolls, a homecoming of traditional crafts. Demonstrations are also offered. Open year-round Mon–Sat 10am–6pm. Sun 12noon–5pm during the holiday season. (828) 350-0307.

EAST ASHEVILLE

Suzanne and John Gernandt's work.

To find yourself at the Gernandt's Studio, travel E from downtown Asheville on Hwy 70 for approximately 4.7 mi. After passing under the Blue Ridge Parkway, travel .5 mi and turn L on Moffit Branch Rd and then an immediate L on Moffit Rd. Travel 1.5 mi, driving by the river, to a stop sign. Take the farthest R up the hill, Eastmore Dr. Take the 2nd L, Welwyn Ln. Studio is in cul de sac at end of lane.

Gernandt Studios 108 WELWYN LANE – When these two artists get to the gates of heaven, all they'll need to do is show their work and walk right in. Suzanne creates woven works that reflect great care and stunning improvisational color. John makes fine furniture —chairs and tables and stands—in which he may use inlays of mahogany or teak or ebony in thoughtful pieces of sycamore or persimmon or poplar. Both artists' work is stagey and beautiful. Open year-round Wed–Sun 10am–5pm and by appointment. (828) 299-4889.

The Road Goes On Forever

Side trips, tidbits, adventures, and treasure hunts

Return to Hwy 70 and turn R. Travel .5 to the Blue Ridge Parkway entrance. Travel N for .5 mi to Folk Art Center.

(34) Folk Art Center BLUE RIDGE PARKWAY - MILEPOST 382 – Home of the historic Allanstand Craft Shop, one of the early retail-cooperatives in the Appalachian region. Hundreds of artful pieces in virtually all media produced by the members of the Southern Highland Craft Guild. A moveable feast of special exhibits in the gallery by individual artisans. The building also houses the Guild's craft library and a theater. Demonstrations are held inside and outside. Spring through fall color. Open Jan–Mar Mon–Sun 9am–5pm. Apr–Dec Mon–Sun 9am–6pm. (828)298-7928. www.southernhighlandguild.org

The Folk Art Center: On the Blue Ridge Parkway and a good place to begin on the way to anywhere.

Return to Hwy 70/Tunnel Rd and turn W toward Asheville. Stuart Nye's is about 2.5 mi on R.

(35) Stuart Nye Hand Wrought Jewelry 940 TUNNEL RD – Thanks to Ralph and Joe Morris, you can see the production of the classic silver dogwood jewelry crafted the way Nye designed it two generations ago, plus 17 other floral and leaf designs. View of working studio. No retail sales here. Open year-round Mon–Fri 8am–12noon & 12:30pm–4pm. (828) 298-7988.

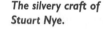

The silvery craft of Stuart Nye.

Guild Crafts is next door to Stuart Nye's.

(36) Guild Crafts 930 TUNNEL RD –A representative offering of Southern Highland Craft Guild and Allanstand at a very accessible and cheery location. Heritage close at hand. Yet another place to feel grateful. Open Jan–Sep Mon–Sat 10am–6pm. Oct–Dec Mon–Sun 10am–6pm. (828)298-7903. www.southernhighlandguild.org

Continue traveling W on Hwy 70/Tunnel Rd for .5 mi. Turn L on Overbrook Rd and then R on Overbrook Place. Barefoot Pottery is on L.

Guidebook Symbols

	Craft Studio	**|1|**	Restaurant
(1)	Craft Gallery	**A**	Lodging
1	Historic Site	**1**	Special Attraction

37 Barefoot Pottery and Gardens 22 OVERBROOK PLACE – Clayworker Chiwa and broommaker husband Andrew Goodheart ply their craft in this charmed, hidden nook. Chiwa brings the spirit of the earth to her pieces, work that dances between functional and sculptural—porcelain vases and stoneware bowls for garden harvests; figurative, gestural work for the soul. Andrew's well-crafted brooms spring to life out of found wood. Charms of all kinds abound here. Open Apr 15–Dec 23 Mon–Tue 10am–4pm. (828) 298-0426.

Return to Hwy 70/Tunnel Rd and turn L, traveling W. Travel 1.4 mi and turn L on Kenilworth Rd. Travel .7 mi on Kenilworth Rd. Look for sign and street # 360 on R and turn R. Tileworks is to L of drive.

38 Asheville Tileworks 360 KENILWORTH RD – This studio covers the subject in a totally delightful way—from arts and crafts relief tiles to groups of tiles for accenting kitchens or fireplaces to custom tile work for most any use. One look at Diana Gillispie's work and you'll be envisioning whole worlds of tile-oriented scenarios. Studio in lovely garden setting. Open Sep–May Mon–Fri 9am–3pm. After 3pm and Sat–Sun by appointment only. June-Aug Mon–Fri 9am–5pm & Sat by appointment only. Good idea to call ahead. (828) 259-9050. brwm.org/ashevilletileworks

Return to Hwy 70/Tunnel Rd and continue W to junction of I-240W, about .2 mi. I-240W connects with downtown Asheville at Charlotte St, Merrimon Ave or Montford Ave exits. To go N take the Weaverville/Hwy 19/23 exit.

To travel to Fairview from here, turn R on Hwy 70 and continue E to junction with I-240E. I-240 E connects with Hwy 74A. Follow signs to Bat Cave and Fairview as I-240 merges back into I-40.

Chiwa's enchanting world, open for discovery.

The expressions of Asheville Tileworks.

NORTH ASHEVILLE

Travel N from downtown Asheville on Merrimon Ave for 2.3 mi to Beaverdam Rd. Turn R. Travel 2.5 mi and George Handy's Studio is on R at intersection with Webb Cove Rd.

The Road Goes On Forever

Side trips, tidbits, adventures, and treasure hunts

George Handy Studio/Gallery 2 WEBB COVE RD – It would be easy enough to fly past George Handy's studio on your way to somewhere else. On the other hand, George Handy's studio is somewhere else. In his work, you will find suggestions of Mayan architecture, African textiles and Inuit artifacts. In one of his pots, mugs, plates, or large wall commissions, a world abounds—organic, earthy and cross-cultural—infused with native spirit—and it is a world (of hallelujahs) not to be missed. Open year-round Mon–Fri 9am–5pm. Sat 9am–12noon. Other hours on Sat and Sun by appointment only. (828)254-4691 or (800)948-2790. www.georgehandy.com

Return to Merrimon Ave and turn L back toward downtown Asheville. Travel about 1.5 mi and turn L on Hillside St. Travel about 3 blocks to Charlotte St and turn L. Macon Ave is about .1 mi on R. Travel .8 mi on Macon Ave and turn L into Grove Park Inn drive. Follow signs to next 4 sites.

A Grove Park Inn Resort and Spa 290 MACON AVE – Conceived by E. W. Grove and brought to reality in 1913 by his son-in-law Fred Seely who constructed it in 11 months from blueprints in his head. The Inn has expanded since then, but it remains a tribute to arts and crafts style. Its original custom-built furniture and hand-hammered copper lighting fixtures came from the Roycroft crafters of New York. Over 500 rooms. The Inn's new 40,000 square foot spa with its rock work and waterfalls ranks in there with the world's best. Open year-round (800)438-0050 ext: 8045. www.groveparkinn.com

Inside this dwelling, George Handy fiddles with the wonderous nature of things.

40 Gallery of the Mountains 290 MACON AVE – Located in the Sammons Wing of the Grove Park Inn. You'll find larger collections of craft elsewhere, but none finer. Hand-dyed and hand-painted silk vests, handwoven coats, wraps, and scarves, pottery, jewelry and woodwork, all assembled and displayed with considerable verve. Open Jan–Mar Mon–Thu & Sun 9am–5pm. Fri–Sat 9am–9pm. Apr–Dec Mon–Tue & Sun 9am–6pm. Wed–Sat 9am–9am. (828)254-2068.

The Grove Park Inn, a marvel of arts and crafts architecture.

Guidebook Symbols

✋ Craft Studio	🍴 Restaurant
① Craft Gallery	Ⓐ Lodging
🔲 Historic Site	⭐ Special Attraction

The nature of art at Grovewood Gallery.

Gabe Cyr's "Gourdian Spirits."

|41| The Grovewood Cafe 111 GROVEWOOD RD – English cottage set among lofty evergreens. Idyllic setting for a romantic lunch or for getting reacquainted with an old friend over dinner. The food just happens to be fabulous, too. Open year round (except the first half of January) Mon–Sat 11am–2:30pm & 5pm until. (828)258-8956.

(42) Grovewood Gallery 111 GROVEWOOD RD – Two floors of furniture, glass, pottery, clothing, and jewelry confirm your suspicion that you have, indeed, reached the epicenter of ground-breaking work. Ask a staff member for information about Grovewood Studios, home to artists represented by the Gallery who do custom work on request. Open Apr–Dec Mon–Sat 10am–6pm & Sun 1pm–5pm. Jan–Mar Mon–Sat 10am–5pm. (828)253-7651. www.grovewood.com

Return to Charlotte St and turn L. Travel .2 mi to Chestnut St and turn L. Gabe Cyr Studio is one block off Charlotte.

43 Gabe Cyr Studio 291 E CHESTNUT ST – Gabe Cyr's soft-bodied figures called "Gourdian Spirits" are so evocative that they've moved some folks to tears. An artful intersection of gourds, patterned fabrics, beads, earthenware, and spiritual imprints of many cultures. Her "altered art" takes many forms —figures, shrines and decorative pieces. Open year-round Wed–Thu 11am–4pm. (828)258-2575.

Travel W on Chestnut St, crossing Charlotte St and then Merrimon Ave. Turn R on Holland St, which is the first street on the R after crossing Merrimon Ave. Mother Moon Pottery on L.

44 Mother Moon Pottery 58 HOLLAND ST – Beka Hedly's stoneware comes in all shapes—vases, bowls, big pots, little mugs and lidded containers, some of which sprout animal heads or birds on their tops or sides. It's obvious that Mother Moon can be very playful. Open May–Aug Mon–Thu 1pm–5:30pm. Sep–Apr Sat 10am–1pm. (828)258-9279.

A "hanger on" at Mother Moon Pottery.

The Road Goes On Forever

Side trips, tidbits, adventures, and treasure hunts

Asheville

Return to Merrimon Ave. To travel downtown, turn R on Merrimon Ave. To travel to Weaverville and other parts N, turn L on Merrimon Ave.

WEST/RIVER DISTRICT

From Haywood St in downtown Asheville, turn R on Patton Ave and travel about 4 blocks to Clingman Ave. Negotiate the prohibited left turn by following signs to connect to Clingman Ave. Travel down Clingman, following it as it makes a split to the L. Next 3 sites are on L.

 Odyssey Center for the Ceramic Arts
236 CLINGMAN AVE – Director Mark Burleson and other artists teach nine-week classes in sculpture, handbuilding and wheel-throwing techniques. Celebrated guest artists also appear for weekend workshops. Call for a class schedule. Or, better yet, drop by and meet up with a bunch of friendly, talented folks. Open year-round Mon–Fri 9am–4pm. (828)285-0210. www.highwaterclays.com

 Highwater Clays 238 CLINGMAN AVE – Mecca for potters. Clay by the pound or by the ton. Glazes covering the entire color spectrum. Not to mention the wheels, brushes, sponges, kilns, grogs, opacifiers, frits and lots of other esoterica of the potter's trade. Open year-round Mon–Fri 8:30am–4:30pm. (828)252-6033. www.highwaterclays.com

Throwing and shaping at Odyssey Center.

Odyssey Gallery 242 CLINGMAN AVE – Former barroom now houses an intoxicating collection of ceramic art. Special exhibits also circulate through this space. All the more reason to become a regular. Open year-round Tue–Fri 12noon–5pm. (828)285-9700. www.highwaterclays.com

Turn R at intersection with Lyman St and then an immediate sharp R onto Roberts St. After visiting studios on Roberts St, return to Lyman St, turn R and then R again on Riverside Dr.

Guidebook Symbols

 Craft Studio   Restaurant
Craft Gallery   **A** Lodging
Historic Site   Special Attraction

Among other things, Julia Stout's steel and stone at Giuilia Studio.

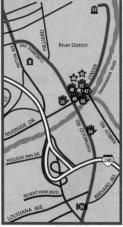

A dance at high temperatures.

48 **Giuilia Art Studio** 140D ROBERTS ST – Artist-in-residence Julia Stout so enjoyed the Italian version of her first name during a year of study in Florence she decided to use it over her studio door. Inside, her work is just as distinctive: cold form steel cut into sculptural shapes—oftentimes the human figure in various yoga postures—caught forever as furniture, wall-hangings or simple sculpture. She is a yoga instructor herself as well as a gifted artist in multiple media that she sometimes mixes. Open year-round Tue–Thu 11am–4pm. (828) 768-2269 and (828)669-2269. www.giuilia.com

49 **Marston Blow Pottery** 123 ROBERTS ST – Pottery and sculpture as the artist says "in the goddess tradition" and there are, indeed, figurines and earthenware that exude a kind of rich and lovely mystique. Marston also offers up bowls and other vessels in deep olives and blues and browns, shades of a summer forest in the Blue Ridge. Open most afternoons year-round 2pm–6pm. (828)257-4077.

50 **Great Southern Glassworks** 9 RIVERSIDE DR – The kind of place where you can learn the difference between a blow pipe and a punty rod. Roddy Capers doesn't mind folks looking over his shoulders (from a safe distance) to study the intricate dance that takes place between artist and glass. Open Oct–May Fri 9am–5pm & Sat call for times. June–Sep usually Mon–Fri 9am–5pm but furnace is sometimes off so call ahead. (828) 255-0187. www.mamboglassrod.com

Continue down Riverside Dr and turn R into Old Cotton Mill parking area at 122 Riverside.

51 **Potter's Mark LTD.** 122 RIVERSIDE DR – When Eileen Black worked as a teacher in New York City she was often stopped for a hall pass since she was only 5 feet tall. Years downstream,

The Road Goes On Forever
Side trips, tidbits, adventures, and treasure hunts

Christopher Mello, the Knome, welds recycled materials into planters and tries them for size in his quirky garden. See for yourself at 9 Riverside Drive.

she still doesn't have to duck under any doorways but her enthusiasm and spirit has, shall we say, gone through the roof. Nowadays she is an experienced and imaginative potter of functional, hand-built dinnerware and her love of life coalesces around her work and particularly around a couple of glazes that mark her lines. Somehow or other she's gotten taller. Open year-round Mon–Fri 10am–4pm & Sat–Sun by appointment only. (828)252-9122. www.pottersmark.com

The prevalent energy at Potter's Mark.

Turn L back on Riverside Dr and R on Lyman St. Travel about .2 mi and turn L into Candle Station. D'eva Sculpture is located at the far end of building.

 D'eva Sculpture 191 LYMAN ST 3A – An enchanting studio with both painting and printmaking at its center. The featured work is Eva Allawos' sculpture—small relief, classical, mythical, charming. You'll find many reasons to need her sculpture. Open year-round Mon–Tue 10am–2pm. Closed on holidays. (828) 273-0470.

In the River District – John Payne's gamely art spills out into public spaces.

To continue to West Asheville, return to Clingman Ave. Turn L as it joins Haywood Rd. Cross the river and continue W on Haywood Rd, following its turns. West End Bakery is on R in the 700 block.

To travel to Museum, continue S on Lyman St to L turn onto Victoria Rd. Museum is just past Asheville-Buncombe Technical Community College.

 Smith-McDowell House Museum 283 VICTORIA RD – A walk through this graceful time-capsuled 19th century home—one of the oldest structures in the city—includes rooms in

Guidebook Symbols

Craft Studio	Restaurant
Craft Gallery	Lodging
Historic Site	Special Attraction

Steebo Designs, what can happen given full-throttle imagination.

period dress and all sorts of periodic events. If you're lucky, you'll happen upon an afternoon tea. An admission fee is charged. Open Jan–Mar Tue–Sat 10am–4pm. Apr–Dec Tue–Sat 10am–4pm & Sun 1pm–4pm. (828)253-9231. www.wnchistory.org

From the Museum, you can return to Clingman Ave and on to West Asheville or you can continue traveling on Victoria Rd to its intersection with Biltmore Ave. Then turn R to go to Biltmore Village or L to return to downtown Asheville.

B **The Parsonage** 439 W HAYWOOD ST – The Parsonage Guest House, recently restored, is located on historic Chicken Hill in the heart of the River Arts District. Because of the neighborly juxtaposition, this small inn is a smidge biased towards artists and their patrons. Inquire at Odyssey Gallery or Highwater Clays. (828)253-3853.

From the River District, continue west on Haywood Rd as it crosses the river and makes a sharp right turn and crosses I-240. Steebo Design is in 300 block.

54 **Steebo Design** 355 Haywood St – Strange things happen to environmental castaways in a studio overrun by stacked-up green frogs and garden creatures, all of which leapt full-blown from Stefan Bonitz's imagination. Open year-round Mon–Sat 12noon–5pm. (828)253-4610. www.steebo.com

55 **West End Bakery** 757 HAYWOOD RD – The meeting place for westenders, a corner bakery that has snuggled neatly into the old town neighborhood, a loungey, unpretentious, good coffee kind of harbor. If you're plotting out your next mountain bike trip, working through statistical variances in kiln temperatures, or trying to assimilate whatever the current administration just said, this is probably the best place to do it. Also salads, sandwiches, killer cinnamon rolls and a building-long outdoor mural that makes any visit to West Asheville worth the trip. Open year-round Tue–Fri 7:30am–6pm & Sat–Sun 8am–3pm. (828)252-9328. www.onhaywood.com

Sally Bryenton's mural at West End Bakery.

The Road Goes On Forever
Side trips, tidbits, adventures, and treasure hunts

To travel to Bernie Rowell's Studio, continue W on Haywood Rd until it intersects with Patton Ave/Hwy 19/23S. Turn L on Hwy 19/23S/Patton Ave, travel 4.9 mi and turn R on Dogwood Rd. Travel 2.5 mi , staying L at blinking light. Turn R at fork on Hooker's Gap Rd. Travel 1 mi to Wintercrest Dr on R. Studio is on hill at end of drive.

 Bernie Rowell Studio 250 HOOKERS GAP –
Using sewn fabrics, beads, painted surfaces, modulated colors and even electronic circuitry, Bernie creates canvas collages that are beautiful to behold. Art quilts. Yet beyond their obvious surface appeal, these many-textured constructions speak directly to the soul. As Bernie says, "Art reflects life. Good art is personal." And while you're there, ask about husband Robert Reitz's custom frames. Open Apr–Nov Thu–Sat 11am–6pm & other days by appointment. (828)667-2479. www.bernierowell.com

Bernie Rowell's textured imagery.

Return to Hwy 19/23 and turn L to go E to return to downtown Asheville.

Leicester and Madison County can be reached by turning L on Hwy 63 off Hwy 19/23 about 2.5 mi after going under I-40.

To travel to the Blue Ridge Parkway, do not turn on to Hwy 19/23 but cross it and travel S on Hwy 151.

At Lothlorien, doors that can open your heart.

SOUTH/BILTMORE VILLAGE

From downtown Asheville, travel S on Hwy 25/Biltmore Ave for 2 mi to Biltmore Village. Traveling S on Hwy 25, turn L on Hwy 81/Swannanoa River Rd just before reaching the Village and travel 1 mi. Lothlorien is on L.

 Lothlorien Woodworking 224 B
SWANNANOA RIVER RD – Once upon a time, two master woodworkers here were carving a life-size St. Francis of Assissi from maple. By now, it graces the church that commissioned it. But stop by anyway. These two talented woodworkers,

Guidebook Symbols

 Craft Studio   Restaurant
 Craft Gallery   Lodging
 Historic Site   Special Attraction

A John Nickerson piece, alive at Vitrum Gallery.

Bellagio

At New Morning Gallery, over 12,000 square feet of grace and good taste.

Mark Strom and Michael Hester, are always up to their elbows in wood, whether doing traditional woodworking, sculpting, or carving. Open year-round Mon–Fri 8am–5pm. Fri pm & Sat by appointment only. (828)258-1445.

Return to Hwy 25/Biltmore Ave and turn L. Travel across the railroad tracks and turn L to park in Biltmore Plaza. Next 7 sites are within walking distance of each other.

(58) Vitrum Gallery 10 LODGE ST – If you've ever wondered why North Carolina has a world-wide reputation for its glass, step inside this evocative, light-filled space. Dazzling pottery and other media, too. Open Jan–Mar 16 Mon & Wed–Fri 11am–5pm & Sat 10am–6pm. Mar 17–Dec Mon & Wed–Sat 10am–6pm & Sun 1pm–5pm. (828)274-9900. www.vitrumglass.com

|(59) Hot Shot Cafe 7 LODGE ST – We're not sure, but we think you have to have a beehive hairdo to be a waitress here.. Breakfast, anytime, and lunch–both served up 1950's style. Featured in The New York Times. Open daily year-round 7:30am–3pm. (828)274-2170.

(60) Bellagio 5 BILTMORE PLAZA – An art-to-wear gallery that showcases dazzling handcrafted wearables, jewelry, home and fashion accessories. This shop is all about texture, color, and form as those things relate to the grace and movement of the human body. Just walking by the windows can stir your imagination. Open Jan–Mar Mon–Sat 10am–6pm & Sun 12noon– 5pm. Apr–Dec Mon–Sat 10am–7pm & Sun 12noon–5pm. (828)277-8100. www.bellagioarttowear.com

(61) New Morning Gallery 7 BOSTON WAY – The "gallery at the top of the stairs" remains as fresh and alluring as the day John Cram opened it more than 30 years ago. Now spread over 12,000 square feet, the store is an icon destination

The Road Goes On Forever
Side trips, tidbits, adventures, and treasure hunts

for regional work. It represents the finest decorative and functional craft created in the mountains with some sublime pieces from outside the area. New Morning, along with the Annual Village Art & Craft Fair in August, which John originally ignited, continue to be anchors of the Asheville craft scene. Open Jan–Mar Mon–Sat 10am–6pm & Sun 12noon–5pm. Apr–Dec Mon–Sat 10am–7pm & Sun 12noon–5pm. (828)274-2831. www.newmorningnc.com

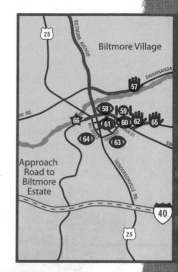

Biltmore Village

Approach Road to Biltmore Estate

62 Blue 1 SWAN ST – Lynn Daniel and Susan West have decided the best jewelry is made in the old tradition—from scratch, one piece at a time. In their cottage in Biltmore Village you can hone in on something to your liking—hand-cut stones arranged in rings and pendants and earrings of yellow, white, rose and green gold, platinum and sterling silver—then collaborate with the artists on a piece of jewelry that is distinctly your own. Written into their work—as with their leaf band and Blue Ridge Mountain ring—is a love of the natural treasures of these hills. Open Jan–Nov Tue–Sat 10:30am–5pm. Dec Mon–Sat 10:30am–5:30pm & Sun 12noon–5pm. (828)227-2583. www.bluegoldsmiths.com

Blue.

63 Legacies 2 BOSTON WAY – In summer, cool off in the backyard with ice cream. Inside, wood carvings, handmade miniatures, candles, and copper fountains, many pieces crafted by the owners. Open Jan–Feb Mon–Sat 10am–5pm. Mar–Dec Mon–Sat 10am–5pm & Sun 12noon–5pm. (828)274-8212.

Village Galleries is across Hwys 25 and 25A from Biltmore Plaza.

64 Village Galleries 32 ALL SOULS CRESCENT – Another reason craft-seekers hold Biltmore Village in such esteem. A spritely and varied collection includes fine art glass, handbuilt ceramics, jewelry, quilts and dolls. The fine art side of the shop features watercolors, silkscreens, original lithographs and limited edition prints. Of particular note are limited prints of Asheville artist and naturalist Sallie

John Lotton's work nicely settled into the warm environment of Village Galleries.

Ellington Middleton. Open Jan–Oct Mon–Sat 10am–5pm. Nov–Dec Mon–Sat 10am–5pm & Sun 1pm–5pm. (828)274-2424. www.villagegalleries.com

Continue traveling .4 mi up Lodge St which becomes Brook St and then Sweeten Creek Rd. Turn L on Fairview Rd and R into first drive on R. Accoutrements is in industrial building to the L.

A visual feast at Interiors Marketplace, Biltmore Station. (828) 253-2300.

Biltmore Estate: George Vanderbilt's dream extended into contemporary times.

 65 Gallery 101/Accoutrements 101A FAIRVIEW RD – Industrial design carried off with arts and crafts flair. Noll Van Vourhis and Lana Garner rescue scrap metal and found objects, transforming them into formidable, yet functional, pieces of furniture that folks just can't stop talking about. Open year-round Mon–Fri 9am–5pm. (828)350-7566.

Return to Biltmore Ave/Hwy 25 and follow signs to Hwy 25A. Biltmore Estate entrance is off Hwy 25A.

 66 Biltmore Estate MCDOWELL ST – George and Edith Vanderbilt's quaint 255-room French chateau built in 1895 by William Morris Hunt, the architectural dandy of the time, is the most prominent, successful, self-supporting historical property in America. Whether wandering the great rooms of the house or the vast gardens designed by Frederick Law Olmsted, prepare yourself for an exhilarating experience. Winery, gardens, restaurants, cafes, retail shops, and more architectural detailing than you are likely to see in one place in your entire life. New to Biltmore is the Inn on Biltmore Estate, a hotel built in the grand style, replete with flourishes which George Vanderbilt, an accomplished

The Road Goes On Forever

Side trips, tidbits, adventures, and treasure hunts

host, would no doubt relish—including a beautifully civilized afternoon tea. An admission fee is charged. Open daily year-round 9am–5pm. Closed on Christmas and New Year's Day. (800) 543-2961 or (828) 274-6214. www.biltmore.com

Asheville Inns and B&B'S

Asheville is blessed with an abundance of historic, captivating inns. Space limitations prevent a full accounting in this book; however, a complete list is available at the Visitors Center of the Asheville Chamber of Commerce. The following is simply a starting point for discovering inns of note. Julia Wolfe's "Old Kentucky Home," the boarding house in her novelists son's stories of "Altamont," no longer operates but you can visit the place anyway (see listing under "Asheville.") No matter which you choose, be sure to call ahead .

ARTS AND CRAFTS
One of Asheville's building booms (1910-1930) coincided with the popularity of arts and crafts architecture. The result is neighborhoods dotted with cozy bungalows and rustic shops. In addition to the American arts and crafts style, represented by the inspirations of Gustav Stickley, Asheville also features homes in the English Romantic style of the movement. Richard Sharp Smith, supervising architect of the Biltmore House was a student of this style. Many homes in the Montford Historic District and shops in Biltmore Village reflect his influence. For a tour of Asheville's arts and crafts history, contact the Preservation Society of Asheville and Buncombe County, (828) 254-2343.

C **Abbington Green B&B** 46 CUMBERLAND CIRCLE – With eight rooms named after London parks and gardens, this Richard Sharp Smith house takes you back to the traditional English B&B's. (828) 241-2454. www.abbingtongreen.com

D **Black Walnut B&B Inn** 288 MONTFORD AVE – (828) 254-3878.

E **Cedar Crest - A Victorian Inn** 674 BILTMORE AVE – Listed on the National Register of Historic Places. (828) 252-1389.

F **Chestnut Street Inn** 176 E CHESTNUT ST – (828) 285-0705.

G **The Colby House** 230 PEARSON DR – Located in the heart of the historic Montford district, The Colby House, circa 1924, offers an elegant and warm retreat. (828) 253-5644. www.colbyhouse.com

H **1900 Inn on Montford** 296 MONTFORD AVE – Another Asheville treasure designed by Richard Sharp Smith, Biltmore's supervising architect, in 1900. Lovingly and thoughtfully restored, Lynn and Ron Carlson continue to provide an atmosphere of warmth and graciousness reminiscent of Biltmore's guilded age. (828) 254-9569 or (800) 254-9569. www.innonmontford.com

Guidebook Symbols

 Craft Studio   Restaurant

Craft Gallery   **A** Lodging

Historic Site   Special Attraction

A historic mansion, saved for a hospitable purpose.

1889 WhiteGate Inn entrance.

I **The Lion and the Rose** 278 MONTFORD AVE – This Queen Anne and Georgian style B&B is another Asheville treasure. And, so is the lavender that lines the walkways. (828)255-ROSE.

J **Old Reynolds Mansion**
100 REYNOLDS HEIGHTS – The 1855 antebellum brick home of Colonel Daniel Reynolds originally sat on 1400 acres of forestland. While only 4 acres remain with the house, the perennial beds and charming courtyard surrounding the 10 guestrooms will leave you wanting for nothing. (828)254-0496. www.oldreynoldsmansion.com

K **Richmond Hill Inn**
87 RICHMOND HILL DR – Facing demolition in the 1980's, the Victorian mansion of Richmond Hill was saved by the Preservation Society, actually moved 600 feet to its present location, and sold to its present owners, the Michels. Stay in the mansion, the Croquet Cottages or in the Garden Pavilion. Inside this architectural treasure, find two restaurants of note: Gabrielle's and the Arbor Grille. (828)252-7313. www.richmondhillinn.com

L **1889 WhiteGate Inn & Cottage**
173 E CHESTNUT ST – A wonderfully restored sprawling wonder in the midst of a magically landscaped downtown location. Innkeepers Ralph Coffey and Frank Salvo provide culinary delights and prize-winning orchids to create an experience you will long treasure. (828)253-2553. www.whitegate.net

M **The Wright Inn** 235 PEARSON DR (828)251-0789.

Beyond Grits

True, you can find plain grits, fried grits, buttered grits, and cheese grits without much trouble. But the larger question is, what else can you find? The restaurants in this section offer up a tantalizing answer—each serving regional (and other) cuisine in its

The Road Goes On Forever
Side trips, tidbits, adventures, and treasure hunts

own heartfelt way. Within the list, and at other exceptional dining establishments in and near Asheville, you will discover some of the most wonderful food this side of the pearly gates.

|●| Café on the Square ONE BILTMORE AVE – High-ceilinged, white-tableclothed space that smiles and sparkles with fine service on a busy corner. (828)251-5565.

|●| Early Girl Eatery 8 WALL ST – Local, organic food at its very best, served in a casual, up-beat atmosphere. (828)259-9292.

|●| Golden Horn Restaurant 48 BILTMORE AVE – Sumptuous Mediterranean fare aided by local produce. (828)281-4676.

|●| Laughing Seed Cafe 40 WALL ST – Long a favorite with the locals for tasty vegetarian fare. (828)252-3445.

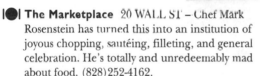

|●| The Marketplace 20 WALL ST – Chef Mark Rosenstein has turned this into an institution of joyous chopping, sautéing, filleting, and general celebration. He's totally and unredeemably mad about food. (828)252-4162.

|●| Pisgah View Ranch RTE 151 IN CANDLER – Platters heaped with apples, sweet potatoes, cornbread, cobblers, and other yummy amazements of this life, served family-style. (828)667-9100.

|●| Rezaz Mediterranean Cuisine 28 HENDER-SONVILLE RD – One of the newest stars on the ever expanding list of Asheville restaurants is Rezaz Mediterranean Cuisine. Featuring owner and Chef Reza Setayesh's American interpretation of Mediterranean favorites. (828)277-2537.

|●| Salsa's 6 PATTON AVE – A terrific combination of Mexican and Caribbean food. A must on your list. (828)252-9805.

ARTS AND CRAFTS REDUX
With the profusion of Craftsman era homes in Asheville, there are numbers of people who've taken to preserving the tradition. In a Biltmore studio called "Floating World," Gerry Brown meticulously builds Arts and Crafts doors with rich period carvings and leaded glass windows. (828) 281-1118.

Guidebook Symbols
 Craft Studio |●| Restaurant
Craft Gallery **A** Lodging
Historic Site Special Attraction

|●| **Terrace Restaurant** AT THE GROVE PARK INN – If the view and the food don't stir you, you may want to check your pulse. (828)252-2711.

FAIRVIEW

Hwy 74A, heading S, can be accessed via the Blue Ridge Parkway, I-40 or I-240 as it merges with I-40.

Travel 5 mi S of the Blue Ridge Parkway crossing and turn R on Emma's Grove. Travel 1.3 mi and bear L at Webb Cove. Travel .5 mi and turn R on Bob Barnwell Rd. Travel 1.3 mi to Cranberry Creek studio on R.

67 Cranberry Creek 423 BOB BARNWELL RD – Masters of traditional basketry who swerved off the road and landed in a really cool place. Everything Greg and Carla Filippelli do— cornucopias, platters, bowls, crescents, and basinets—has a random beauty that started at the original point of swerve. Open year-round Mon–Sat 10am–6pm & Sun 1pm–5pm. (828)628-2177.

Return to Hwy 74A. Turn R. Travel 3.5 mi. Turn R on Smith Farm Rd. Gallery/workshop is .5 mi in old chicken barn at end of drive.

68 Appalachian Designs 14 SMITH FARMS RD – Hearty, hand-hewn, yellow pine beds, tables and chairs that look at home in a bunkhouse or a townhouse. Lang Hornthal learned his craft out west and brought it to the Carolinas. We're glad he did. His workshop and gallery are in a renovated chicken house, the perfect setting for viewing his rustic creations—from watching the logs being stripped the old-fashioned way with a drawknife to playing Goldilocks among the beds. The beautiful views are free. Open year-round Mon–Thu 8am–5pm. Fri 8am–1pm. Fri afternoon & Sat–Sun by appointment only. (828)228-9994. www.appalachiandesigns.com

Return to Hwy 74A and turn L, heading back toward Asheville. Travel 2 mi and turn R on Miller Rd. Marketplace is in 1st building on R.

69 Blue Ridge Arts and Crafts Marketplace 9 MILLER RD – A rustic marketplace for a group

Greg Filippelli caught in the act of weaving at Cranberry Creek.

At Appalachian Designs, beds made to fit perfectly in your house of dreams.

Rambling quarters for the studios of artists.

The Road Goes On Forever
Side trips, tidbits, adventures, and treasure hunts

of local artists one block from historic Drovers Road (Hwy 74A). This rambling arts-and-crafts-style house holds several studios in addition to a gallery. Even more studios are in the workshop out back and in the warmer months, pick-up-and-go music jams. Open June 15–Dec 15 Mon & Fri–Sun 10am–5pm. (828)628-4875.

Return to Hwy 74A and turn R. Travel about 6.6 mi back to the Blue Ridge Parkway or I-40 or to downtown Asheville via Hwy 70.

ALEXANDER & REEMS CREEK

From downtown Asheville, travel N on Hwy 19/23 (or Merrimon Ave or scenic River Rd/Hwy 251) for approximately 6.5 mi. Exit on New Stock Rd, turn L off exit ramp and travel 2.5 mi and turn L on Monticello Rd. Travel 1.7 mi and turn R on Hwy 251/River Rd (French Broad Overview By-Way.) Travel 1.2 mi and turn L, crossing river. Travel 1.1 mi on Fletcher Martin Rd. Turn L on Curtis Miles Rd and then another immediate sharp L. Travel .2 mi, turn R on Haney Rd and Studio is .5 mi on R.

 Dancing Dragonfly Pottery 83 HANEY RD – Troy Amastar's studio alone is worth a detour off any beaten path. A unique construction of timber frame with straw and cob (adobe) walls, her work space holds so many fascinations you'll be hard-pressed to move on to whatever's next. Chief among the fascinations is Troy's line of work–pottery that brims with color and life. Open year-round Mon–Sat 10am–7pm. (828)683-3405.

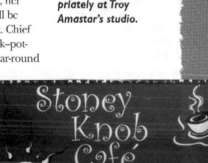

If you see a dragonfly, you're stopped appropriately at Troy Amastar's studio.

Return to Fletcher Martin Rd. Turn R and travel back and under Hwy 19/23. Turn L on Business 19/Merrimon Ave. Travel .4 mi and Stoney Knob Cafe is on L.

|🍴| Stoney Knob Cafe & Patio 337 MERRIMON AVE – Take a little break from trailblazing and get into the moment—namely dining alfresco at this funky, spirited cafe. From the farmer's market to table, nightly gourmet specials remind you of the starving artist within clambering to get out. Occasional live music—call ahead. Open year-round Tue–Sat 8am–8pm & Sun 9:30am–3pm. Closed Mon. (828)645-3309.

Just a lot of fun near old Stoney Knob.

Guidebook Symbols

🖐	Craft Studio	🍴	Restaurant
🔵	Craft Gallery	🅐	Lodging
🔲	Historic Site	⭐	Special Attraction

Everyone works at Ox-Ford Farm.

Turn L on Merrimon Ave. Travel .2 mi. Turn R on Reems Creek Rd. Go .6 mi and turn R, just after crossing Reems Creek Bridge.

72 | Weaverville Milling Company Restaurant

1 OLD MILL LANE – The classic grain mill was in operation from 1912-1965. It's now a hearty restaurant serving up tasty meals with a twist. Specials include roast pork tenderloin with apple nut dressing. Crafts for sale in the loft. Open daily for dinner at 5:30pm except Wed. Closed first three weeks of Jan. (828)645-4700.

Continue traveling Reems Creek Rd to intersection with Ox Creek Rd. Turn R and Inn is .5 mi on R.

N Ox-Ford Farm B&B 75 OX CREEK RD –

This place is the very embodiment of country life. The stone and frame farmhouse dates from the 1880's, the sweeping views from atop the surrounding meadows are eternal. The working farm is home to pedigree sheep, beef cattle, peacocks, ducks, chickens, and an occasional adopted wild turkey. (828)658-2500.

Return to Reems Creek Rd and turn R. Vance Birthplace in on R, about 5 mi from intersection with Merrimon Ave.

Vance Birthplace as it was and is.

73 Vance Birthplace REEMS CREEK RD – A

two-story pioneer log house and out-buildings, some reconstructed, mark the site where North Carolina's Civil War governor Zebulon Vance was born. Spring and fall, artisans in period costume demonstrate early craft-making, especially quilting and woodworking. Open Apr–Oct Mon–Sat 9am–5pm & Sun 1pm–5pm. Nov–Mar Tue–Sat 10am–4pm. (828)645-6706.

Continue traveling on Reems Creek Rd until it ends. Turn L at T intersection and immediate R on blackberry Inn Rd. In less than 1 mi turn L at church on McDaris Cove Rd. Studio is 1.5 mi on L.

Kathy Triplett's teapots: surely they talk when we leave the room.

74 Kathy Triplett McDARIS COVE RD – A stu-

dio with an attitude. Everywhere you look charmed and prissy teapots strut their great stuff. From clay, this woman assuredly creates a joyous deco wonderland. Open year-round Thu–Fri 12noon–4pm. (828)658-3207.

The Road Goes On Forever

Side trips, tidbits, adventures, and treasure hunts

*Return to Merrimon Ave/Business 19. To travel into Weaverville,
turn R. To return to Asheville, turn L.*

WEAVERVILLE

*From downtown Asheville, travel N on Hwy 19/23 or
Merrimon Ave/Hwy 25 for about 10 miles and follow
signs to Main St. Next 6 sites are within walking
distance of each other.*

0 **The Secret Garden B&B** 56 N
MAIN ST – Historic Weaverville
residence, Secret Gardens B&B boasts
a picturesque 60-foot veranda, three
rooms with private baths and sitting
rooms. Gourmet candlelit breakfasts
and afternoon libations in the sunlit
solarium will prepare you well for
exploring the quaint village and its many treasures. (800)797-8211. www.secretgardenNC.com

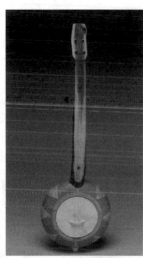

*On the cusp of
downtown Weaverville.*

75 **Mangum Pottery** 16 N. MAIN ST – Rob and
his wife Beth are establishing their own universal
language in clay: witty, playful slab-formed
vases, tables, clocks and musical instruments;
elegant wheel-thrown teapots in raku crackle
or mixed media. Open Jan–Apr Mon–Fri
9am–5pm. May–Dec Mon–Fri 9am–5pm &
Sat 10am–4pm. (828)645-4929.
www.mangumpottery.com

76 **Sunnyside Café** 18 N MAIN ST –
Head for the sunny-side of the street,
where Chefs Jack and Patty Keeran marry
local organic produce with savory entrees
like pecan-crusted mountain trout. Oh,
yum. Open year round. Lunch Mon–Fri
11:30am–2pm. Dinner Tue–Sat 5:30am–
9pm. (828)658-2660.

77 **Well-Bred Bakery and Café** 26 N MAIN
ST – Where you would be found every
morning if you ruled the universe. Organic,
freshly-baked gourmet treats served in casual
surroundings of a neighborhood bakery. Open
year-round Tue–Fri 7am–6:30pm. Sat 9am–5pm.
Sun 10am–3pm. (828)645-9300.

*The playful artistry of
Rob and Beth Mangum.*

Guidebook Symbols

Craft Studio		**I●I** Restaurant	
(●1) Craft Gallery		**A** Lodging	
1 Historic Site		Special Attraction	

The source of old things: Preservation Hall.

Another really good and lively gourd put to good use.

|78| Preservation Hall 55 N MAIN ST – Darcey and Capri Williams have converted the oldest commercial building still in use in Western NC (circa mid-1800's) into an emporium offering architectural antiques and materials from old homes and buildings as well as a gallery which features work from Appalachian artisans. Three floors of great finds. Open year-round Tue–Fri 9:30am–5:30pm. Sat 9am–2pm. Sun–Mon by appointment. (828)645-1047. www.preservation-hall.com

P **Inn on Main Street** 88 S MAIN ST – A garden walk bordered by herb and organic vegetable gardens endears this Victorian inn to any visitor. Innkeeper Dan Ward has created custom tiles to bring a dash of color to everything. (828)645-4935 or (877)873-6074. www.innonmain.com

Q **Dry Ridge Inn** 26 BROWN ST – Built in 1849 as a parsonage for a nearby revival camp-ground. Today it's a welcome sanctuary. Innkeepers Howard and Kirsten Kusenbery have installed a baby grand in the parlor and a gourmet cook in the kitchen. Seven rooms. (828)658-3899. www.dryridgeinn.com

Return to Hwy 19/23 and travel N to continue studio trail in Barnardsville and Mars Hill and to connect to Circle the Mountain Trail S of Burnsville.

To travel back to downtown Asheville, turn S on Hwy 19/23.

BARNARDSVILLE

From Hwy 19/23 N of Weaverville, take Barnardsville Rd exit (Hwy 197). Travel E (R if you're traveling from Asheville) for 4.6 mi. Turn L on Riddle Rd. Studio is located at 2nd drive on R.

79 **Brave Eagle Gourds** 29 RIDDLE RD – So little time, so many gourds. Welcome to the lively works of Virginia Saunders, a hand of inspiration that reaches out and grabs the first good gourd it comes to. Open year-round Mon & Wed–Sat 10am–4pm. (828) 626-2419.

The Road Goes On Forever
Side trips, tidbits, adventures, and treasure hunts

Return to Barnardsville Rd and turn L. Travel .9 mi. and turn L on Whitmore Branch Rd. Travel .2 mi and turn L on Dock Branch Rd. Travel .8 mi to end of road. Studio is in the garden at the back of house.

80 **Heart Song Artworks** 141 DOCK BRANCH RD – Gina Canter's studio and gallery have everything to do with her Cherokee, Celtic and Appalachian folk paintings, as well as her limited edition prints and greeting cards. Her paintings reveal the legends and lore of the Appalachian region; many of the sites she portrays are in the immediate region and accessible to visitors. Open year-round Wed & Sat–Sun 10am–5pm or by appointment. (828)626-2457. www.heartsongartworks.com

Gina Canter's Heart Song Artworks, fairly full of song.

Return to Barnardsville Rd, turn L and travel about 1.5 mi. Turn R into Hawk & Ivy drive.

R **The Hawk & Ivy Holistic Country Retreat B&B** 133 N FORK RD – The country retreat of James and Eve Davis situated close by national forest lands and the Ivy River. This welcoming haven includes a guest cottage and gift shop. The innkeepers' ever-expanding garden has the express purpose of nourishing body and soul— fresh berries, fruits and flowers—and, most everywhere, original art from talented folk in the region. (828)626-3486. www.hawkandivy.com

Proven retreat for the body and soul.

Return to Hwy 19/23. To travel to Asheville, head S. To connect with studios and galleries off Hwy 19 in Mars Hill area, travel N on Hwy 19/23 and follow signs to Hwy 19 as road changes. See listings for Mars Hill area. To connect to Circle of the Mountain Trail, continue N on Hwy 19 to listings south of Burnsville.

S **Center for Massage and Natural Health Residential Retreat** 530 UPPER FLAT CREEK RD – A healing arts retreat. Located on 25 acres of rolling hills, the center includes log barns, a turn-of-the-century grist mill, a koi pond, and walking trails that gently wind through the property. (828)658-0814. www.centerformassage.com

Guidebook Symbols

	Craft Studio		Restaurant
	Craft Gallery		Lodging
	Historic Site		Special Attraction

LEICESTER

Leicester can be reached by traveling N on Hwy 63 off of Hwy 19/23/Patton Ave in West Asheville. To reach Cat's Studio, travel 3 mi on Leicester Hwy/Hwy 63 and turn R on Mt. Carmel Rd and travel 1.7 mi. Turn L on Old Leicester Rd and travel 1 mi. Turn R on Bear Creek Rd and travel .8 mi. Cat's drive is on R—look for rabbits on gatepost.

(An alternative route to Leicester is through Alexander. Follow directions to Dancing Dragonfly across French Broad and continue traveling on Fletcher Martin Rd to L turn onto Alexander Rd—about 1.2 mi from river. Travel 3.3 mi and turn L on Bear Creek Rd. Cat's is 2.9 mi on L.)

The jazzy, masterful work of Cat Jarosz.

 Cat's Stoneware Studio 1177 BEAR CREEK RD – In a small barn with a kiln shed attached, Cat Jarosz creates masterful pottery—dinnerware, coffee pots, pitchers, platters—distinguished by a ribbed texture and subtle glazes. Artful and universally functional as well. Open year-round Mon & Tue 2pm–6pm. Call after 2pm for appointments on other days. (828)683-1755 or (828)683-3747.

Turn R out of drive and travel 2.9 mi to Alexander Rd. and turn L. Travel 1.8 mi and turn R on Leicester Rd. Travel 2 mi and turn L on S Turkey Creek Rd. Travel 2.8 mi to Potato Branch split, turning L at split. Paved road turns into dirt road. After the road changes to dirt take first L (next to brick silo) onto small dirt drive. Travel .4 mi to end and studio is on R.

82 Turkey Creek Woodcrafters 309 POTATO BRANCH RD – Woodcrafter Jeff Frank works at his trade in the midst of his organic farm, surrounded by goats, sheep, chickens, and turkeys. He crafts custom furniture of walnut, oak, maple and cherry from rocking chairs to reproductions, including rustic mountain furniture that's extremely hard for the human heart to resist. Open year-round Mon–Fri 9am–5pm. Sat by appointment. (828)683-0030. www.turkeycreekwoodcrafters.com

Return to Leicester Rd and turn L. Travel 1.2 mi and turn L on N Turkey Creek Rd. Travel 1.5 mi. N Turkey Creek Rd turns into Early's Mountain Rd. Veer R on Early's Mountain Rd (which then becomes Big Sandy Mush Rd). Travel 3 mi. Jones Pottery is on R.

The Road Goes On Forever
Side trips, tidbits, adventures, and treasure hunts

Jones Pottery Ltd. 209 BIG SANDY MUSH RD – With his roots in the region, Matt Jones makes storage jars, pitchers, teapots, tableware and garden planters inspired by traditional alkaline-glazed Carolina pieceware of the 19th and 20th centuries. His work is often striped and toned with earth-colored glazes, extraordinarily inviting to the eye and hand. Not only is the pottery hand-built, so is the kiln from which it is born and the studio/showroom next door. Open year-round Mon–Fri 9am–5pm & Sat–Sun by appoinment only. (828) 683-2705. www.jonespottery.com

Honorably striped, Matt Jones' traditional Carolina pieceware.

Take L back onto Big Sandy Mush Rd and travel 1 mi. Take L on Sandy Mush Creek Rd and go 1.1 mi. Take L on Early View and Madison Tile Works is first house on R, about .2 mi on Early View Rd.

 Madison Tile Works 62 EARLY VIEW RD – Madison MacLaren has been working in clay for more than 30 years and her handbuilt tiles are still as fresh and exuberant as ever. Her work winds up as gifts and memorials and in all sorts of home and commercial settings and it all emanates from the spacious studio which she and her husband built in this mountain glen. Open year-round Mon–Fri 10am–5pm but always good to call ahead. (828) 683-1824.

A source of exuberance made in Tile Works.

Take L back on Sandy Mush Creek Rd and travel 1.5 mi. Turn L on Hwy 63 and drive 8 mi. Take R on Hwy 209 N toward Hot Springs and drive 1.8 mi. Turn L on Caldwell Mountain Rd and travel 2.1 mi. Turn L on Meadow Fork Rd and drive .7 mi. Take L on Beasley Cove Rd and go .4 mi. Studio drive on R.

HOT SPRINGS

 dORY 444 BEASLEY COVE RD – Dory Brown and her busband built their home in the 70's

Guidebook Symbols

 Craft Studio   Restaurant
 Craft Gallery   Lodging
Historic Site Special Attraction

dORY Brown's spiral garden, another unfolding of deep enthusiasm.

and have been adding enticements ever since— a pond reflecting ever-changing views, permaculture gardens and, coming soon, alternative energy. In the midst of all this, Dory designs and creates some truly exceptional jewelry and metalcraft, in large part influenced by her work and study at Haywood Community College and at Penland. In short, there are some high level reasons for stopping by. Open year-round Thu–Sat 10am–6pm. (828)622-7145. www.futuristicallyarchaic.com

Take R back on Meadow Fork Rd and travel 8.1 mi. Turn L on Hwy 209 and drive 7.6 mi. The Yellow Teapot and the Bridge Street Café are on L.

⟨86⟩ The Yellow Teapot 81 BRIDGE ST – A cooperative gallery featuring pottery, paintings, soap, fiber pieces and other lively expressions of local artisans. And, as you might imagine from the name, the art of tea-sipping is generally a work in progress. A handy place to check in on workshops and other art-related goings-on. Open year-round Mon & Wed–Sun 10am–6pm. (828)622-9727. www.yellowteapot.com

|87| Bridge Street Cafe and Inn 145 BRIDGE ST – What cinches the deal is the locally grown organic vegetables and herbs used in the brick-oven pizzas and other dishes. Not to be missed: dining on the deck overlooking Spring Creek. Open Apr–Nov Thu–Sat 5:30am–10pm. Sun 11am–2pm & 5:30am–9pm. (828)622-0002. www.bridgestreetcafe.com

T Duckett House Inn and Farm 433 LANCE AVE (NC 209) – The 1900 Victorian house borders Spring Creek and is within a shout of the Appalachian Trail and a short hike to the hot springs for which Hot Springs was named. In other words, centrally located between trail and apres trail. Six guest rooms, tent camping, and garden fresh meals. (828)622-7621. www.bbonline.com/nc/ducketthouse

U Tree Spirit B&B 93 FRISBEE ST – A lovely and welcoming four guest-room B&B featuring

Spring Creek, known by its clearness and clatter.

The Road Goes On Forever
Side trips, tidbits, adventures, and treasure hunts

the products of Tree Spirit Herbals. The whole of the experience has to do with taking a breath. (828)622-9631. www.hotspringsnc.org/treespirit

Hwy 209 becomes Hwy 25/70 in Hot Springs. Travel about 4 mi N and E on Hwy 25/70. Lonesome Mountain Designs is on R as Hwy 25/70 makes sharp turn to R.

The relaxing sound of rushing water at the Tree Spirit B&B.

 Lonesome Mountain Designs 5150 HWY 25/70 – In an old building literally draped over a creek and adjacent to the scenic Laurel River, Kristen Derrick and Greg Adams create mosaics inspired by the waters that rush past them. Garden pieces, benches, birdhouses & feeders— all infused with the river's energy. They also craft canvas and leather bags and other custom sewn pieces. A good place, in general, to absorb the jumpy ions of racing water. Open Apr–Oct Thu–Fri 10am–3pm & Sat–Sun 10am–6pm. Other times by appointment only. (828)656-2288.

 Mountain Magnolia Inn & Retreat 204 LAWSON ST – 130-year-old Victorian home restored so beautifully "This Old House" featured it. Extensive gardens and dinner on weekends. (828)622-3543. www.mountainmagnoliainn.com

Continue on Hwy 25/70, traveling R as it turns sharply. Travel 10 mi and merge R on Business 25/70 which then becomes Main St in downtown Marshall. Travel 1.7 mi and park. Zuma's is on R across from the courthouse.

Good coffee, well-flanked.

MARSHALL

Marshall is about 20 mi NW of Asheville, via Hwy 19/23N to Hwy 25/70. Follow signs into downtown.

Zuma Coffee 10 S MAIN ST – Joel Friedman's coffee shop in historic downtown Marshall, across the street from the stately Madison County Courthouse, has fast become a hub of community activity and general news gathering. Grab a fresh-baked muffin or cookie while you're doing your coffee-cream-sugar-and-did-you-hear-about-Aunt-Betsy thing. Open year-round Mon–Fri 7am–5pm & Sat 9am–2pm. (828) 649-1617.

Guidebook Symbols

Craft Studio		Restaurant
Craft Gallery		Lodging
Historic Site		Special Attraction

Continue down Business 25/70 for .8 mi. Take L on Hwy 213 E and travel 9.1 mi. Turn L on Main St at first traffic light. Purple Mountain Gallery is on L.

MARS HILLS

Mars Hill is located near the intersection of Hwy 19/23N and Hwy 213 (about 20 mi N of Asheville.).

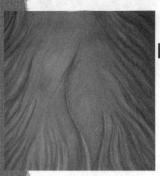

The question of the day at Purple Mountain: Why not enjoy every spare moment?

(90) Purple Mountain Gallery 37 S MAIN ST – Brothers Bryce and Tate Barnes have rounded up a collection of paintings, sculptures, pottery and photography from both local and out-of-the-region artists. With its coffee bar and the occasional evening music jams, the gallery is a good place to relax and enjoy everything that's happening in the immediate vicinity. Open year-round Mon–Thu 7am–12noon. Fri 7am–9pm. Sat 7am–6pm. (828)680-9520.

91 Rural Life Museum MARS HILL COLLEGE CAMPUS – Ivy-covered stone building once part of the college, now dedicated to preserving mountain farm and craft culture. Visually compelling recreations of hearth and home, exhibits of farm and craft implements and techniques, historic photographic murals, all supported by scholarly documentation. Open Mon–Fri 2pm–4pm during the school year. (828)689-1424.

Todd Barrow's art.

Return to Hwy 213, turn L. Travel 1.1 mi. Merge N on Hwy 19/23. Travel 1.8 mi. Follow 19 N when it splits toward Burnsville. Travel .2 mi. Turn R on California Creek Rd. Travel .5 mi and Spun Song is on L.

92 Spun Song Studio 520 CALIFORNIA CREEK RD – Weaving (much of it with silks) and woodworking—that pretty much describes the artful goings on of this husband and wife team. The Rines also display the work of talented friends —fiber art and fine woodwork, among other things. Open year-round Thu–Sat 10am–6pm. Sun–Wed by appointment only. (828) 689-2572.

Continue traveling S on California Creek Rd until it merges into Beech Glenn Rd. Turn L into parking area for ballpark and community center. Studio is across parking area next to white house.

The Road Goes On Forever

Side trips, tidbits, adventures, and treasure hunts

Rustic Raven 2938 BEECH GLENN RD –
Todd Barrow knows something about rustic
furniture. He also (and hence the name) knows
a thing or two about ravens. He crafts art furniture—beds, mirrors, tables, chairs, lamps, railings—from indigenous trees and sometimes
adds found objects like deer antlers. A couple of
his chairs have brightened the covers of
Architectural Digest and *Southern Accents*.
Open most of the year Tue–Thu 10am–6pm.
Best to call ahead. (828)689-9672.
www.brwm.org/rusticraven

*Darlene Berndt's
Sculpture renderings.*

*Return to Beech Glenn Rd, turn R and travel about 1.3 mi to
Walker Branch Rd. Turn R. Travel 2 mi , following signs around
two turns to discover two dinosaurs contemplating you from the L
side of the road.*

*Stresing Art: diverse
and energetic.*

 Stresing Art Gallery 371 HAMBURG RD –
It's the dinosaurs in the garden that are a dead
giveaway you've found the Stresings. Continue
on up the drive to the gallery and try to stay
focused on your current mission: to appreciate
the far-ranging talents of Lou and Earl Stresing,
with work spanning wood-carvings, art lamps,
glass art, and paintings, not to mention the
occasional Stegosaurus. Open year-round
Tue–Sun 10am–5pm. (828)689-4231.

*Return to Beech Glenn Rd, turn R and travel .9 mi to Hwy 19
Turn L to travel to Asheville. Turn R to travel to Burnsville and
parts N, the Circle the Mountains Trail.*

SOUTH ASHEVILLE SPUR

*Travel 1.3 mi S of Biltmore Village on Hwy 25 and turn L on West
Chapel Rd. Travel 1 block and turn R on Rose St. Travel another
block and turn L on Azalea St. Dar's is 2nd house on L.*

 Dar's Digs 10 AZALEA ST – A cast of colorful
characters painstakingly (and ever so finely)
rendered in clay: a jester, a dancer, a boy bowing
his head. Ceramic sculptures, polymer dolls and
handwoven scarves and jewelry. The creative
fount is Darlene Berndt. Open year-round Tue
& Sat 10:30am–5pm. (828)277-6380.

Guidebook Symbols

🖐	Craft Studio	🍴	Restaurant
Ⓛ	Craft Gallery	🅰	Lodging
🔢	Historic Site	⭐	Special Attraction

At the Cohen's, elegant frames for nature's best work.

Pottery with a nine-generation history of good use.

Turn L back on Hwy 25 and travel 3.7 mi. Turn L on Mills Gap Rd and travel .2 mi. Turn R on Sweeten Creek Rd and travel 1.9 mi. Turn L on Cedar Ln and travel .2 mi. Turn L on Locust Ct. Cohen's is 1st house on R.

 Ruthie and Mike Cohen 197 LOCUST CT – About the jewelry, Ruthie says the idea is to make fine frames for "nature's good show." And for their stagey, elegant work there's a lot happening—whether it's stone canyon agate, imperial jasper, opals or branch pearls. "We look for the fire in the stones," she says. After which, there's the fire in their own imagination, a hearth that is always stoked with wonder, joy, and laughter. Open year-round Wed–Fri 12noon–4pm. (828)687-7830. www.jewelryadventureclub.com

Return to Hwy 25, turn L, traveling S on Hendersonville Hwy/Hwy 25 for 2.9 mi. Brown's is on L.

 Brown's Pottery 2398 HENDERSONVILLE HWY – The oldest traditional face jug producing family in America—in point of fact, one of the oldest pottery families in America, now into its ninth generation of continuous operation. The original Brown's Pottery began in England and crossed the pond in the early 1700's. The family continues to dig clay for cookware from the same pit Grandpa used, though some things have changed—a face jug Grandpa Brown sold for $2.50 recently sold for $65,000 and some of the family's work is displayed at the Smithsonian and at the American Museum of Folk Art. Open year-round Mon–Sat 10am–6pm. (828)684-2901. www.brownspottery.com

Turn R back on Hwy 25/Hendersonville Hwy and travel back toward Asheville for approximately 2 mi back to the Blue Ridge Parkway. Head S on the Parkway to Hwy 191. Follow signs to NC Arboretum when exiting Parkway.

HWY 191 NEAR PARKWAY

Follow above directions from Parkway. Alternative routes to the NC Arboretum is Hwy 191 S from West Asheville, E from I-26 or N from Hendersonville.

The Road Goes On Forever
Side trips, tidbits, adventures, and treasure hunts

The North Carolina Arboretum
100 FREDERICK LAW OLMSTED
WAY – A 426-acre facility that's part
of the University of North Carolina.
Explore a bounty of trails and gardens, including an Appalachian Quilt
Garden and new Craft Garden—
providing natural dye and fiber plants
used in basketry, broom-making,
paper-making and other fiber arts.
Handcrafted wrought iron gates welcome you to formal paths. More treasures await in the greenhouses. Among
the showy plants of interest, one of
the finest bonsai collections in the
South. An admission fee is charged. Open year-
round Mon–Sat 9am–5pm & Sun 12noon–5pm.
(828)665-2492. www.ncarboretum.org

*Beautiful wrought iron
gates found at the NC
Arboretum.*

*Return to Hwy 191 and turn R, traveling south for 1 mi. Turn L
on Clayton Rd and Evan's Pottery is about .2 mi on L.*

 Evan's Pottery 101 CLAYTON RD – A
collection of Appalachian everyday ware,
featuring methods and shapes generations old.
Colorfully glazed handmade pottery by Evan
Brown, a 6th generation potter. Open Apr–Dec
Mon–Sat 9am–5pm. (828)684-6842.

*Return to Hwy 191. Turn L. Travel .5 mi and Pisgah Forest
Pottery is on L.*

 Pisgah Forest Pottery 1720 BREVARD RD –
Established by Walter Stephen in 1926, these
cabins of craft are practically a national shrine
to pottery-making. The dinnerware and mugs
are long famous for their turquoise, wine, jade,
and crystalline glazes. The folks here mix their
own clay on the property and fire up a kiln
stoked with pine wood. Tom Case answers the
bell. Open year-round Mon–Sat 9am–5pm.
(828)684-6663.

*To travel to Asheville, turn R on Hwy 191. Follow signs back to
downtown. To return to the Blue Ridge Parkway, turn R on Hwy
191. Follow signs back to the Parkway. To travel to Hendersonville
and String of Pearls Trail or Brevard and the Cascades Trail, turn
L on Hwy 191 and follow signs to either town.*

Guidebook Symbols

Craft Studio		Restaurant
Craft Gallery		Lodging
Historic Site		Special Attraction

The Urban Trail

Story of a City

Who knew that, in one short walk of thirty stops, across a distance of about two miles, one could experience so much about what makes the mountain city of Asheville so beautiful. Chances are, when dreamers, benefactors, and artists first talked about an urban trail for Asheville, they had no idea how variegated and textured it would become. Slip on the Birkenstocks, grab a trail guide (available at Pack Place where the trail begins), and prepare your mind and heart for an adventure in "Ohmigosh, I had no idea."

Just in case you thought this walk was all about obscure local politicians, dead lawyers and sour-faced ex-mayors, consider this partial cast of characters:

• Master storyteller William Porter, known to his readers as O.Henry, moved here to marry Asheville-born Sarah Coleman.

• Epic twentieth century novelist Thomas Wolfe, author of *Look Homeward Angel*, wrote about the people of Asheville and the places from his childhood you will see along the trail.

• Stone Sculptor Frederic Miles immortalized neighborhood florist Cyrus Deake by including his face in a wrap-around frieze at the Drhumor Building.

• Elizabeth Blackwell, the first female M.D. in America, also studied under an Asheville doctor.

• Architect Douglas Ellington brought

Parisian art deco effervescnce to such buildings as City Hall, First Baptist Church and the S&W Cafeteria.

• Jimmy Rogers, who some consider to be the father of country music, lived in the Flat Iron Building before recording Blue Yodels One, Two and Three.

• Dr. Edwin Wiley Grove, inventor of Grove's Chill Tonic, builder of the Grove Park Inn, and the opulent Grove Arcade, which has now been restored and is bristling with commerce and life.

• Raphael Guastavino, whose graceful self-supporting tile domes distinguish Grand Central Station, Carnegie Hall, the chapel at West Point and one of the most precious and beautiful buildings in Asheville, the Basilica of St. Lawrence.

• Charlton Heston, who as a budding actor in 1947, directed and starred in the Asheville Community Theater's rendition of Tennessee Williams' *The Glass Menagerie.*

• James Vester Miller, an African-American brick mason whose work in the municipal building is mesmerizingly beautiful.

These and dozens of other fascinating men and women illuminate the journey through Asheville's past. Created by artisans, many from the region, the public sculptures express their own poetry of invention. Along the way, you'll also get to know the city's contemporary landscape, dotted with shops and restaurants, galleries and gathering places of an irresistible charm.

String of Pearls

The towns and hamlets and waysides that form a loopy handle south of Asheville have cottoned to the hopes and cares of travelers for more than two hundred years. Each is a destination unto itself, fully blessed with a history and a character both distinct and evocative. ⋮⋮ There is an enormous heritage of art and craft on this trail, eclipsed only by the scale of hospitality so evident along the way. ⋮⋮ From Asheville to Black Mountain, you'll drive through the Swannanoa Valley, a basin beneath the Great Craggies which back into the Blacks and Mount Mitchell, highest of all Eastern peaks. But down along the streets of brick buildings in Black Mountain, there is mostly a slow-motion gawkery going on. A stop by a blacksmiths shop or a jeweler can turn into a conversation as panoramic as a ride on the Parkway.

⋮⋮ Route 9, a North Carolina Scenic Byway, wiggles across the Continental Divide (3,048 feet) and drops through deep mountain farm meadows into Bat Cave, then Chimney Rock and Lake Lure. These small towns carry the names of their own extraordinary geologies–Bat Cave for its caves under the mountain,

Along the way, a flowering of genuine hospitality.

An open invitation to browse

Chimney Rock for the granite spike and nature preserve open for visitors since 1916. **⋮⋮** Further on in Columbus and Tryon, the art of hospitality unfolds much as the land does. Here there are plantation houses, the temperate climates of the Isothermal Belt flowering out camellias and azaleas, the inns and horsetrails of Tryon, the ripple of racing silks on steeplechase day, the hand-thrown pottery of a gentle world. **⋮⋮** Turning north, you move toward the welcoming main streets of Saluda, Flat Rock and Hendersonville, towns anchored in the history of 19th century America: Saluda with its diverse craft community, influenced and inspired by strong Penland ties; Flat Rock with its Charleston connections, grand inns, hills of Connemara and elegant craft; and Hendersonville, apple capital, home of jamborees and hoedowns and sidewalk sales, food fairs and lush galleries. **⋮⋮** A string of pearls. A drive through the mountains. A josling of memories. A sweet journey into slowed-down, art-filled places that welcome your company. Take your time. Fill your heart. Enjoy the trip.

String of Pearls

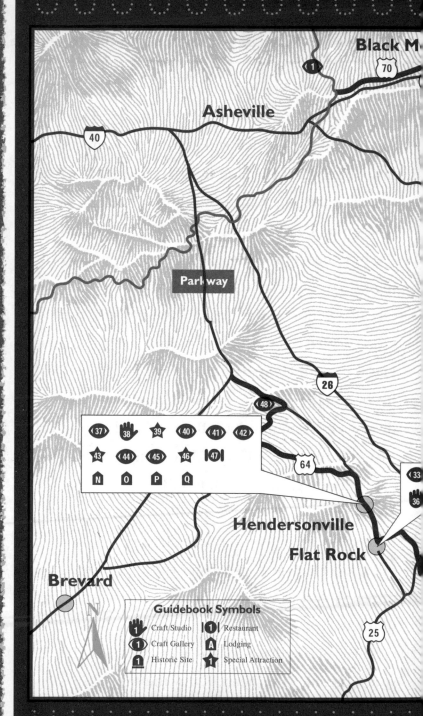

Black M

Asheville

Parkway

Black M

70

1

40

26

48

64

33

36

Hendersonville

Flat Rock

Brevard

25

Guidebook Symbols

Craft Studio · Restaurant
Craft Gallery · Lodging
Historic Site · Special Attraction

To envision this tour, hang a necklace of villages and towns down the map draping it around Mt. Pisgah and Mt. Mitchell at the top and letting it gracefully fall towards South Carolina stopping just shy of the border. Once you've got this image in your head, you'll be ready to lower the rumble seat, toss your picnic basket in the back and tally-ho, forthwith.

Hospitality reigns supreme. From Black Mountain to Chimney Rock to Columbus to Tryon to Saluda to Hendersonville–you'll rarely be far from a welcoming inn or bed & breakfast. They all have long and genial histories of making travelers (and especially art-seekers) feel at home.

Although you could cover this ground in two or three days moving like the wind, due to the length of conversations and breadth of hospitality you're about to encounter, the better calculation would be to square the hypotenuse of whatever it was you were originally thinking.

The Folk Art Center: An inspiring collection of artful pieces.

PARKWAY MILEPOST 382

1 Folk Art Center BLUE RIDGE PARKWAY, – Home of historic Allanstand Craft Shop, one of the early retail co-ops in the Appalachian region. Hundreds of artful pieces in virtually all media produced by members of the Southern Highland Craft Guild. A moveable feast of special exhibits in the gallery by individual artisans. The building also houses the Guild's craft library and a theater for seasonal productions. Demonstrations outside and inside, spring through fall color. Open daily year-round. Apr–Dec 9am–6pm. Jan–Mar 9am–5pm. (828) 298-7928.

Travel east on Hwy 70 for 10 mi into Black Mountain.

BLACK MOUNTAIN

Hwy 70 becomes State St in Black Mtn and Art Center is on R as you enter downtown.

2 Black Mountain Center for the Arts 225 W STATE ST – An inventive re-use of a historic city building, including the jail area, where instead of a crook you might just find a cook conducting a class. With a busy schedule of exhibits and performances, it's a beehive of creative expression. Learn how to build a dulcimer, bellydance, make wheel-thrown pottery, write fiction, play the banjo, take tai

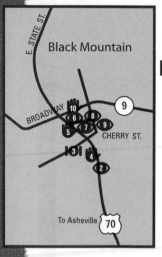

The Road Goes On Forever

Side trips, tidbits, adventures, and treasure hunts

chi, study acting, and get into perspective drawing. Open year-round Mon–Thu 10am–5pm. Fri 10am–8pm. Sat 1pm–4pm. (828)669-0930.

Continue down State St and park on either State St or Cherry St. The next 7 sites are within walking distance of each other. The bakery is just off State St on Church St.

|3| Black Mountain Bakery 102 CHURCH ST – Something in the time-space continuum goes haywire when you walk in this place. Blink, and suddenly two hours have disappeared. Blame it on the java and other-worldly goodies like raspberry coffeecake and oatmeal raisin breakfast pie. Open year-round Tue–Sat 8am–4pm. (828)669-1626.

Song of the Wood: Source of celestial tones "set free".

4 Song of the Wood 203 WEST STATE ST – Hammered dulcimers started from scratch and ending in song or as Jerry Read Smith describes, "celestial tones set free to tell their stories." Jerry's dulcimers and bowed psaltries may wind up in the hands of players from all over the world, but the help and advice is down-home friendly. Also mountain dulcimers, celtic harps, and instrumental music on CD. Open year-round. Mon–Sat 10am–5pm. (828)669-7675.
www.songofthewood.com

5 Visions of Creation 114 CHERRY ST – A crafter of dreamlike jewelry originally from Colombia, South America, Robert Vengocchea designs pendants and rings that often juxtapose precious stones of contrasting colors. He particularly likes a description of his work that would have Dr. Seuss and Salvadore Dali coming together to design fine art jewelry. That's pretty close, but there's only one Robert Vengoechea and his visions speak, quite beautifully, for themselves. Commission work is a specialty of the house. Open Jan–Apr Fri–Sat 12noon–5pm. May–Dec Mon & Wed–Thu 11am–5pm. Fri 11am–6pm. Sat 10am–6pm. Sun 1pm–5pm. Do call ahead. (828)669-0065.
www.visionsofcreation.com

A Vengoechea original at Visions of Creation.

Guidebook Symbols

👋	Craft Studio	|●|	Restaurant
(1)	Craft Gallery	A	Lodging
1	Historic Site	⭐	Special Attraction

Conversational art at Seven Sisters Gallery.

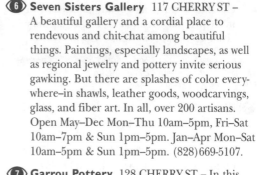

⑥ Seven Sisters Gallery 117 CHERRY ST – A beautiful gallery and a cordial place to rendevous and chit-chat among beautiful things. Paintings, especially landscapes, as well as regional jewelry and pottery invite serious gawking. But there are splashes of color everywhere–in shawls, leather goods, woodcarvings, glass, and fiber art. In all, over 200 artisans. Open May–Dec Mon–Thu 10am–5pm, Fri–Sat 10am–7pm & Sun 1pm–5pm. Jan–Apr Mon–Sat 10am–5pm & Sun 1pm–5pm. (828)669-5107.

⑦ Garrou Pottery 128 CHERRY ST – In this gallery, father and son, John and Derrick Garrou, show their value-priced, globally-useful pottery in myriad shapes. Without one of their apple bakers, your kitchen is simply woefully incomplete. Open Jan–Mar Thu–Sat 10am–5pm. Apr–Dec Mon–Sat 10am–5pm. (828)669-0222. www.blackmountainnc.com

Splashings of Garrou Pottery

⑧ Cherry Street Gallery 132 CHERRY ST – A plethora of craft–glass, pottery, jewelry, iron, wood–from within and without the mountain region. Once you start looking, you'll wonder where the time goes. Dennis Harvey's been wondering that for the last 9 years. Open Apr–Dec Mon–Sat 10am–5pm & Sun 12noon– 4pm. Jan–Mar Mon & Thu–Fri 12noon–5pm. Sat 10am–5pm. Sun 12noon–4pm. (828)669-0450.

⑨ The Old Depot 207 SUTTON AVE (Across street Cherry St Gallery) – A nonprofit arts and crafts gallery with over 75 craftspeople represented. Baskets, pottery, train whistles, weaving, and more. Open Apr–May Tue–Sat 10am–5pm. June–Dec 23 daily 10am–5pm. (828)669-6583. www.olddepot.org

Return to car and go one block to Broadway. Black Mountain Iron Works is on Broadway between State St and Sutton Ave.

⑩ Black Mountain Iron Works 120 BROADWAY – Outdoor sculpture on the lawn here is a sure draw. Dan Howachyn and Tekla provide demonstrations on most Saturday afternoons. Forged iron pieces for home and garden,

The Road Goes On Forever
Side trips, tidbits, adventures, and treasure hunts.

Tekla's work—Black Mountain Iron Works.

including "yard whimsies" of grand charm. Practical pieces for the hearth. Open year-round. Summer Mon–Sat 10am–6pm & Sun 1pm–5pm. Winter Mon–Fri 12noon–5pm & Sat 10am–5pm. (828)669-1001. www.blackmountainiron.com

Black Mountain B&B's

At the Red Rocker Inn:
*Crossing the threshhold
of relaxation.*

A **Black Mountain Inn** 718 W OLD HWY 70 – Historic B&B in a restored stagecoach stop. Three acres of lovely grounds to explore. (800)735-6128. www.blackmountaininn.com

B **Monte Vista Hotel** 308 W STATE ST – Owned by the Phillips Family for over 80 years, the regal old hotel continues to serve up meals daily and welcome appreciative guests who return each year. (828)669-2119. www.montevistahotel.com

C **Red Rocker Inn** 136 N DOUGHERTY ST – A fixture in Black Mountain for 105 years. Rocker therapy at its best. Even the meals are relaxing. (828)669-5991. www.redrockerinn.com

D **The Inn Around the Corner** 109 CHURCH ST – A lovingly restored 1915 four-square Victorian. Five regular rooms and two luxury suites make up the accommodations. (828)669-6005.

From Broadway in Black Mountain, travel S toward Bat Cave on Rt 9 for approximately 7.5 mi. Lavender's Handcrafts is on R.

11 **Handcrafts by Lavender** 1918 HWY 9 – A cottage by a stream where Eula Mae displays quilts she makes along with afghans, stoles, and throws. Warm pieces and excellent company, not to mention a lifetime of mountain stories. Open daily year-round 8:30am–9pm. (828)669-2198.

*Continue on Rt 9 to Bat Cave, about 10 mi.
Turn L on Hwy 64/74A toward Chimney Rock and Lake
Lure. Travel 2.6 mi to Chimney Rock.*

CHIMNEY ROCK

*Entering Chimney Rock on Hwy 64/74A from the Bat Cave
direction, Chimney Rock Woods is on R as you enter village.*

Guidebook Symbols

 Craft Studio   Restaurant
 Craft Gallery    Lodging
 Historic Site   Special Attraction

The cherished view at Chimney Rock Park.

A good thing at Edie's.

The peace of Lake Lure.

 Chimney Rock Woods 531 MAIN ST – Thomas Hebb–carver extraordinaire. Put a tree in his path and watch out. Bears and other mountain critters are likely to emerge–you get the idea. Mar–Dec Tues–Sat 11am-5pm, Sun 11am–4:30pm, Jan–Feb Fri–Sat 11am–5pm, Sun 11am–4:30pm. (828)625-2544.

Chimney Rock Park is .1 mi on R.

13 Chimney Rock Park HWY 64/74A (MAIN ST) – An early advertisement called Chimney Rock "the most stupendously interesting scenic objective in the South." Today's promotional material is a bit more understated, but the privately-owned park is no less alluring in its natural drama. In fact, you may have already seen it in the film "Last of the Mohicans." Almost a thousand acres, including cliff and forest trails, 400-foot Hickory Nut Falls, and overlooks of considerable magic. An admission fee is charged. Open daily year-round 8:30am–4:30pm (until 5:30pm during Daylight Savings Time) for ticket sales. Park remains open 90 minutes after ticket plaza closes. Closed Thanksgiving, Christmas, and New Year's Day. (800)277-9611. www.chimneyrockpark.com

Turning Point Gallery is .1 mi on R past Chimney Rock Park.

14 Turning Point 396 MAIN ST – Turn, turn, turn. For Bob Burns, each and every season for the last 25 years has been the season for turning vases, bowls, and candle holders. When he's not turning, he's creating mosaics, puzzles and toys. Open Mar–Dec Mon–Tue 10am–6pm. Thu–Sat 10am–6pm. Sun 11am–7pm. Jan–Feb daily 10am–6pm. (828)625-9738.

Continue on Main St. Edie's Good Things is .2 mi on L.

15 Edie's Good Things 371 MAIN ST – Corrugated tin walls and sycamore shelves display the work of forty peerless craftspeople. But the most exquisite piece of work is Edie herself. Celebrating fine crafts and their makers is a kind of religion to her. You'll be a member of the congregation before you leave. Open daily

The Road Goes On Forever

Side trips, tidbits, adventures, and treasure hunts

Apr–Dec 9am–6pm. Jan–Mar Fri–Sat 9am–5pm & Sun 9am–2pm. (828)625-0111.

Chimney Rock Inns and B&B's

16 Esmeralda Inn, Restaurant and Gardens 910 MAIN ST – The Esmeralda Inn had served as a beacon of hospitality in Chimney Rock since 1890. Sadly, in 1997, fire destroyed the main lodge. But like a phoenix rising from ashes, the inn came back to life thanks to the hard work and determination of owners Ackie and Jo Anne Okpych. This legendary place was once a hideaway of such stars as Clark Gable, Gloria Swanson, Douglas Fairbanks and Mary Pickford. The floor in the lobby played a role in the movie "Dirty Dancing." Fourteen rooms with mountain views. Open daily Apr–Nov. Dec & Feb–Mar Thu–Sat. Closed Jan. Restaurant hours of operation are Mon-Sat or Thu–Sat 11:30am–12:30pm & 5:30pm–8:30pm. Sun brunch 11am–2pm. (828)625-9105. www.esmeraldainn.com

Grab a picnic lunch and enjoy some river time beside the Rocky Broad.

E Wicklow Inn 307 MAIN ST – A riverside inn with a hint of an Irish accent located in the shadow of Chimney Rock. (828) 625-4038. www.thewicklowinn.com

F The Dogwood Inn and Gift Shop 339 MAIN ST – Built in the 1890's and used as a stagecoach stop between Asheville and Charlotte. Open Mar–Dec. (828)625-4403. www.dogwoodinn.com

A lakeside view of Lake Lure Inn.

Continue E on Hwy 64/74A to Lake Lure, approximately 2 mi.

LAKE LURE

G Lake Lure Inn AT THE BEACH – Still as elegant as it must have been when Franklin D. Roosevelt, F. Scott Fitzgerald and Emily Post took refuge here. Restored with a bit of 1920's panache and Victorian furnishings. Open year-

National Geographic has called Lake Lure one of the most beautiful man-made lakes in the world.

The veranda at the Lodge on Lake Lure.

round. Serving dinner daily except Mon. Sun brunch 11am–2pm. Reservations suggested. (828)625-2525.

17 Point of View Restaurant SHORELINE OF LAKE LURE AT THE OLD MARINA – The timeless beauty of the lake will undoubtedly steer your appetite toward the ever-present mountain trout on the menu. (828)625-4380.

H Lodge on Lake Lure 361 CHARLOTTE DR – Among many delights is a windowed porch above the lake where, if you blink twice, you can easily confuse your view with Banff or some landscape in Northern Italy. A boathouse below for departures by single canoe, motored ensemble, or flotilla. (800)738-2785 or (828)625-2789. www.lodgeonlakelure.com

Continue traveling E on Hwy 64/74A/Rt 9 and follow Rt 9 S when it turns R off Hwy 64/74A, approximately 2 mi from lake. Travel 9 mi to Hwy 108W and turn R, traveling 4 mi to Columbus.

COLUMBUS

On Hwy 108 in center of town, Polk County Courthouse is on L (as you travel from the E.)

18 Polk County Courthouse 1 COURTHOUSE SQUARE – This 142-year old antebellum Greek Revival courthouse is the oldest active courthouse in Western North Carolina. Open year-round Mon–Fri 8:30am–5pm. (828)894-3301.

Continuing on Hwy 108, turn L on Walker Ave, travel .1 mi and turn R on Peniel Rd. Travel 5.9 mi to Little Mountain Pottery on R.

The Road Goes On Forever
Side trips, tidbits, adventures, and treasure hunts

Little Mountain Pottery 6372 PENIEL RD –
Having been around the world and back again
working with folk potters, Claude and Elaine
Graves have tried to "capture North Carolina in
clay and glaze." You can watch them at work and
judge for yourself as you admire their stoneware
and salt-fired pieces as well as clay sculpture and
whimsical work. Open year-round Mon–Sat
10am–4pm. (828)894-8091.

Return to Columbus, turning L on Walker and L on Hwy 108.
Travel 2.5 mi to community of Lynn.

LYNN

From Hwy 108 in Lynn, as you travel W, turn R on Story Rd.
Studio is on R in top floor of historic building. The top floor opens
at street level on Story Rd. Limited parking on upper road.

 Mills-Mosseller Studio 1205 LYNN RD – In
the sanctuary of a 1914 church, Hand-hooked
rugs of considerable merit. Sales by commission
only, including to the Smithsonian Institute,
governor's mansions, and the Little White
House in Georgia when the Roosevelts were
there. It's a treat to visit with Ronald Mosseller,
a second-generation crafter. Open year-round
Wed 1:30pm–4:30pm, Thu 7am–9:30pm & Sat
9:30am–12:30pm. (828)859-5336.

Return to Hwy 108 and turn R. Mimosa Inn is on L.

Mimosa Inn ONE MIMOSA LANE
(Off Hwy 108 toward Columbus) – Situated
on the site of the Mills Plantation, a stop for
travelers for 200 years. Rebuilt in 1916 after a
fire destroyed the original building. Nine
rooms. (828)859-7688.

Continue on Hwy 108 into Tryon, approximately 1.5 mi.

The craft of Saluda
Forge (now doing
business in Tryon).

TRYON

Turn R off Trade St (Hwy 108) on Ola Mae Way.
The next two sites are at top of hill, about .1 mi.

 Saluda Forge 73 OLA MAE WAY –
Bill Crowell sculpts and forges table
bases and room screens that show off the

Guidebook Symbols

	Craft Studio		Restaurant
	Craft Gallery		Lodging
	Historic Site		Special Attraction

hand-painted tiles of his wife, Kathleen Carson, who has the studio next door. He also designs and forges other functional and decorative hardware for the home. Open year-round Mon–Sat 10am–5pm. (828)749-1713. www.saludaforge.com

22 Simply Irresistible! A One-of-a-kind Gallery 66 OLA MAE WAY – Kathleen Carson features her own hand-painted tiles as well as work of her husband, Bill Crowell. Also iron work, embroidered linens, and the glass work of some talented friends. Open Tue–Wed & Fri–Sat 10am–6pm & Thu 10am–9pm. (828)859-8316. www.tileandiron.com

Return to Trade St and turn R and park. The next 4 sites are within easy walking distance of each other.

23 Tryon House 86 N TRADE ST – Crafts and gifts. Town mascot Morris hangs out here, in every imaginable incarnation, including the original–as a toy horse. Open year-round Mon–Sat 9:30am–5pm. (828)859-9962.

24 Silver Fox Gallery 78 N TRADE ST – A stunning, contemporary gallery that would make any silver fox proud. A roster of talented resident artists keep Bonnie and Jim Rash's gallery ever-fresh and exciting. Jewelry, fine crafts, paintings, and sculpture. Open year-round Mon–Thu 10am–5pm. Fri–Sat 10am–8pm. Sun 1pm–4:30pm. (828)859-2259. www.silverfoxartgallery.com

25 Wood N Art Gallery 10 MAPLE ST (OFF N TRADE ST) – Woodwork, jewelry and other well-conceived crafts by folks in the region. The proprietor and craftsman B. Van Vlaenderenis is the originator of much of it. He will happily enlighten you on the subject of intarsia, or pictures in wood. Demonstrations daily. Open year-round Tue–Sat 10am–5pm. (828)859-6300.

26 The Upstairs Gallery 49 S TRADE ST – A contemporary gallery of fine art and crafts.

Sharon Tesche's "Dancing Ladies" in The Upstairs Gallery.

The Road Goes On Forever

Side trips, tidbits, adventures, and treasure hunts

The seasonal exhibits of regional and southeastern artists have enriched the Tryon community for more than 25 years. A true treasure. Open Sep–June Tue–Sat 11am–5pm. (828)859-2828. www.upstairsgallery.org

In your car, turn R on Pacolet St and L on Chestnut St. Next site is in lower level of Tryon Arts Center with parking on Melrose Ave.

27 Tryon Crafts, Inc. 34 MELROSE AVE – Offering instruction in a wide variety of crafts including pottery, needlework, lapidary work, enameling, stained glass, and quilting. Craft shop open Mon–Fri 9am–2pm. Craft classes offered Mon–Sat. (828)859-2323. www.tafcenter.org

Return to Trade St and turn L, following Hwy 108 to split with Hwy 176. Turn L on Hwy 176 N toward Saluda.

SALUDA

Travel 8.3 mi from intersection in Tryon on Hwy 176 toward Saluda. Karen Newgard Pottery is on L on hillside.

28 Karen Newgard Pottery 7449 HWY 176 – Contemporary cave-paintings on salt-fired porcelain: the couches, cats and living rooms of our 20th century lives carved in relief on useful objects. Pottery outside the box and worth every minute of your time. Open year-round Mon–Fri 10am–5pm & Sat–Sun by appointment only. (828)749-3242.

Continue on Hwy 176 for .3 mi and turn R on Ozone Dr. (toward I-26) Travel 1 mi and Gallery is on R.

29 Saluda Mountain Crafts Gallery 1487 OZONE DRIVE – Wood, pottery, quilts and jewelry from local and regional artists handsomely displayed. Follow your instincts to the fine furniture upstairs and the fine fudge next door. Open year-round Mon–Thu 10am–5pm. Fri–Sat 10am–6pm. Sun 11am–5pm. (828)749-4541. www.saludamtncrafts.com

Karen Newgard's pottery.

Guidebook Symbols

Craft Studio	Restaurant
Craft Gallery	Lodging
Historic Site	Special Attraction

Turn L back on to Ozone Dr and return to Hwy 176. Turn R on Hwy 176 toward downtown Saluda. Travel .2 mi and bakery is on L.

|30| Wildflour Bakery, Inc. 173 E MAIN ST – The bread has no preservatives, but don't worry because you'll eat the whole loaf before you leave the parking lot. Lunch favorites include pocket veggie sandwiches that look like old-fashioned apple jacks. Open year-round Mon & Wed–Sat 8:30am–3pm. Sun 10am–3pm. (828) 749-9224.

Turn L on Hwy 176, continuing into downtown Saluda. Next two sites are .1 mi on R.

31 Heartwood Contemporary Crafts 21 E MAIN ST – Explore the Penland-Saluda connection. Funny how good craftspeople and good galleries find a way of getting together. Pottery, jewelry, furniture, handwovens, iron-work and windchimes that resonate with your soul. Open year-round Mon–Fri 10am–5pm. Sat 10am–6pm. Sun 12noon–5pm. (828) 749-9365. www.heartwoodsaluda.com

not in Trusting Too Big

Everything's plumb: a chair and pottery at Heartwood Contemporary Crafts.

|32| The Purple Onion 16 MAIN ST – Well on its way to becoming a legend, Susan Casey offers up simple yet sophis-ticated dining in

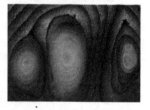

the casual atmosphere of the Purple Onion. A great place for a meal or simple cup of java. Drop by on Thursday or Saturday evening and take in some live music. Open year-round Mon–Tue & Thu–Sat 11am–3pm & 5pm–9pm. (828) 749-1179. www.purpleonionsaluda.com

Saluda B&B's

The Oaks B&B.

J The Oaks B&B 10 GREENVILLE ST (OLD HWY 176) – Enjoy the grace of the Victorian age with elaborate architecture, ornamental interiors, and croquet. Full breakfast. Open Apr–Dec 15. (800) 893-6091.

The Road Goes On Forever
Side trips, tidbits, adventures, and treasure hunts

K **The Orchard Inn** ONE MILE SOUTH OF SALUDA ON HWY 176 – The prototype for an inn Norman Rockwell might have painted with early Americana furnishings, bric-a-brac, table settings throughout, and the cordiality of drawing rooms. A friendliness that belies description, worth the drive from Saluda, or Alaska, to get here. (800) 581-3800.

Continue driving N on Hwy 176 (also called Spartanburg Hwy.) Travel 7 mi and turn L on Blue Ridge Rd. Travel 1.7 mi on Blue Ridge Rd to Hwy 25 (Greenville Hwy) in Flat Rock.

FLAT ROCK

At the intersection of Blue Ridge Rd and Hwy 25 in Flat Rock, turn L and the Gallery is immediately on your L.

(33) Hand in Hand Gallery 2720 GREENVILLE HWY – David Voorhees creates elegant and decorative porcelain reminiscent of a garden path; Molly Sharp works with silver, gold, brass and copper to create evocative jewelry. This talented couple also hosts the work of guest artists on a regular basis. Open Jan–Apr Tue–Sat 10am–5pm. May–Aug Mon–Sat 10am–6pm & Sun 1pm–6pm. Sep–Dec 23 Mon–Sat 10am–5pm & Sun 1pm–5pm. (828) 697-7719. www.handinhandgallery.com

Turn back N on Hwy 25 (Greenville Hwy) and travel .3 mi. Turn L on Little River Rd. Entrance to Carl Sandburg Home is .2 mi on L.

34 **Carl Sandburg Home** 1928 LITTLE RIVER RD – A National Historic Site, the home of poet Carl Sandburg during his later years. The house is built in low-country plantation style. Books and memorabilia. Open daily year-round 9am–5pm. Closed Christmas. (828) 693-4178. www.nps.gov/carl

Carl Sandburg's home Connemara.

Return to Hwy 25 and turn L (north) and travel .2 mi. Church is on L.

35 **St. John in the Wilderness** HWY 25 (GREENVILLE HWY) – Built in 1833 as the chapel for a country estate, it later

Guidebook Symbols

🔨	Craft Studio	🍴	Restaurant
🏺	Craft Gallery	🏠	Lodging
🏛	Historic Site	⭐	Special Attraction

The Glass Kitchen's cooking.

became the first Episcopal church in Western North Carolina. And, some 10 years before the Emancipation Proclamation, slaves and white families worshipped side by side in the church's pews.

To travel to Glass Kitchen, turn L on Erkwood Dr. just past the church and travel to intersection with Kanuga Rd, approximately 1 mi. Turn L on Kanuga Rd. and make immediate R on Drake and the Glass Kitchen is on L.

36 **Glass Kitchen** 1207 KANUGA RD – Meanwhile, down by the furnace, Christopher and Lissa Juedemann divide their attention between stained glass projects, fused glass ovals and bowls, one-of-a-kind glass beads, and other things having to do with the loveliness of light passing through glass. In the spring their studio becomes an outpost surrounded by thousands of wildflowers. All this beauty deeply informs the art that comes, full-blown, out of the kitchen. (828) 692-5111. www.glasskitchen.com

From Glass Kitchen, return to Hwy 25 and travel north for 1.5 mi to Made in the Mountains on L.

Flat Rock Inns and B&B's

L **Highland Lake Inn - A Country Retreat** HIGHLAND LAKE RD – Gourmet cuisine, homegrown vegetables and flowers from the gardens and greenhouses. Combining the up-to-date with the gentle element of times gone by. Serving breakfast, lunch, and dinner. Call for times and reservations. (828)693-6812 or (800)762-1376. www.hlinn.com

M **Woodfield Inn** 2905 GREENVILLE HWY – The oldest inn in continuous operation in NC. Meals to please those from either side of the Mason-Dixon line served in antebellum dining rooms. Open year-round Mon–Sat 7am–10pm. (828)693-6016. www.innspiredinns.com

Peacocks on the roam at Highland Lake Inn.

The Road Goes On Forever

Side trips, tidbits, adventures, and treasure hunts

HENDERSONVILLE

Next site is 1.5 mi. N of St. John in the Wilderness on Hwy 25 on the L (and .4 mi S of Hwy 176 on Hwy 25).

(37) Made in the Mountains 927 GREENVILLE HWY – Potter and silk painter Donna Kassab has created a lovely space to sell her work and that of others. Pottery, woodturnings, pressed wildflower notecards, and unusual fiber jewelry. Open year-round Tue–Sat 10am–5pm. (828)697-0630.

Made in the Mountains – a wide-ranging gallery.

Turn L out of Made in the Mountains. Travel N on Hwy 25 for .4 mi. Turn R on Hwy 176E/Spartanburg Hwy. Travel .8 mi. Turn L on Old Spartanburg Hwy. Travel .2 mi, turn L on Bradshaw. Travel .5 mi to R turn on Gilbert. Pottery is on L at end of Gilbert, about .4 mi.

(38) Clay Trade/ Annie-Laurie Designs 1230 GILBERT ST – A pottery studio located on the historic Johnson Airfield is no accident. Steve and Annie Laurie Turner have been potters for years and when this location became a possibility, they didn't hesitate. Enjoy their colorful tableware and maiolica pottery, but leave time to check out their 1940 Cub aircraft (and if you are really lucky, a ride.) Open May–Dec Fri–Sat 12noon–4pm. Good idea to call first. (828)696-3743.

Steve and Annie Laurie's colorful maiolica pottery.

Retrace your tracks to Hwy 176/Spartanburg Hwy and turn R into Historic Hendersonville. Watch for Main St. signs and park in downtown area around 3rd Ave.

HISTORIC HENDERSONVILLE

The next 8 sites are within walking distance of each other. The Curb Market is one block W of Main and 2nd. The others are all on Main St.

(39) Henderson County Curb Market 221 N CHURCH ST – Flowers, preserved foods, fresh cakes, woven goods, and wood carvings. Open Jan–Mar Tue & Sat 9am–1pm. Apr–Dec Tue, Thu & Sat 8am–2pm. (828)692-8012.

Guidebook Symbols

Craft Studio   Restaurant

Craft Gallery   Lodging

Historic Site   Special Attraction

40 **A Show of Hands** 242 N MAIN ST – Jiles and Polly Lovin feature arts of the Appalachians in their downtown gallery with more than 50 potters represented. There's also jewelry, soap, woodcarvings, candles, and fiber. Open year-round Mon–Sat 10am–5pm. (828)698-7673.

41 **Touchstone Gallery** 318 N MAIN ST – Beautifully selected, ofttimes whimsical art and craft created by contemporary American artists. A gonzo-gift-giving-kind-of-place where you'll find work of enchantment for any age. Open Jan–Mar Mon–Sat 10:30am–6pm. Apr–Dec Mon–Sat 10:30am–6pm & Sun 12noon–NOON–5pm. (828)692-2191.

As seen in Touchstone Gallery

A Show of Hands noble resident.

Work at Wickwire Gallery.

42 **Wickwire Fine Art/Folk Art** 330 N MAIN ST – An abundance of fine art, folk art, and crafts displayed with grace. A place so visually stimulating, interesting and pleasureable it can adjust your attitude before you know it. All of a sudden, you're thinking, "Wow." Shirley and Dave Palmer-Hill have a winning way with customers and artists alike to bring about this alchemy. Do you agree? Open Jan–Apr Mon–Thu & Sat 10am–6pm. Fri 10am–8pm. May–Dec Mon–Thu & Sat 10am–6pm. Fri 10am–8pm. Sun 1pm–4pm. (828)692-6222.

43 **Mineral and Lapidary Museum of Henderson County** 400 N MAIN ST – This museum is a dream–come–true for Larry Hauser. And he had a lot of help from the

The Road Goes On Forever
Side trips, tidbits, adventures, and treasure hunts

other members of the Henderson County Gem and Mineral Society to bring it to life. An amazing place. While you're into it, ask about the geode–cracking. Open year-round Mon–Fri 1pm–5pm & Sat 10am–5pm. (828)698-1977. www.mineralmuseum.org

(44) Divine Stained Glass–Studio and Gallery 430 N MAIN ST – Leaded, stained, and etched glass for windows, skylights, transoms and such. Materials and ongoing classes. Open year-round. Mon–Sat 10am–5pm. (828)693-1227.

(45) The Arts Center 538 N MAIN ST – Home to four resident artists with ever-changing exhibits of 2-D and 3-D art as well as special events. The Arts Center is aptly named. Open year-round Tue–Fri 1pm–5pm & Sat 1pm–3pm. (828)639-8504. www.theartscenterofhc.com

And you wouldn't want to miss it.

(46) Mast General Store 527 N MAIN ST – An Appalachian tradition since 1883, the Hendersonville location of the old-time mercantile is a wonderful reminder of times just too good to leave behind. Features traditional housewares and candies, casual clothing and outdoor gear as well as footwear for all four mountain seasons. Open Easter–Dec Mon–Sat 10am–6pm & Sun 1pm–6pm. Jan–Easter Mon–Sat 10am–5pm & Sun 1pm–5pm. (828)696-1883. www.mastgeneralstore.com

(47) Larks On Main 401 N. MAIN STREET – In a Roaring Twenties bank building, where vault now shelters cabernets, the owners have taken to integrating craft whenever and wherever possible. Scalloped pockets in the walls display glass or pottery or other works during the year. Architectural details, too, are deliciously styled—iron railings, light fixtures and a mobile in the courtyard—all by area artists. Wonderful cuisine, including tapas, emanates from the wood-fired grill. And, yes, the wood is apple (as you might expect). Lunch and dinner seven days a week. (828) 694-1030.

Mast General Store from 1883.

Guidebook Symbols

 Craft Studio   Restaurant

 Craft Gallery   **A** Lodging

Historic Site   Special Attraction

THE CENTER FOR CRAFT, CREATIVITY & DESIGN
BROYLES RD

If there was a front door to craft in Western North Carolina, this would likely be it. Please come right on in.

This center with the rather long name exists to integrate craft, creativity and design into lifelong learning programs. It accomplishes that mission, as part of the University of North Carolina, through research, education and community collaboration. But for the moment, consider another purpose: renewal of your own mind and body by visiting the crafts on display in the Center's exhibit space and by taking off on the Rudnick Nature Trail that starts at the back door.

First, the crafts: inspiring work, lush and unexpected, by professional craftspeople in Western North Carolina, as well as by students and faculty of the area's colleges and universities—changing six times a year.

Next, the trail: a great stroll into three distinctive eco-systems— a wildflower meadow, a trillium bog, and a hardwood and rhododendron forest. It winds through almost 50 acres, crossing mountain streams and rambling past public art features like benches designed as a result of a juried competition. The trail, cared for by Carolina Mountain Club, will continue to grow through the years in beauty and in its treasury of public art.

In addition, the Center offers a series of monthly tea-talks, receptions for new exhibits, and conferences at the adjoining Catherine Kellogg Center, all of which you can readily discover by visiting the Center on-line at www.craftcreativitydesign.org.

Open year-round Mon–Fri 1pm–5pm.
(828)890-2050.

The Road Goes On Forever

Side trips, tidbits, adventures, and treasure hunts

Continue traveling N on Main St. Turn L on Hwy 64W (Brevard Rd). Travel 4.5 mi, turn R on Broyles Rd. Travel 1.2 mi. Turn L into Kellog Center, bearing R as drive splits inside gate.

(48) The Center for Craft, Creativity, and Design BROYLES RD – *See sidebar on pages 158.* Open year-round Mon–Fri 1pm–5pm. (828)890-2050. www.craftcreativitydesign.org

Turn L back on Broyles Rd and travel .2 mi. Bear R on S Rugby Rd. Travel 1mi and turn L on Haywood Rd/Hwy 191N. Travel approximately 3 mi to intersection with Hwy 280. Brevard is to L (W) and I-26 is to R (E).

Hendersonville B&B's

N Inn on Church Street 201 CHURCH ST – A lovingly restored home with 21 guestrooms. This downtown inn features tiled baths with original tubs, hardwood floors, and luxurious beds. The dining room boasts a chef who uses only the finest Angus Beef and local organic produce to create gourmet fare. (800)330-3836. www.innspiredinns.com

O The Apple Inn 1005 WHITE PINE DR – With majestic oaks and hemlocks surrounding this century-old home, you'll feel quite secluded. The grounds also feature hundreds of azaleas, dogwoods, laurels, and perennial beds. (828)693-0107. www.appleinn.com

P The Poplar Lodge 2350 HEBRON RD – Once an inn, now a beacon for patrons of fine dining and lovers of life in general. Roaring fireplaces in the winter and mountain breezes in the summer. (828)693-8400.

Q The Waverly Inn N MAIN ST – Hendersonville's oldest inn features 14 rooms named after local flora, to include Birdfoot Violet, Ox-eye Daisy, and Closed Gentian. Walking distance to downtown. (800)537-8195. www,waverlyinn.com

Guidebook Symbols

 Craft Studio   Restaurant

Craft Gallery   Lodging

Historic Site   Special Attraction

Biltmore and Craft

An Artful Industry

When Mr. George Vanderbilt and his architect, Richard Morris Hunt, set out to build a European chateau in Asheville, it quickly became apparent that they would need European craftspeople to do the work.

In all, there were over 1,000 individuals who contributed to the actual building of the great house, including stonecutters, woodworkers, masons, sculptors, carvers, carpenters, tile-makers, glaziers, blacksmiths, painters, and their apprentices. They traveled into the mountains from faraway places–from England, Spain, Italy, France, Ireland, Austria–and from European neighborhoods and enclaves in New York and Philadelphia.

Edith and Cornelia Vanderbilt.

Many stayed well beyond the five years it took to craft Biltmore House. They stayed to work on an even larger canvas – the cityscape of Asheville, a mountain town which had, in the mean-time, quadrupled in size and become a magnet for tourists of every station. Their contributions live on in

It took five years and hundreds of workers to complete the Biltmore House.

Biltmore Industries.

architecture, public and private; in bungalows, in cathedrals, in city buildings, in streetscapes, stone carvings, and iron-work.

In the midst of this turn-of-the-century boom period, a quiet renaissance began to emerge in silvaculture and native handcraft due, once again, to the sweeping stewardship of George and Edith Vanderbilt. For while George organized the first forestry school in America, Edith organized Biltmore Industries, a training school for young men and women in mountain crafts—particularly wood carving and the weaving of woolen homespun cloth.

The industry continued, moved from Biltmore Village to the grounds of Grove Park Inn, for nearly 70 years. During its heyday, when 40 looms clapped in sliding rhythm, the products of the business spun an international reputation. Colorfully dyed bolts of woolen cloth became wastecoats and jackets, some warming the shoulders of ambassadors and presidents. One particular dye, in fact, earned the name "Coolidge Red." In the early eighties, these looms ceased their artful industry. But the mountain craft renaissance ignited by the Vanderbilts continues to light a path for contemporary artists and their devoted followers.

Detail of the stone facade of Biltmore House.

Cascades Trail

Water is a constant, reassuring presence on the Cascades Trail. It tumbles, trickles, courses, and pools all along this breathtaking route. 〰 At the start, Hwy 276 and the Davidson River are woven together as neatly as a schoolgirl's braid. Crisscrossing back and forth through Pisgah National Forest, they chase each other all the way to the outskirts of Brevard. 〰 In the summer months, this picturesque town plays host to hundreds of music students from around the world, and thousands of visitors who come to see them perform at the renowned Brevard Music Center. 〰 Going toward Cedar Mountain, the French Broad River takes up where the Davidson left off, accompanying you to a virtual potter's row of notable galleries and studio spaces. It's here, in the wet clay, in the buckets of liquid glaze, that one realizes how water is just as elemental to a turned pot or vase as it is to each of us. 〰 The road to the resort communities of Sapphire, Cashiers and

Mountain Forest Studio — Brevard's oldest pottery.

The Craft of Falling Water

Highlands cuts across rivers, creeks, and runs before dropping into the Cullasaja Gorge. ⟨⟨⟨ Waterfalls abound here, chief among them Dry Falls, which you can walk behind and not get wet (well, almost), and Bridal Veil, which probably qualifies as the first ever drive-through waterfall. The narrow highway, with its hairpin turns and sheer drop offs can be treacherous, but it is arguably one of the single-most beautiful roads in the country. We urge you to enjoy the views and the stops along this route, but with appropriate caution. ⟨⟨⟨ The road and the water, like old friends, will part ways for the final leg of the journey to Franklin. When you are done, you will have gained an appreciation for the rich crafts tradition that thrives in this region. ⟨⟨⟨ You will also discover that water, in its own way, is the most patient of all crafters. Slowly, over millions of years, it has carved the very faces of these mountains.

Cascades Trail

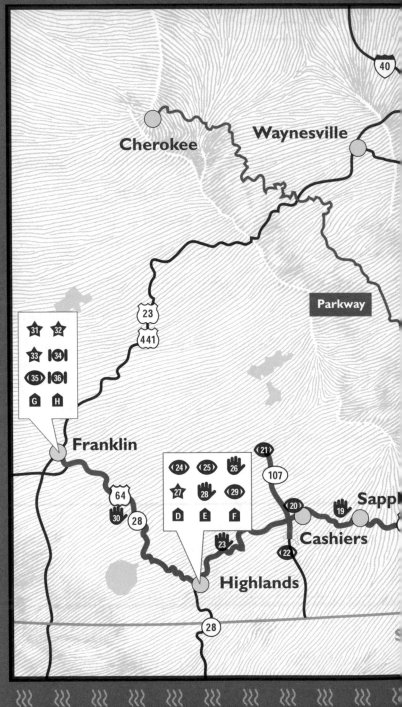

Cherokee

Waynesville

40

Parkway

23

441

31	32
33	34
35	36
G	H

Franklin

21

107

24	25	26
27	28	29
D	E	F

20

19

Sapp

Cashiers

64

30

28

23

22

Highlands

28

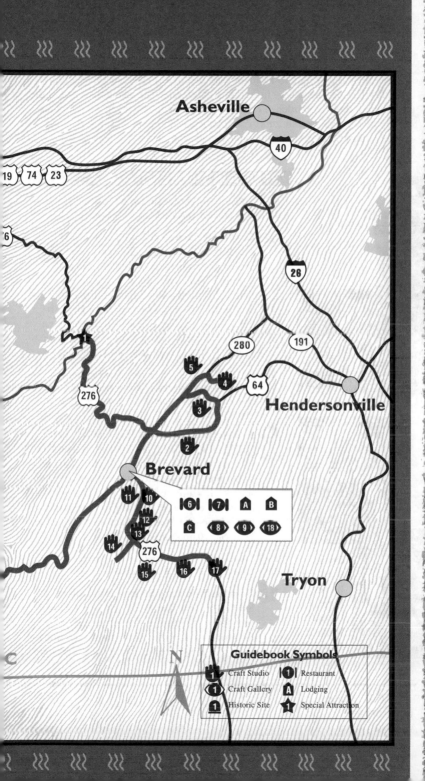

Asheville

40

19 74 23

26

280 191

5

4 64

3 **Hendersonville**

2

276

Brevard

11 10

6 7 A B

C 8 9 18

12

13

14

276

15 16 17

Tryon

C

N

Guidebook Symbols

Craft Studio   Restaurant

Craft Gallery   A Lodging

Historic Site   Special Attraction

The crafts of the Cascades are concentrated along one main route between Brevard and Franklin. There's a collection of fascinating studios near Brevard on Rt. 276 and galleries of note in both towns as well as in the resort town of Highlands, etched on a steep slope between Brevard and Franklin.

You can drive the Brevard to Franklin road in a day or two through beautiful countryside, stopping to peer into studios (and waterfalls) along the way. On the other hand, there are worlds of craft to discover, people to meet, good food to relish, trails to explore and inns to sample. As relatively short as this road trip may be, it invariably stretches out once you get into it.

PISGAH FOREST AREA

From the Blue Ridge Parkway, take exit to Hwy 276. Follow Hwy 276 toward Brevard. Cradle of Forestry is 4 mi on L.

1 Cradle of Forestry HWY 276, PISGAH NATIONAL FOREST – The new interpretive center harmonizes nicely with its peaceful setting. Inside, learn the story of Gifford Pinchot, Carl Schenck, and the birth of the American forestry movement through short films and engaging exhibits. Admission fee is charged. Open daily mid-Apr–Oct 9am–5pm. (828) 877-3130. www.cradleofforestry.com

Return to Hwy 276, turning L toward Brevard and travel approximately 12 mi to intersection of Hwy 276 and Hwy 64. Follow Hwy 64E (continuing straight at traffic light) for 2.2 mi. Southern Expressions is on R.

2 Southern Expressions 2157 NEW HENDERSONVILLE HWY – This husband and wife team harvested white and yellow pine on site to build simple, attractive gallery and studio spaces. He's a potter. She's a weaver. Their work is truly an expression of their southern roots. Open June–Oct Mon–Sat 9am–5pm. Nov–May Mon–Sat 10am–5pm. (828) 884-6242.

Turn R back on Hwy 64 and travel 4 mi to King Rd. Turn L and travel .8 mi to BernWell Pottery on L.

Dennis Bern and Wendy Elwell, i.e., BernWell Studio and Gallery.

3 BernWell Pottery Studio and Gallery 324 KING RD– Four hands at work: hers creating practical, yet beautiful, dinnerware; his creating dramatic pieces for preparing and presenting food. Working together for 20 years, they have

The Road Goes On Forever
Side trips, tidbits, adventures, and treasure hunts

developed much-sought-after specialties–his
hardwood ash glazes, her wide palate of colors.
Open year-round Mon–Sat 10am–5pm.
(828)883-8300. www.bernwellpottery.com

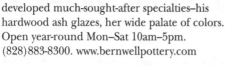

Leftwich Art.

*Leaving BernWell's, turn L on King Rd and travel 2.1 mi to
intersection with Hwy 280. Turn R and travel 2.2 mi to
Brickyard Rd and turn R. Travel .7 mi to Bane Rd and
make R. Driveway for Leftwich Pottery is .1 mi on R.*

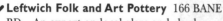

4 Leftwich Folk and Art Pottery 166 BANE
RD – An expert on local glaze and clay lore
as well as other matters geological, Rodney has
brought mountain life into the light with his
cutout sketches on pots and vases. Kim's work
provides a whimsical folk perspective. Open
year-round Tue–Sat 10am–4pm. (828)890-3053.

*Return to Hwy 280 and turn L. Travel 1.6 mi to McGuire Rd
and turn R. Studio is .6 mi on R at end of road.*

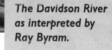

*The Davidson River
as interpreted by
Ray Byram.*

5 Ray Byram Studio 239 MCGUIRE RD –
Welcome to the working studio of a painter and
printmaker. Take a look at how the artist carefully transforms his original paintings into seri-
graphs. Open year-round Tue–Wed 10am–
4pm. (828)877-6509. www.RayByram.com

*Return to Hwy 280 and turn R. Travel 4 mi back to intersection
of Hwy 276 and Hwy 64 and continue through light on Hwy 64W
toward Brevard. Travel 3.5 mi to intersection with Main St (Hwy
276S), turn L and find a parking spot.*

Guidebook Symbols

	Craft Studio		Restaurant
Craft Gallery		Lodging
Historic Site		Special Attraction

BREVARD

From intersection of Hwy 276 and Hwy 64, all of these downtown stops are easily accessible.

The Red Wolf Gallery, including namesake art within.

|6| **Bracken Mountain Bakery** 34 S BROAD ST – No directions necessary, just follow your nose. Fresh-baked breads and pastries made from organically grown stone-ground flours milled in North Carolina. Darn good coffee, too. Open May–Oct Mon–Fri 8am–5pm & Sat 8:30am–5pm. Nov–Apr Tue–Fri 8am–5pm & Sat 8:30am–5pm. (828)883-4034.

|7| **Grammy's Bistro** 1 E MAIN ST – A good place to fortify yourself for the trail. Gourmet sandwiches, wraps and vegetarian fare make for a delightful spread. Open year-round Mon 11am–3pm. Tue–Fri 11am–3pm & 5:30am–9pm. Sat 11:30am–3pm & 5:30am–9pm. Sun 11:30am–2:30pm. (828)862-4746.

(8) **Red Wolf Gallery** 3 E MAIN ST – Step into the old hotel building, with its tin ceiling, take one quick look around, and the name of the gallery will be forever etched in your memory. Sculpture, paintings, ceramics, wood, fiber—all of it outstanding work by regional artists. Open Apr–Dec Mon–Sat 10am–5pm. Feb–Mar Mon–Sat 10am–4pm. Sun hrs June–Aug. (828)862-8620.

(9) **Number 7 Arts, Fine Arts & Crafts Cooperative** 7 E MAIN ST– Inside you'll find a small community gallery which serves as an outreach program for the Transylvania County Arts Council, energetically representing Brevard's many talented local artists. Open Jan–Nov Mon–Sat 10am–5pm. Dec Mon–Sat 10am–5pm & Sun 1pm–4pm. (828)883-2294. www.number7arts.com

Drive 2 mi (from intersection of Broad and Main) S on Hwy 276.

The Road Goes On Forever

Side trips, tidbits, adventures, and treasure hunts

Each year thousands of children and adults slide down 60 feet of pitched granite, propelled by 11,000 gallons of water a minute. It's called Sliding Rock and it is located in the middle of the Davidson River just outside Brevard.

HWY 276 SOUTH/BREVARD

Driving S on Hwy 276 from Brevard, cross the French Broad River and make L on Wilson Rd. Make immediate R on Crestview Dr. Studio is 3rd house on L.

 Twin Willows Studio 15 CRESTVIEW DR – An up-to-your-elbows studio where Ann DerGara, a talented and prolific painter and printmaker, creates her magic. You're welcome to watch her make monoprints and monotypes from original works on her very large etching press. Open Apr–Nov Mon–Fri 11am–4pm or call for appointment. (828)877-5275.

Twin Willows.

Make L turn back on Hwy 276. Travel .3 mi. Pottery is on R.

 The Duckpond Pottery 2398 GREENVILLE HWY – You won't find a pond, but you will find a treehouse pottery perched on the banks of the French Broad River. Nick Friedman woodfires his stoneware vessels and tiles, all of which are worthy of adoption–just take your pick from his collection. Open mid-Apr–Dec Mon–Sat 10am–6pm & Sun 12noon–6pm. (828)883-4512. www.duckpondpottery.com

Turn R back on Hwy 276, travel .5 mi to studio on L.

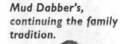 **Mountain Forest Studio** 2991 GREENVILLE HWY – The 100-year-old farmhouse is almost as charming as Mary Murray, the talented potter who works here. Beautiful flower gardens out front set the stage for what you'll find inside. Locals know to stop by on Sundays: that's the day Mary's sister, Susan, tends the gardens (and answers questions.) Open year-round Mon–Sat 10am–5pm & Sun 1pm–5pm. (828)885-2149.

Mud Dabber's, continuing the family tradition.

Turn L on Hwy 276. Travel 1.2 mi to gallery and studio on L.

Mud Dabber's Pottery and Crafts 4201 GREENVILLE HWY – Continuing the family tradition which they began in the 1970's, eight members

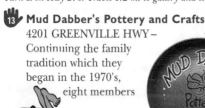

Guidebook Symbols

Craft Studio		Restaurant	
Craft Gallery	A	Lodging	
Historic Site		Special Attraction	

BREVARD MUSIC CENTER
Beverly Sills still remembers her time at the Center. "In Brevard there was a woodworker who created miracles in black walnut. In our living room, is a gigantic coffee table created by him. We may change: it doesn't. That is Brevard—a never-ending wonder of music-making." Call for a summer festival schedule. (828)884-2011.

Expressive Judith Duff Artwork..

of the Dodson family and five good friends sell their work in the historic Powell Store (another outlet is in Balsam.) Son John E. and wife Carol make pots and fire them on-site. Ask for the full story on their logo. Open year-round Mon–Sat 10am–6pm & Sun 1pm–6pm. (828)884-5131. www.muddabbers.com

Look for Island Ford Rd directly across Hwy 276 out of the Mud Dabbers parking area. Travel 1.8 mi on Island Ford Rd and turn L immediately after Honey Locust Dr. Forge is .2 mi on L.

 Bear Forge Blacksmithing 1034 ISLAND FORD RD – From haunting life-sized red wolves to safari-animal heads to large ornamental ironwork and small utilitarian tools, Richard Merrill has mastered the forge and "kicked it up a notch." If you can conceive it, Richard can create it. Open year-round Mon–Fri 9am–5pm & Sat 12noon–5pm. (828)884-5548.

Return to Hwy 276 and turn R. Travel 3.3 mi and turn R on E Fork Rd. Travel 1.4 mi to Happy Acres, turning L. Make an immediate R into drive. Studio is on L at end of drive.

 American Folkart 233 HONDAH RD – Gourds come in all shapes and sizes and so does the art. Karen Dittman sticks to the traditional–brightly colored, plump lady gourds and santas that make you chuckle. She continues her themes on canvas and birdhouses. Open May–Dec Mon–Fri 12noon–5pm. Call for weekend hours . Jan–Apr Thu–Sun 12noon–5pm. (828)862-4830. www.karendittman.com

Return to Hwy 276 and turn R. Travel 2 mi and turn R on Cedar Lane. Travel .4 mi. Studio on R.

 Cedar Mountain Artworks 450 CEDAR LANE – While pursuing her MFA, Judith Duff took a pottery class and "never got it out of my mind." Lucky for us. Her Shinto glazes and artist's eye combine to create inspired work. Her newest work, woodfired and influenced by her Japanese study and travel, is so evocative and deep that you are sure to become an admirer. Open year-round Mon–Sat 10am–5pm except Thanksgiving and Christmas Day. (828)884-5258. www.judithduff.com

The Road Goes On Forever

Side trips, tidbits, adventures, and treasure hunts

Moses saw the promised land from Mt. Pisgah. Inspired by this biblical reference, George Vanderbilt gave the highest peak on his estate the same name. Part of this land became the foundation for Pisgah National Forest.

Return to Hwy 276 and turn R. Travel 1.5 mi and turn L on Cascade Lake Rd. Travel .1 mi and turn R on Reasonover Rd. Travel 2.5 mi and turn R into drive, following signs to studio.

 17 The Glass Feather 2300 REASONOVER RD – Nestled in acres of wildflower gardens at 3,000 feet, the Travises' fused glass studio commands awesome views of Cedar Mountain. The view inside is no less admirable–a nature-inspired collection of plates, platters and bowls. Bring a sandwich and enjoy the hospitality. Open June–Aug Wed–Sat 10am–5pm. Call for other times. (828)885-8457. www.glassfeather.com

Return to Hwy 276, turn R and travel back to Brevard, about 13 miles.. Turn L on Broad St (also Hwy 64W) travel 2 blocks. Turn R and then L on S. Caldwell St. Gallery is on L.

 18 Transylvania County Arts Council
321 SOUTH CALDWELL ST – The artists, residents and visitors of Transylvania County are indeed fortunate to have such a lovely space, a renovated church, to showcase the jewels of the area. Open Jan–May Mon–Fri 10am–4pm. June–Aug Tue–Fri 10am–4pm & Sat 11am–3pm. Sep–Dec Mon–Fri 10am–4pm & Sat 11am–3pm. (828)884-2787. www.tcarts.org

Brevard B&B's

A The Inn at Brevard 410 E MAIN ST – Once a private home, this elegant historic inn now provides gracious accommodations and fine food for guests fortunate enough to be in the neighborhood. (828)884-2105. www.InnatBrevard.8M.com

B The Red House Inn 412 PROBART ST – A rambling, well porched patriarch built before Lincoln was president with a history as courthouse, post office, private school, stagecoach stop and various and sundry other things. (828)884-9349.

C Chestnut Hill B&B
400 BARCLAY RD –

The gardens of Glass Feather.

A WALK IN TIME
A trip to the Cradle of Forestry just isn't complete without strolling its trails and two paved loops of history. The Biltmore Campus Trail ambles past buildings from America's first forestry school established in 1898. The buildings play host to craft demonstrations April 22–October 31 Fri-Sun. The surprise on the Forest Festival Trail is a 1915 steam train once used to haul timber from these mountains.

Guidebook Symbols

 Craft Studio	Restaurant
Craft Gallery	Lodging
Historic Site	Special Attraction

The tranquility of this historic B&B provides a welcome respite from the sum total of everything else you've encountered on your journey. Open Apr–Oct. (828) 862-3540. www.bbonline.com/nc/chestnuthill

Return to Hwy 64W and travel approximately 19 mi to Sapphire.

SAPPHIRE AND CASHIERS

From Toxaway Lodge/Motel take Hwy 64W for .2 mi. The Pottery Shop is on R.

 19 The Pottery Shop HWY 64W – Inside this charming white-frame, one-room building which started life as a gas station during the 1930's, you will find functional earthenware with pastel glazes created by potter Jan Lee. Everything's a great gift and it can be especially nice if you're the recipient. Open May 20– Oct 31 Mon–Sat 10am–5pm. (828) 966-9398.

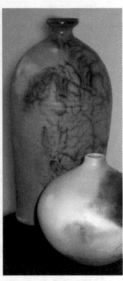

The Pottery Shop.

Continue traveling on Hwy 64W for 9.2 mi. Turn R at traffic light at the intersection of Hwy 64 and 107 onto Hwy 107N. Cashiers Commons is group of shops on R.

20 Southern Hands CASHIERS COMMONS HWY 107N – A broad spectrum of decorative accessories and crafts, both regional and national. Open Apr–Dec Mon–Sat 10am–5pm. (828) 743-5499.

A welcome greeting at Southern Hands.

Turn R back on Hwy 107N and travel 5.1 mi. Gallery on L.

 21 Main Street Folk Art & Furnishings HWY 107N – Susan's handmade baskets decorate locally-crafted furniture. Other artists contribute to an impressive, ever-changing presentation of folk art pieces, bird carvings, and wooden lamps. Well worth the side trip down 107. Open May–Dec Mon–Sat

The Road Goes On Forever

Side trips, tidbits, adventures, and treasure hunts

The highest point on the Blue Ridge Parkway (6,053 ft. at mile 431), Richland Balsam is home to plant life that was stranded here when the glaciers retreated. As a result, you can check out spruce and fir that are typically found in the upper reaches of Canada.

11am–5pm. Jan–Apr call for appointment. (828)743-2437.

Return to Cashiers and continue on Hwy 107, traveling .5 mi past intersection with Hwy 64. Gallery is on L.

(22) White Moon Art Gallery 889 LAUREL KNOB RD – Karen Weihs—owner, artist, author —puts her evocative oil and acrylic paintings alongside the work of guest artists and crafters, including other original canvases, sculptures, baskets and more. An intersection of good work. Open May–Dec Mon–Sat 11am–5pm & Sun 12noon–4pm. (828)743-3588. www.weihs.com

Return to intersection of Hwy 64 and 107 and turn L on Hwy 64W. Travel 4 mi and turn R on Norton Rd. Travel 2.5 mi and turn L on Quail Ridge Rd. Studio on corner.

(23) Quail Ridge Gallery 22 QUAIL RIDGE RD – Working studio of woodturner Paul Poole. Watch as he transforms maple, walnut and their relatives into vessels and more. Open year-round Mon–Sat 9am–2pm & 4pm-5pm. (828)743-9001.

Return to Hwy 64W and turn R.

Quail Ridge Gallery.

HIGHLANDS

From intersection of Norton Rd and Hwy 64W, Travel for approximately 4.7 mi. Gallery is on R on summit of ridge.

(24) Summit One Gallery 4152 CASHIERS RD – Mary Adair Leslie will be the first to tell you that she loves selling art. Her beautiful gallery reflects her enthusiasm and fine eye, sharpened by a museum background. She represents some of the region's finest craftspeople and fine artists. Open Mar–Dec Mon–Sat 10am–5pm & Sun 1pm–4pm. Jan–Feb Wed–Sat 10am–5pm. (828)526-2673. www.summitonegallery.com

Drive on Hwy 64W 2 mi to Highlands. Turn L to Cottage Row.

(25) Me and My Sisters 37 COTTAGE ROW – Visit the sisters' cottage where all the soft sculpture, cornhusk flowers, gourd lamps, ornaments and angels are handcrafted by members of the Angert family. Open Apr–Dec Wed–Sat 11am–5pm. (828)526-9367.

The sisters' porch.

Guidebook Symbols

 Craft Studio   Restaurant

Craft Gallery   Lodging

Historic Site   Special Attraction

Continue on Hwy 64W into Highlands. Travel 1.3 mi and turn R on Pinecrest Rd. Travel 200 yds and turn R at turn in road. Studio on R in barn with silver roof.

 Pinecrest Pottery Studio

105 PINECREST RD – Pat Taylor has chosen a majestic forest cathedral as the setting for his pottery studio and gallery. In such an inspired setting, it's a wonder his pots don't take wings and fly. But, earth, fire, and water keep his work grounded and waiting for you. Open May–Sep Thu–Sat 10am–5pm. Sep–Oct Sat–Sun 1pm–5pm. (828)526-1995.

Return to Hwy 64W, turning R toward Highlands. Travel .5 mi and turn L on Carolina Way. Shop on L.

 The Custom House 442 CAROLINA WAY – A complementary blend of American crafts from all over (see map in back of store) and lamps, lamps and more lamps, for both inside and out. Open Apr–Nov Mon–Sat 10am–5pm. Dec–Mar Mon–Sat 11am–4pm. (828)526-2665.

Return to Hwy 64W and turn L into Highlands. Travel .1 mi. At intersection, follow Hwy 28 straight across and travel 1.1 mi. Turn R on Cook Rd. Travel .2 mi and veer R on Picklesimer Rd. Home studio is .25 mi on R.

 Marge Rohrer Originals 200 PICKLESIMER RD – Marge and David design and weave the fabrics they then use to create classic garments and accessories. Their color-filled studio is a great place to open your eyes and heart. Open May–Dec Wed–Sat 10am–5pm. Jan–May Thu–Sat 10am–5pm and by appointment. (828)526-4198.

Return to Highlands. Turn L on Hwy 64W at intersection of Hwys 64 and 28. Go through town. Wright Square is .3 mi on L.

 Southern Hands 1 WRIGHT SQUARE ON MAIN ST– Cascading display of furnishings and high quality regional crafts. Try, but you won't see everything the first time around. Open

The Road Goes On Forever

Side trips, tidbits, adventures, and treasure hunts

While in Highlands don't forget to ask shop keepers, "What's the deal with the dogs?"

Mar–Dec Mon–Sat 10am–5pm & Sun
11am–5pm. (828)526-4807.

*Continue on Hwy 64W, turning L out of parking at Wright
Square. Travel 10 mi to Weavery.*

Highland Area B&B's

D **Main Street Inn** 270 MAIN ST – For people
who prefer homey comfort and a sumptuous
breakfast served up with the elegance of fine
linens. (828)526-2590. www.mainstreet-inn.com

E **Colonial Pines Inn** 541 HICKORY ST –
Only half a mile from Main Steet, this inn is set
off to itself by two acres of giant rhododendrons
and hemlocks. Berry gardens in season. Open
daily May–Oct. Weekends only Nov–Apr.
(828)526-2060. www.colonialpinesinn.com

F **4 1/2 Street Inn** 55 4 1/2 ST– Beautiful
grounds and antiques grace this welcoming,
historic home, genteely operated by two
former Atlantans. Open Mar–Dec.
(828)526-4464. www.4andahalfstinn.com

HIGHLANDS TO FRANKLIN

*On Hwy 64W, from Highlands travel 10 mi to Muggins Weavery,
approximately half way between Highlands and Franklin.*

30 **Muggins Weavery** HWY 64W – Halfway
between Highlands and Franklin. Looms
crowd the floor of the Muggins' studio and
gallery; spools of colorful yarn line the walls.
Be very careful turning into the gravel parking
area; Muggins sits at a blind curve. Open
year-round Mon–Sat 10am–4pm. Closed Tue.
(828)369-8564.

FRANKLIN

*Continue traveling on Hwy 64W/28 into Franklin,
approximately 7.4 mi. When Hwys 64/28 split, follow
Hwy 28 to downtown Franklin, turning L on Main St, approximately 1.3 mi from intersection of Hwys 28 and 64, and L. again
on Depot St for another .3 mi. Ann's Needle Depot is .2 mi on L.*

Guidebook Symbols

Craft Studio	Restaurant
Craft Gallery	Lodging
Historic Site	Special Attraction

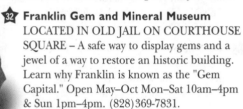

31 Ann's Needle and Hook Depot 495 DEPOT ST – At Ann's, an average, ordinary person can grow into quilting, rug-hookery, silk ribbon embroidery, colonial knotting, and teddy bear creation, among other things–and just generally become a more enlightened human being. It's all a matter of color, fabric, and pattern, along with an abundance of good-natured encouragement. Pottery, stained glass, basketry, and homespun flannels and wools for sale. Open year-round Mon–Fri 9am–5pm & Sat 10am–4pm. (828) 524-9626.

From Ann's, turn R back on Depot St and turn L on N-E Main St. Park in the vicinity of the courthouse square. The sites below are all on Main St. and within walking distance of each other.

32 Franklin Gem and Mineral Museum LOCATED IN OLD JAIL ON COURTHOUSE SQUARE – A safe way to display gems and a jewel of a way to restore an historic building. Learn why Franklin is known as the "Gem Capital." Open May–Oct Mon–Sat 10am–4pm & Sun 1pm–4pm. (828) 369-7831.

33 Macon County Historical Society and Museum 36 W MAIN ST – Textile displays of weavings (1817-1972) and other artifacts from Macon County are as rich as the space that houses them. Open year-round Mon–Fri 10am–4pm & May–Oct Sat 11am–4pm. (828) 525-9758.

34 Frog and Owl Kitchen 46 E MAIN ST – Jerri Fifer describes what's offered in this convivial, high ceilinged space as "European food with mountain flair." Literally translated, that could mean chicken tarragon with cheese grits, gingered beef tips with barley, squash bisque, or some other equally wondrous intercontinental inspiration. Open year-round Tue–Sat 11am-2:30pm for lunch. Thu–Sat 5:30pm-? for dinner. (828) 349-4119.

Continue through town on Main St. and turn L, following signs for Hwy 441 and 28S. At first traffic light, look for gallery in Palmer St Shopping Center on R.

The Road Goes On Forever

Side trips, tidbits, adventures, and treasure hunts

(35) Michael Rogers Gallery 18 PALMER ST –
Magnificent mountain views, as seen from the
Appalachian Trail, captured in watercolors by
Michael. Open year-round Mon–Fri 10am–5pm
& Sat 10am–2:30pm. (828)524-6709.
www.sharethebeauty.com

Michael Rogers' sensitive landscapes of the Carolinas.

Return to HWY 441 and turn R. Café is 1 mi. on R.

|36| Gazebo Creekside Cafe 103 HERITAGE
HOLLOW DR – In the mood for a refreshing
mid-day meal? You can't beat the Gazebo. Open
daily Apr–Oct 10am–4pm & Fri 'til 10pm. Nov–
Mar Mon–Sat 10am–3pm. (828)524-8783.

Franklin B&B's

G The Franklin Terrace 159 HARRISON AVE –
Two blocks from Main Street. Originally built as
a school in 1887, now known for its sweeping
porches and intimate guest rooms romanced
with period antiques. (828)524-7907 or
(800)633-2431. www.franklinterrace.com

H Snow Hill Inn 531 SNOW HILL RD – Nine
rooms, gourmet breakfasts, evening desserts,
14-foot ceilings, and antiques, all in a renovated
1914 schoolhouse with 360 -degree views.
(828)369-2100. www.bbonline.com/nc/snowhill

Guidebook Symbols

 Craft Studio |O| Restaurant

 Craft Gallery   Lodging

 Historic Site   Special Attraction

Haywood Community College

Nurturing Excellence

The allure of the production crafts program at Haywood Community College is summed up in the tired, but proud smiles so often found on the faces of its students. "They are doing what they love," says Gary Clontz, clay instructor and department chairperson. Approximately 60 students are enrolled in the seemingly all-consuming, seven-quarter program. At the end of that period, the instructors hope they've helped the students craft something of lasting value: a lifelong profession.

"We provide a service to craftspeople that no one else is offering," says Clontz, who has been with the school since 1974. "We try to balance the teaching of technical crafts skills with business skills–like how to access the market and start a small business."

But does attention to such practical matters as bookkeeping and marketing interfere with the artistic side of the student's education? As

From top to bottom: Everyone helps build a kiln, a pause in weaving, a critique in the wood shop.

Laurie Fae glazes a large platter

Catherine Duncan, former curator of the Southern Highland Craft Guild says, "The work is consistently innovative with the highest caliber of craft being produced anywhere in the country." Many graduates, in fact, go on to become active exhibiting members of the Guild and frequently participate in Guild fairs.

That the work remains outstanding from year to year is testament to the school's instructors. In addition to Clontz, the faculty includes Robert Blanton, instructor in jewelry; Robert Gibson, design and photography; Catharine Ellis, fiber; and Wayne Raab, wood. Graduates become walking testimonials when asked about the two years spent with these patient teachers. "The whole time you're there, the instructors treat you as if you're a professional craftsperson," says Sarah Wells Rolland, a 1989 graduate. "We were so well taken care of it was almost frightening to leave."

But leave they do, and often to a promising future. "When I arrived at Haywood, I'd never touched clay," remembers Rolland. "By the time I graduated, I was wholesaling and marketing my work."

The thread room.

Shadow of the Smokies

In the 1880s, the first trains arrived in the mountains, and with them visitors from all over the world. Resorts sprang up within a carriage ride of each railway stop. Fanciful places like the Eagle's Nest. White Sulphur Springs. The Balsam Manor Inn. The Randolph House. And the Yankee Hipps Hotel. ▲ They arrived in cars, pulled by locomotives, coming from cities where industry was worshipped, to find a world still unaffected by combustion engines, machinery, and electricity. A world where mass production was a matter of doing one thing—well. Where even the most common of objects arrived without peer—each carrying the personality of its maker. The curve of a chairback. The pattern of a basket. The weave of a blanket. ▲ These visitors to the mountains found something they'd lost in their mad dash toward progress and the dazzle of the future. And they soon found themselves champions of its preservation. ▲ This tour begins where the railroad, coming up from Georgia, made its first stop after cresting the mountains, at the tiny station in

Passions in repose at Collene Karcher's
marble studio near Sylva

Objects Without Peer

Balsam. A short distance further on is the town of
Waynesville, still welcoming visitors with the same
homespun charm and good will as it did a century
ago. Cross Soco Gap and you will alight in a
place whose craft heritage predates our country.
The spirit of the American Indian remains
unbowed in the objects you will find here.
Ceremonial masks and pottery. Finely detailed
wood sculpture. Baskets of river cane, split white
oak, and honeysuckle vine. Following the train
track from Bryson City, you will come to a place
that feels like a homecoming. In Dillsboro, visitors
abandon their cars for the pleasures of ambling
along tidy streets. Its avenues are filled with places
where craft isn't just sold, but is joyously conjured
up before your very eyes. And here, if you're so
inclined, you can still ride the rails behind a steam
locomotive. Stay in the Shadow of the
Smokies, and you eventually land at a point where
so many others have come before you. It's a place
where a handmade object can, in its own simple
way, balance the progress of an entire century.

Shadow of the Smokies

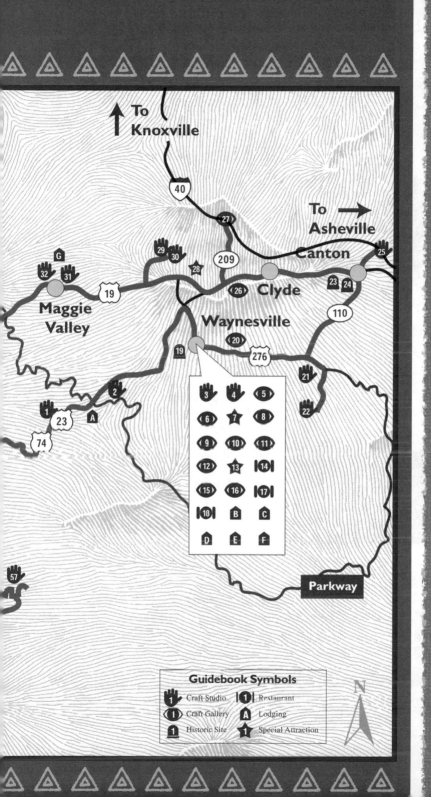

One of the most attractive features of the loop is its compactness. Not only is it short–maybe 100 miles–it also has a high craft-to-miles-traveled ratio. "Shadow" can be easily entered from the east (Asheville), from the south (Atlanta via 441) or from the north (Knoxville via I-40). There are high concentrations of crafts in Waynesville, Cherokee, and Dillsboro but, anywhere on this loop, you'll be close by something of charm, merit, or beauty. A perfect weekender's loop–in two days you can cover an immense amount of ground and pretty well visit most or all of the sites listed.

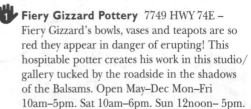

SOUTHWEST WAYNESVILLE

Exit the Blue Ridge Parkway at Balsam, mile marker 443. Turn R on Hwy 23/74 exiting the Parkway. Travel 4 mi. Pottery on R.

1 Fiery Gizzard Pottery 7749 HWY 74E – Fiery Gizzard's bowls, vases and teapots are so red they appear in danger of erupting! This hospitable potter creates his work in this studio/gallery tucked by the roadside in the shadows of the Balsams. Open May–Dec Mon–Fri 10am–5pm. Sat 10am–6pm. Sun 12noon– 5pm. Jan–Apr call for appointment. (828)631-1582. www.fierygizzard.com

An eruption of color at Fiery Gizzard Pottery.

Turn L back on Hwy 23/74 (going back in the same direction) and travel 2.5 mi. Turn R at sign to Balsam. Follow signs to Inn, approximately .4 mi from Hwy 23/74. Turning R on Cabin Flats.

A Balsam Mountain Inn 68 SEVEN SPRINGS DR – Opened in 1908 to serve the highest railway depot east of the Rockies, this three-story inn offers an abundance of porches, rockers and wonderful food. It boasts few modern conveniences—like room phones and TV—and that's just fine. Home to "Art in the Mountains", a dandy exhibition of local art, craft and music. Reservations are advised for accomodations and meals. Open daily year-round 9am–10pm. (828)456-9498. www.balsaminn.com

The graceful porches of the Balsam Mountain Inn.

Return to Hwy 23/74 and turn R. Travel .8 mi to Mud Dabber's on R.

2 Mud Dabber's Pottery and Crafts 20767 GREAT SMOKY MOUNTAIN EXPRESSWAY – Brad comes by his passion for clay honestly. His parents, John and Sylvia, started the family clay business in the 1970's. Brad, who has recently added a wood–fired kiln, builds expressive sun masks, mysterious wood spirits and mischievious gnomes. You'll also find the work of brother John and other family members. Open year-round Mon–Sat 10am–6pm & Sun 1pm–5pm. (828)456-1916.

Turn R on Hwy 23/74 and travel approximately 6.7 mi into Waynesville. Take Hwy 276 exit off Hwy 23/74. Turn R off exit ramp and travel .8 mi. Turn R on Branner Ave. Rug Braider's is on L in Holly Square shopping area.

 Rug Braider's Niche, Etc. 55 BRANNER AVE – In a few years, you'll be able to trace the renaissance of colonial-style rug braiding back to this tiny storefront. Here Ron and Linda Bledsoe use 100% wool to coil mesmerizing rugs. And, since once a teacher always a teacher, these school system retirees offer regular work-shops to pass on what they've learned. Open daily year-round 1pm–7pm. (828).452-9707.

Continue on Branner .2 mi to intersection with Depot. Turn R. Gallery is on R and is on the grounds of the service station.

Metal Art Gallery and Sculpture Garden 136 DEPOT ST – Hmm. Decisions, decisions. Buy a metal sculpture or get my oil changed? You can do both at Grace's gallery, conveniently co-located with her husband's gas station. In truth, it's all quite charming, as is Grace's sculp-ture. The way she works with metal isn't cold or industrial; it's rooted in the natural world with interpretations of fish, frogs, lizards and roosters that would make worthy inhabitants of any home. Open year-round Mon–Fri 8am–5pm. Sat–Sun by appointment. (828)456-8843 .

Continue down Depot St. Gallery is in next block on R

(5) SPACE 254 DEPOT ST – A young-hearted gallery of collectibles and art pieces–mosaics, paintings, handmade scarves, and wares– along with some architectural "found objects" and genuine hospitality. Open June–Dec Mon–Sat 10am–6pm. Jan–May Wed–Sat 10am–6pm. (828)456-4652.

Turn off Depot St onto Commerce St (almost directly across from SPACE). Gallery and Coffeehouse .1 mi on R.

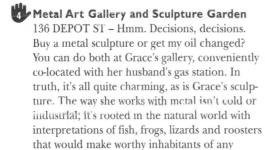

Mud Dabber Magic!

Guidebook Symbols

Craft Studio   Restaurant
Craft Gallery   Lodging
Historic Site   Special Attraction

6 Iron Horse Gallery and Panacea Coffee House 66 COMMERCE ST – Lynda and Jim Pierce have created a handsome space in Frog Level where you have permission to croak over the sheer fact of being alive amongst some very fresh work, including paintings and pottery, for your home. Jazz clouds the air and the smell of coffee may drift you next door where the java and soups rival those of any other place you've ever been. Open year-round Mon–Sat 10am–5:30pm. (828)456-8008. www.piercepottery.com

DOWNTOWN WAYNESVILLE

Return to Depot St, turning R. Travel to Main St, approximately .2 mi. Turn R onto N Main St and park. The following eight sites are on N Main St and are within walking distance of each other.

7 Waynesville Book Company 184 N MAIN ST – A fine place to stock up on regional and local books and maps, not to mention the tidbits on the local history, heritage, and natural features you can glean from the friendly proprietor, Kent Stewart. Open year-round Mon–Sat 10am–5:30pm.

8 Burr Studio and Gallery 136 N MAIN ST – Dane Burr continues to find unforgettable faces and characters in handfuls of clay. When in doubt, there's always the genius of turning whatever it is upside down and making it into an owl. He and his wife MaryEtta, an accomplished potter, welcome folks with warmth and artistry, including their friend Jim Michelson who drops by to paint small and lovely watercolors. Open June–Dec Mon–Sat 10am–5:30pm. Jan–May Mon–Sat 10am–5pm. (828)456-7400.

Enjoy a smile or two at Burr Studio and Gallery.

9 Deja View Gallery 132 N MAIN ST – You may have seen something like this before, but, really now, you haven't seen this: the large-format-camera whisper detail of Jon Bowman's photography of the Smokies and Blue Ridge or the blended atmosphere of pottery, paintings, quilts, jewelry and mountain-inspired gifts. Open Jan–Mar Tue–Sat 10:30am–5pm. Apr–May Mon–Sat 10am–5:30pm. June–Dec Mon–Sat 10am–6pm. (828)452-9787

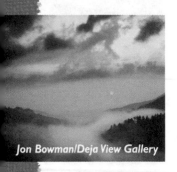

Jon Bowman/Deja View Gallery

The Road Goes On Forever
Side trips, tidbits, adventures, and treasure hunts

Within the borders of Haywood County, there are 19 peaks of over 6,000 feet.

10 **Hardwood Gallery** 102 N MAIN ST A working studio and gallery where wood sculptor Dennis Ruane carves elegant scenes and figures out of trunks and stumps you could pass by on a forest ramble without a thought. Some inlaid pieces, masks and wall hangings, all silky smooth and great looking. Also functional bowls, spoons, and salad sets. Open May–Dec Mon–Tue & Thu–Sat 10am–5:30pm. Jan–Mar Thu–Sat 10am–5:30pm. Call for appointments at other times. (828)456-3500. http://home.earthlink.net/~aluaden/

11 **Twigs and Leaves** 98 N MAIN ST – Here abouts, art dances with nature. Two floors of nature-related creative work–wrought iron, glassware, earthenware, furniture and art–representing over a hundred craftspeople, with 80 percent of them living and working in the region. David Erickson and Kaaren Stoner, a ceramist known for leaf motifs in her work, renovated a 19th century building. After all that, they decided to settle in above the store. Open Feb–Mar Tue–Sat 10am–5:30pm. Apr–Dec Mon–Sat 10am–5:30pm. Jan Wed–Sat 10am–5:30pm. (828)456-1940. www.twigsandleaves.com

The soft, dynamic shapes of Hardwood Gallery.

12 **Whitewoven Studio/ CrossCurrents Gallery** 84 N MAIN ST – A bright and cozy Main St. shop features expressive weavings of Sheree White Sorrells, particularly rugs and wall-hangings, but also original concepts in table linens, hand-bound books, art clothing and other things. Her evocative pieces emerge from the seven handlooms (which you can see) though, as she says, "A simple piece of cloth–that's the beginning of everything." Also home accessories and furniture from other artists, often scattery and whimsical. Open year-round Mon–Sat 10am–5:30pm. Sun 1pm–5pm. (828)452-4864. www.rugweaver.com

Twigs and Leaves–art and nature.

13 **Mast General Store** 63 N MAIN ST – Yet another wonderful tentacle of the original Mast

---

Guidebook Symbols

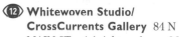

	Craft Studio		Restaurant
	Craft Gallery		Lodging
	Historic Site		Special Attraction

General Store in Valle Crucis, circa 1883. This old-time mercantile offers up outdoor gear, casual clothing and hiking apparel along with traditional housewares and candies. The historic emporium is a wonderful reminder of times too good to leave behind. Open Easter-Dec Mon–Sat 10am–6pm & Sun 1pm–6pm. Jan-Easter Mon–Sat 10am–6pm & Sun 1pm–6pm. (828)452-2101. www.mastgeneralstore.com

The irrepressible goodies of Whitman's Bakery.

|14| **Whitman's Bakery** 18 N MAIN ST – The true seat of power in Waynesville isn't in city hall. It's at the tables of this popular establishment. Expansive lunch menu and comfortable booths encourage lingering. It's impossible to get in or out without passing two huge glass cases of goodies. Shame on them. Open year-round Tue–Sat 6am–5:30pm. (828)456-8271.

(15) **T. Pennington Art Gallery** 15 N MAIN ST – Sights in Waynesville and Asheville are subjects of this artist's colored pencil creations. Originals, and signed and numbered prints available in custom frames. Open year-round Mon–Sat 10am–5pm. (828)452-9284. www.tpennington.com

(16) **Blue Owl Studio and Gallery** 11 N MAIN ST – Antique postcard photos are the basis for the hand-colored prints you'll find in Garey Wagner's studio and gallery. Historic hotels, public buildings, and scenic vistas evoke childhood memories of these mountains. Twelve area potters are also well-represented here. Open June–Dec Mon–Sat 10am–5:30pm & Sun 12noon–5pm. Jan–May Tue–Sat 10am–5pm. (828)456-9596.

Hand-colored prints at Blue Owl Studio and Gallery.

Continue to drive further up Main St. Turn R on Church St. Lomo Grill is on R.

|17| **Lomo Grill** 44 CHURCH ST – This beautifully restored space comes with tin ceiling and exposed brick walls. Upstairs at the Grill, garden-grown herbs and farmer's market vegetables complement local hormone-free beef, lamb and trout entrees. Downstairs, exotic

The Road Goes On Forever

Side trips, tidbits, adventures, and treasure hunts

breads and lunches are the specialties. Feb–Dec 16 Mon–Sun 11am–3pm & 5:30pm–9pm. (828)452-5222. www.lomogrill.com

Turn R on Haywood St. Soco Moon is .1 mi on R.

|⑱| Soco Moon Tea House and Emporium

319 N HAYWOOD ST – Another great place to set aside your worldly concerns. Open year-round Mon–Fri 8am–4pm & Sat 9pm–midnight. Call for appointments. (828)456-5133.

Waynesville Area Inns and B&B's

B **Haywood House B&B** 675 S HAYWOOD ST – Built in 1906, and attentively restored by Lynn and Chris Sylvester, this local landmark was once the home of W.C. Allen, author of several nonfiction volumes, including *History of Haywood County* and *Stories of Our State.* The downstairs, with its original built-in hutches, bookshelves and paneling, is a shrine to oak. Open daily year-round Mon–Sun 4:30pm–7pm. (828)456-9831. www.haywoodhouse.com

C **The Yellow House on Plott Creek Rd** 89 OAK VIEW DR – Perennial gardens, bird gardens, herb gardens—all-in-all, a very mellow yellow. Open May–Dec Mon–Sat 10am–7pm & Sun 10am–2pm. (828)452-0991. www.theyellowhouse.com

The Yellow House on Plott Creek.

D **Suyeta Park Inn B&B** 31 SUYETA PARK DR – An 1890's grand hotel sitting on a bluff in downtown Waynesville surrounded by gardens and lovingly restored by three generations. What could be finer? (828)456-5266. www.suyetapark.com

Check-in at the Suyeta Park Inn.

E **Old Stone Inn** 109 DOLAN RD – Families have come back to the same room, the same week of the year, for decades. Some things just get better with time. Rustic accommodations and heaven-sent food. Call for reservations for dinner. Open Apr–Dec. (828)456-3333. www.oldstoneinn.com

F **The Swag Country Inn** 2300 SWAG RD – Conveniently located in the middle of nowhere, the Swag is perched 5,000 feet up and miles

Guidebook Symbols

🖌 Craft Studio		◯	Restaurant
◯ Craft Gallery	Ⓐ Lodging
▣ Historic Site	⚑ Special Attraction

from the nearest worry. Sixteen amenity-laden rooms, 50-mile views, and four-star meals. Open Apr 28–Nov 15 Mon–Fri 7am–10pm. (828)926-0430. www.theswag.com

Baskets, pottery, and garden art at Wood 'n Craft.

EAST OF WAYNESVILLE

Return to Main St, driving S. Turn L on Hwy 276 (Pigeon St) and Museum is on R.

19 **N.C. Handicraft Museum** IN THE SHELTON HOUSE AT THE CORNER OF HWY 276 AND SHELTON ST – Built in 1875, this museum features Indian artifacts, handwoven coverlets and quilts, and the work of master potters from an earlier time. Open year-round Tue–Fri 10:30am–4pm. (828)452-1551.

Continue traveling S on Hwy 276 for 4.1 mi. Gallery on L.

20 **Wood 'n Craft** 4061 PIGEON RD – This airy, light-filled cabin features a variety of craft. Baskets, pottery, garden art are well represented, as is the artwork of Jean Mayhew, proprietor. Open Apr 15–Dec 15 Mon–Sat 10:30am–5pm. (828)–648-2820.

SMOKY MOUNTAIN FOLK FESTIVAL
The toe-tapping, leg-slapping, fast-dancing, story-telling cultural history of Haywood County comes to life every Labor Day weekend at the Smoky Mountain Folk Festival. Held on the historic stage of Stuart Auditorium on Lake Junaluska, this high-energy event is one of the mountain's best kept secrets. (800) 491-6803

The Road Goes On Forever

Side trips, tidbits, adventures, and treasure hunts

Continue on Hwy 276 approximately 2.2 mi. Pottery is on R at intersection of Hwys 276 and 110.

 Cliffside Outfitters and Pottery 6388 CRUSO RD – Outfit yourself with a warm vest or some comfortable trail pants, invest in a custom-made knife, and enjoy choosing your soon-to-be favorite coffee mug from Mitzi Warren's latest kiln firing. Open Feb–May Wed–Sat 10am–5pm. June–Jan Mon–Sat 10am–5pm. (828)648-0790.

Continue S on Hwy 276, traveling .9 mi. Turn R on Mundy Field Rd. Travel .3 mi and turn R on Dix Creek Rd. Travel .4 mi and turn R on Smokey Cove Rd. Travel .3 mi and turn R into drive. Studio is on R side of driveway.

 Rolland Studio and Gallery 324 SMOKEY COVE RD – Nestled on a hillside not far from the famed Cold Mountain, Sarah Rolland has created a bustling pottery with shapes and glazes that command attention. She fearlessly builds stoneware in dramatic, organic forms. Another hoorah! for Haywood Community College's Craft Program! Open year-round Mon–Fri 9am–3pm & Sat by appointment. Good idea to call ahead. (828)648-0770.

Return to Hwy 276 and travel .4 mi N back to intersection with Hwy 110. Turn R on Hwy 110 (Pisgah Dr) and travel 5.3 mi to Canton. Turn R on Hwy 19/23 N and travel .2 mi. Turn L on Academy St and L again on Park St. The Museum/Visitor's Center is on R and Theatre on L.

The teapot world of Sarah Rolland.

23 Canton Area Historical Museum 36 PARK ST – A good glimpse into this historic papertown's past and a good place for information on its present. Open year-round Mon–Fri 9am–4pm. (828)646-3412. www.cantonpapertown.com

24 Colonial Pathways Theatre 53 PARK ST – This 105-year-old theatre has been lovingly restored and placed on the National Register of Historic Places. Open year-round Mon–Fri 7am–4pm. (828)235-2760. www.cantonpapertown.com

Guidebook Symbols

Craft Studio | Restaurant
Craft Gallery | Lodging
Historic Site | Special Attraction

To continue on main trail, continue traveling on Park St/Hwy 19/23 for 5.6 mi. to exit at Jones Cove Rd. Turn L at end of exit ramp, travel .1 mi and turn L on campus. Drive to top of hill, turn R at stop sign and look for Production Crafts Building on R.

Side Spur to Sabbath-Day Woods

To take loop to Sabbath-Day Woods, take two immediate L's from Park St in Canton to get back on Main St. Follow Main St until Newfound Rd turns off to R. Take Newfound Rd and travel about 2.5 mi. Cross over I-40 and turn L on Freedom Dr. Workshop and gallery on R.

 Sabbath-Day Woods 722 FREEDOM DR – Desmond Suarez, a second-generation furniture designer and maker, uses mortise & Tenon joints, dove-tail drawers and hand rubbed oil finishes to craft Shaker and Arts & Crafts style furniture pieces that are sure to become heirlooms. Open year-round Mon–Fri 9am–5pm. (828)235-9444. www.sabbath-daywoods.com

Heirloom furniture from Sabbath Day Woods.

Return to Hwy 19/23/Main St in Canton. Travel W toward Clyde, approximately 5.6 mi from Museum/Visitor's Center to exit at Jones Cove Rd.

CLYDE

From Jones Cove Rd exit on Hwy 74/19/23S, turn L at end of exit ramp, travel .1 mi and turn L on campus. Drive to top of hill, turn R at stop sign and look for Production Crafts Building on R.

 Haywood Community College 185 FREEDLANDER DR – This school, known throughout the country for its distinguished craft program, invites passers-by to stop and enjoy a view into working studios. Student craft work, always of a high caliber, is often on display. (828)627-4670.

Haywood Community College features craft production.

Return to Hwy 19/23/74, turning L going S. Travel approximately 1.3 mi to Hwy 209 for Frog Holler Organiks Side Spur. Continue traveling on Hwy 19/23/74 for main trail.

Side Spur to Frog Holler Organiks

From intersection of Hwy 19/23/74 and Hwy 209, exit to Hwy 209 and watch carefully for signs and follow 209 for 3.5 mi as it heads north. Turn L at Citgo on Ironduff Rd, traveling 1.1 mi to fork in road. Keeping R at fork, travel .9 mi to Downs Cove and turn R. Travel .3 mi and turn R on Sterling Way. Keep R into parking area.

The Road Goes On Forever

Side trips, tidbits, adventures, and treasure hunts

(27) Frog Holler Organiks and Il Fiore Gardenhouse Gallery 110 STERLING WAY – Gardens, greenhouses, gallery–goodies galore. And the setting's not bad either. A 24-hr call ahead will get you a delectable made-to-order meal served up on the premises. Open May–Oct Thu–Sat 10am–5pm. (828)627-0811.

Return to Hwy 209 and travel S back to Hwy 19/23/74 , approximately 3.5 mi.

Happenings at Frog Holler?

LAKE JUNALUSKA

Travel W on Hwy 19/23/74 for .3 mi past exit for Hwy 209 and bear R as Hwy 19 splits R from Hwy 23. Travel W on Hwy 19 approximately 1.3 mi and turn R on West Lakeshore. Inn is 1 mi on L. Note overlook!

(28) Lambuth Inn 55 LAMBUTH DR AT LAKE JUNALUSKA – An architecturally enchanting retreat and inn above Lake Junaluska listed on the National Register. Private reservations welcome most of the year. Just down the street from the Harrell Center Heritage Museum, displaying historic crafts. Seasonal rates. Dining. (828)452-2881. www.lakejunaluska.com

Flying Cat's Work.

Return to Hwy 19 and turn R, traveling W. Travel 2.8 mi to intersection with Hwy 276N.

AROUND MAGGIE VALLEY

Traveling from Lake Junaluska, at the intersection of Hwy 19 and Hwy 276, turn R on Hwy 276 and travel 2 mi. Turn R on Utah Mountain Rd and travel .5 mi. Turn L on Windy Hill Lane. Studio on R.

(29) Flying Cat Pottery by Kim Dryden WINDY HILL DR – Yes, there is a story here. Kim Dryden or her studio-mate Susan will be happy to clue you in. And Kim will also be glad to introduce you to her functional stoneware and porcelain pottery. Another fine graduate of the Haywood Community College Craft Program. Open Mar–Dec 22 Mon–Fri 10am–5pm. (828)734-0542.

(30) Flying Cat Pottery by Susan Phillips WINDY HILL DR – Susan Phillips, a graduate of the craft program and the weaving program at

Guidebook Symbols

 Craft Studio   Restaurant

Craft Gallery   Lodging

Historic Site   Special Attraction

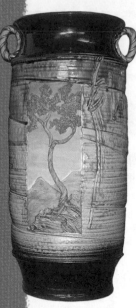

The artful beat of a different drummer.

Pitter the Potter's statuesque menorah.

Haywood Community College, turns out raku pottery and functional stoneware as well as sculptural stoneware with hints of her weaving background. Open Mar–Dec 22 Mon–Fri 10am–5pm. (828) 734-0542.

Return to Hwy 19, turn R and continue for 2.6 mi in to Maggie Valley. Pottery is on R in log cabin.

 Different Drummer Pottery 2614 SOCO RD – Wheel-thrown functional porcelain and the landscape tilework of Terance Painter plus the work of other area potters. After you inquire about the name, support Terance's march and take home one of his tiles or pots. You'll also find his fine stoneware pottery in use at Cataloochee Ranch. Open year-round Mon–Sat 9am–5pm. (828) 962-3850.

Continue traveling W on Hwy 19 for approximately 3.1 mi. Pottery on R.

 Pitter the Potter HWY 19 – There are two accomplished potters here, Dennis Pitter, and his wife, Linda. Both share a passion for craft and conversation. You can learn a lot. Open daily year-round 10am–6pm. (828) 926-7676.

Continue traveling on Hwy 19 toward Cherokee for approximately 7.3 mi to Bearmeat's Indian Den.

 Cataloochee Ranch FIE TOP RD OFF HWY 19 – A 1,000-acre guest ranch that's really its own little mountain-top world. Family-style meals featuring Southern Appalachian specials served in a rustic lodge. How do people feel about this special place? Read the guest book. Open Apr–Oct Mon–Sun Breakfast 8am–9pm. Lunch 12:30pm. Dinner 6pm & 7:30pm. Reservations recommended. (828) 926-1401.

CHEROKEE

Approximately 7.3 mi. on Hwy 19 from Maggie Valley, Bearmeat's Indian Den is on L.

 Bearmeat's Indian Den 4210 WOLFTOWN RD – David Smith has assembled an enviable collection of handcrafted Native American

---

The Road Goes On Forever

Side trips, tidbits, adventures, and treasure hunts

MUSEUM OF THE CHEROKEE INDIAN
History, crafts, artifacts and stories. It's the perfect listing in a guide book like this.

artwork. You can also find a smattering of other Appalachian handcrafted goodies. And fresh produce. Enjoy the porches surrounding David's place as you ponder and browse. Open Jan–May Mon–Sun 9am–5pm. June–Dec Mon–Sun 9am–7pm. (828) 497-4052.

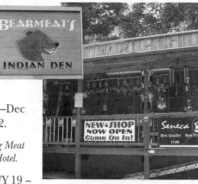

Continue W on Hwy 19 approximately 5.2 mi. Big Meat House of Pottery is on L across from Casino and Hotel.

34 Big Meat House of Pottery HWY 19 – Big Meat family members have been potters for generations. In addition to traditional low-fired coil pottery that turns into wedding vases

Hand-crafted Native American artwork and lots of porch.

and medicine bowls, you'll also see authentic and high quality masks, pipes, knives, basketry and beaded jewelry. If you are lucky, you might hear some stories. Open May–Oct Mon–Sat 9am–5pm. (828) 497-9544.

Continue W on Hwy 19 to intersection with Hwy441N for approximately 1.4 mi. Turn R on Hwy 441N. Medicine Man's is on R next to Ponderosa Steak House, .4 mi.

35 Medicine Man Crafts HWY 441N – Owner Kay Sharpe's devotion to craft and her encouragement of local craftspeople is much in evidence. Pay notice to the wood sculptures and ask about their makers. Open daily year-round 9am–5pm and until 8pm during summer. (828) 497-2202.

Continue N on Hwy 441N. The Museum is immediately on L.

36 Museum of the Cherokee Indian TSALI BLVD AND HWY 441N – Complete history of the Cherokees from ice age to present: treaties, language, artifacts and stories. Open June–Aug Mon–Sun 9am–8pm. Sep–May 9am–5pm. Closed Thanksgiving, Christmas and New Years Day. An admission fee is charged. (828) 497-3481. www.cherokeemuseum.org

Guidebook Symbols

 Craft Studio   Restaurant

 Craft Gallery   Lodging

Historic Site   Special Attraction

Something to wear at Qualla Arts and Crafts.

Crafts Gallery is across Tsali Blvd from Museum.

(37) Qualla Arts and Crafts Mutual TSALI BLVD AND HWY 441N – They call themselves "the most outstanding Indian-owned and operated cooperative in America." You'll soon discover why. Inside a lush and beautiful gallery, you will find river cane, split oak and honeysuckle vine baskets of peerless quality, along with ceremonial masks, low-fired pottery and wood carvings. Open Fall Mon–Sat 8am–6pm & Sun 9am–5pm. Winter Mon–Fri 8am–4:30pm. Summer (June 13–Aug 24) Mon–Sat 8am–7pm & Sun 9am–5pm. (828)497-3103.

Continue N on Hwy 441N. Indian Village is on L. You will see signs at intersection of Tsali Blvd, and Hwy 441.

A freestanding part of Oconaluftee Indian Village.

38 Oconaluftee Indian Village HWY 441 N – Travel back to 1750 and see Cherokee Indian life as it was, not how it's been portrayed in movies and television. The earliest forms of American craft—pottery, basket making, wood carving and weaving—are demonstrated and sustained here by members of the Eastern Band of Cherokee Indians. Open May 15–Oct 25 9am–5:30pm. An admission fee is charged. (828)497-2111. www.oconalufteevillage.com

39 Unto These Hills Outdoor Drama HWY 441 – An outdoor drama of the Eastern Band of Cherokee Indians and their brave leaders, Junaluska, Tsali and Sequoyah, who fought for the survival of a great creature. Open mid-June–Aug Mon–Sat evenings. Tickets reserved in advance or purchased at the box office. (828)497-2111.

One of nine log buildings at Mountain Farm Museum.

Continue traveling N on Hwy 441N. Next two sites are located at entrance to Great Smoky Mountain National Park, approximately 3 mi from Unto These Hills Theatre.

40 Mountain Farm Museum IN THE GREAT SMOKY MOUNTAINS NATIONAL PARK AT 1194 NEWFOUND GAP RD – Discover the ways and wiles of early farm life in this collection of nine old log buildings. Open daily year-round sunrise to sunset. (828)497-1904. www.nps.gov/grsm

The Road Goes On Forever
Side trips, tidbits, adventures, and treasure hunts

Mingus Mill is .5 mi from Museum on Hwy 441 N.

 Mingus Mill IN THE GREAT SMOKY MOUNTAINS NATIONAL PARK AT 1194 NEW-FOUND GAP RD Experience the thud, clank and spin of grinding corn. Open daily Apr–Oct 9am–5pm. (828)497-1904.

Turn and travel back down Hwy 441N to intersection with Hwy 19. Turn R on Hwy 19 and travel 10 mi to Bryson City.

BRYSON CITY

Hwy 19 becomes Main St in Bryson City. Elizabeth Ellison's studio and gallery on R.

Elizabeth Ellison Watercolors
155 MAIN ST – Elizabeth Ellison's watercolors have a mystical feel to them even as they are tethered to the natural world around her. Earthy and of her beloved place–the wilder side of the Appalachians–her paintings will infuse you with mountain spirit. Widely exhibited, Elizabeth often teams up with her nature writer-husband, George Ellison, as illustrator. Open year-round Mon–Sat 10am– 4:30pm. Good idea to call ahead. (828)488-8782. www.elizabethellisonwatercolors.com

Continue on Hwy 19/Main St, following signs to Hwy 74. Turn L on Hwy 74 and travel 14 mi toward Sylva.

Bryson City B&B's

The Historic Calhoun Country Inn 35 EVERETT ST – Fifteen rooms featuring hand-made quilts, antique and period furniture, including the rockers on the front porch. The Hyde family, who now own and operate the inn where their mother used to work, have restored it–embracing regional connections by naming each room after literary greats including Thomas Wolfe, Wilma Dykeman and Horace Kephart. Check out what's in the library while you sample the fresh breads, homemade jams and cobblers, or sourwood honey and biscuits. (828)488-1234. www.calhouncountryinn.com

MODERN DAY WARRIORS
Well before members of the Eastern Band of the Cherokees were American citizens, before they could vote or hold a passport, individuals from the tribe were giving up their lives in defense of this country. A veterans' monument, dedicated in 1993, now quietly bestows respect near the Tribal Council House in Cherokee.

An Elizabeth Ellison watercolor.

Guidebook Symbols

Craft Studio	Restaurant
Craft Gallery	Lodging
Historic Site	Special Attraction

Randolph House Country Inn 223 FRYE-MONT ST. This 1895 12-gabled mansion fills up regularly with folks who then fill up themselves with homemade breads, vegetables harvested from the nearby gardens, and mountain trout from local waters. (828)488-3472. www.randolphhouse.com

Nantahala Village Mountain Resort 9400 HWY 19W – Originally established in 1948, this retreat offers over 50 cabins and a beautiful newly-constructed lodge. Enjoy fresh local mountain trout while dining in front of a stone fireplace in a black-walnut-floored and wormy-chestnut-paneled restaurant. Open Mar–Dec. (828)488-2826. www.nvnc.com

DILLSBORO

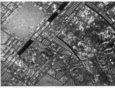

The bright facets of Riverwood Menagerie.

Brant Barnes at Riverwood Pottery.

At intersection of Hwy 441/74 and Hwy 23/441, turn S toward Dillsboro (and Franklin.) Travel 1 mi and make immediate L (after crossing bridge) on River Rd. Turn L on Craft Circle. The following four sites are located on Craft Circle and are within walking distance.

43 Riverwood Menagerie 54 CRAFT CIRCLE – Find yourself surrounded by stained glass in a multitude of shapes and colors. Get caught up watching Ivor Pace create new work and you'll want to hang around. Open daily year-round Mon–Sun 10am–5pm. (828)586-9083.

44 Riverwood Pottery 60 CRAFT CIRCLE – Brant Barnes loves to cook. So most everything he offers works in the kitchen, even his vases. His wife, Karen, is the creator of the beads and wall sconces. Good vibrations abound. Open May–Dec Mon–Sat 10am–5pm. Jan–Apr Tue–Sat 10am–5pm. (828)586-3601.

The Oaks Gallery, aptly named.

45 Oaks Gallery 29 CRAFT CIRCLE – The only thing that overshadows the work in this intimate gallery is the 300-year-old oak towering over it. Especially fine bowls, woven scarves and shawls, kitchenware and jewelry sold by people who care. Susan Leveille, proprietor, continues a long family tradition of supporting crafts, and their makers, in these mountains.

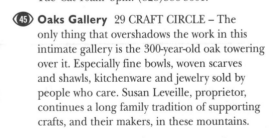

The Road Goes On Forever

Side trips, tidbits, adventures, and treasure hunts

Open Apr–Dec Mon–Sat 10am–5pm. Jan–Mar
Thu–Sat 10am–5pm. (828)586-6542.

 Riverwood Pewter Shop 17 CRAFT CIRCLE
– A fascinating process wherein pewter is
hammered into molds to make plates, platters
and bowls. The product is simple elegance. Ruth
McConnell carries on a tradition her father
learned while visiting his aunt, the legendary
Lucy Morgan, at Penland in the 1930's. Open
Apr–Dec Mon–Sat 10am–5pm. Jan–Mar Sat
10am–5pm. (828)586-6996.

*Hand-hammered
pewter-ware from
Riverwood Pewter Shop.*

*Return to Hwy 23/441 and turn R. Travel .2 mi back across river
and turn R on Haywood Rd (Hwy 23 Bus.) Take immediate R on
Webster St. Dogwood Crafters is on L.*

 Dogwood Crafters 90 WEBSTER ST – Looks
like a rustic log cabin but is actually one of the
most extensive collections of cottage craft anywhere. See if you can find the back. Open mid-
Mar–May Mon–Sun 9:30am–5:30pm. June–Aug
& Oct Mon–Sun 9:30am–9pm. Sep & Nov–Dec
Mon–Sun 9:30am–5:30pm. (828)586-2248.
www.dogwoodcrafters.com

Turn L on Front St. Mountain Pottery is on L.

Mountain Pottery 150 FRONT ST – Rick
Urban, an art director who escaped from
Madison Avenue, has successfully eluded capture
for over 21 years by posing as a contented potter.
Watch this former ad guy at his wheel or treat
yourself to the work of the 75 other potters
whose work is displayed in this cheerful, sun-
filled place. Open Apr–Dec Mon–Sat 10am–6pm
& Sun 12noon–5pm. (828)586-9183.

*Just one of the thou-
sands of spectacular
views along the way.*

Guidebook Symbols

 Craft Studio |**1**| Restaurant

Craft Gallery   **A** Lodging

Historic Site   Special Attraction

Return to Haywood Rd (Hwy 23 Bus) and turn R. Travel 1.5 mi and you will find yourself on Main St in Sylva.

Dillsboro B&B's

K **Squire Watkins Inn** 657 HAYWOOD RD –
This circa 1895 house is known as one of
Dillsboro's finest examples of Queen Anne
architecture. The hospitality is just as pleasantly
arranged. (828)586-5244.
www.bbonline.com/nc/squirewatkins.com

L **Jarrett House** HAYWOOD RD – A Dillsboro
institution since 1882. Hosts Jim and Jean
Harbarger have been doing the innkeeping
since 1975. Just the place to feast on a dinner
of country cured ham, fresh vegetables, hot
biscuits and vinegar pie (like pecan pie without
the pecans. You can then retire to the front
porch, sit a spell, and watch passers-by.
(828)586-0265.

SYLVA

*From Dillsboro travel on Haywood Rd (Hwy 23 Bus) for 1.5 mi
and you will find yourself on Main St in Sylva. Park on Main St
for the following four sites.*

*Classical shapings at
Karcher Stone Crossing.*

49 **Annie's Naturally** 506 W MAIN ST –
Serving all-natural, organic European breads
and pastries fresh-baked each day, this bakery
has a host of treats awaiting you. Open year-
round Tue–Sat 7am–6pm. (828)586-9096.

50 **LuLu's on Main** 18 MAIN ST – A restaurant
with many fans, both local and regional,
including *Southern Living* which chose it as one
of their favorites. Continental cuisine–soups,
salads and entrees–guaranteed to sway you over
to its growing list of devoted clientele. Open
year-round Mon–Sat 11am–9pm.
(828)586-8989.

51 **City Lights Bookstore** 3 E JACKSON ST –
(Half a block north of Main Street) Browse
shelves laden with notable books of our time,
study over imaginative items from regional
artisans, and listen closely to the proprietors
as they guide you through both books and

The Road Goes
On Forever
Side trips, tidbits,
adventures, and
treasure hunts

directions to the many treasures of this region. Open year-round Mon–Sat 9am–9pm. (828)586-9499. www.citylightsnc.com

 Spring St. Café 3 E JACKSON ST – (under the bookstore) For fresh and healthy, eclectic and homestyle food, you'll do well to dine at this upbeat downtown cafe. From Jamaican Jerk BBQ to Babaganouj to buttermilk biscuits, local produce takes on wildly different personas. Don't miss the homemade herbed goat cheese. Open year round Tue–Sat 11am–9:30pm & Sun 10:30am–2:30pm. (828)586-1800. www.springstcafe.com

Fresh fixins:
Spring Street Café.

Another example of classical shapings at Karcher Stone Crossing. Karcher studio (below).

Continue traveling N on Main St/Hwy 23 Bus and turn L as Bus 23 bears L. Travel about 2 mi to junction with Hwy 74 and bear R heading N. Turn L immediately on Steeple Rd and again L on Skyline Dr. Make immediate R on Beta Rd. Karcher Studio is .3 mi on R.

Karcher Stone Crossing 260 BETA RD – What's a sculptor, classically trained in Rhode Island and Italy, doing in a 100-year-old chestnut barn near Sylva? Don't ask. Just marvel at the figurative pieces she wrests from 1600-pound blocks of Alabama marble. Other startling works in bronze, alabaster, blackstone and wood. Open Apr–Oct Tue–Sat 10am–5pm or by appointment. (828)586-4813. www.collenekarcher.com

Guidebook Symbols

Craft Studio   Restaurant
Craft Gallery   Lodging
Historic Site   Special Attraction

Some of nature at Nature's Work.

Return to Hwy 74 and turn R and then exit immediately following signs back to Bus 23 and Cullowhee. Travel about 2 mi back to junction with Hwy 107 to Cullowhee. Turn L on Hwy 107 and travel .8 mi and turn L on Citrus Dr. (Watch for Nature's Work sign on L).

 Nature's Work

31 CITRUS DR – What have we here?! A stunning assortment of furniture and accessories finely crafted from salvaged wood. A small gallery space features the work of woodworker Robert Brown plus local artisans' metalwork, photography, stained glass and furniture. Open year-round Tue–Sat 11am–4pm. (828)586-9541.

Return to Hwy 107 and turn L. Travel 4.3 mi to Western Carolina University.

CULLOWHEE

Traveling from Sylva on Hwy 107, turn L at Western Carolina University campus. The Mountain Heritage Center is in the H. F. Robinson Administration Building . Park directly to R of building.

55 Mountain Heritage Center WESTERN CAROLINA UNIVERSITY – A museum of Southern Appalachian history and culture which oftentimes features craft demonstrations to illustrate the importance of craft-making in this mountain region. Open June–Oct Mon–Fri 8am–5pm & Sun 2pm–5pm. Jan–Dec Mon–Fri 8am–5pm. (828)227-7129. www.wcu.edu/mhc

Chair caning–a tradition in our mountains.

Return to Hwy 107. Turn L and travel 3.5 mi and turn L on Caney Fork Rd. Enter second drive on R, which is approximately .7 mi from Hwy 107. Studio at end of drive.

The Road Goes On Forever

Side trips, tidbits, adventures, and treasure hunts

Heritage Series by Susan Lingg

624 CANEY FORK RD – Susan's irrepressible sense of awe and whimsy find full expression as she brings paint to her hand-made paper canvases. You'll be enchanted with the results. Open Nov–Sep Mon–Tue & Thu–Sun 10am–5pm. (828) 293-5556. www.watercolorsby-susan.com

Part of Susan Lingg's Heritage Series.

Return to Hwy 107 and turn L. Travel 1 mi and turn R on Moody Bridge Rd. Go 1.3 mi to the end of Moody Bridge Rd. Studio is at end of road.

 Plum Orchard Forge 1267 MOODY BRIDGE RD – Yep, there really is a forge at the end of this road. And a blacksmith who is a self-described frustrated jeweler. After years at the forge making large commissioned pieces, David Brewin now crafts custom light-switch plates, fish hooks and other small forged items. Open year-round Mon–Fri 8am–5pm. (828) 293-3151. www.plumorchardforge.com

Cullowhee B&B

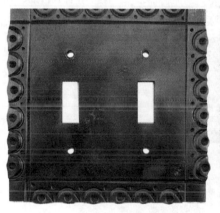

M **The River Lodge B&B** 619 ROY TRITT RD – Built from hundred-year-old handhewn logs rescued from barns and cabins in the northern part of the state, the River Lodge offers warm hospitality on the banks of the Tuckasegee River. (828) 293-5431. www.river-lodge-bb.com

Product of Plum Orchard Forge.

Guidebook Symbols

Craft Studio		Restaurant
Craft Gallery		Lodging
Historic Site		Special Attraction

John C. Campbell Folk School

The Art of Sharing

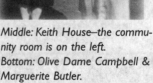

Middle: Keith House—the community room is on the left.
Bottom: Olive Dame Campbell & Marguerite Butler.

John C. Campbell Folk School is maybe the only school you'll ever find where you can take a course entitled "Hand-planed bamboo fly rod," "Hammering a tune on the hammered dulcimer," or "Making a tear-drop fiddle." It's a place where you can butt things, fuse things, throw things, hook things, join things, and splatter things, then step back and clog til the cows come home. And it is as it should be, on this small piece of earth near Brasstown where, in a true collaboration, the community founded a school based on the ideas brought forward by John and Olive Dame Campbell.

The Campbells had come to the mountains of the South in 1908, as humanitarians, to study the region and its people. As John interviewed farmers about their practices, Olive collected ancient ballads and a variety of contemporary handcrafts.

After John died in 1919, Olive and her friend Marguerite Butler traveled to Europe to look at Danish "schools

for life." They came back to the U.S. determined to offer the same kind of opportunity in Appalachia. With land donated by a local family and the sincere support of the nearby mountain people, an institution was born in 1925.

"Higher learning" at Campbell Folk School, from its beginnings, has been seated in the soul. As Director Jan Davidson puts it, the school "seeks

Top: Folk School weaving class, 1951.
Bottom: Woodcarving students. 1950.

to bring people toward two kinds of development: inner growth as creative thoughtful individuals, and social development as tolerant, caring members of a community."

Come to the Folk School any time of the year, and you will find families and friends speaking excitedly in the dialects of craft: kiln temperatures, woofs and warps, slumps and fuses, mortices and tenons, dove-tailing and hand-gouging. After a weekend or week-long class in traditional and contemporary arts and crafts, cooking, gardening and nature studies, students return home and take with them something of what John and Olive intended. Something about themselves, tucked away, in a suitcase or knapsack, in the shape of a quite wonderful object of their own hand.

Making a chair the old way.

The Lake Country

In the first half of this century, a series of dams were constructed on the Hiawasee, Nantahala and Little Tennessee rivers. In addition to creating electricity, the dams transformed what were once dry hollows and coves into a series of many-fingered lakes that give the trail its name. ✂ The lakes brought with them both opportunity and heartache. Homes, churches, and farms were lost to the rising waters. But one thing could not be washed away: the strong sense of community so firmly rooted in the small towns and villages that populate the region. ✂ The crafts along the trail are those of a community. You'll find handiwork in finely stitched lace and forged iron, and you'll also hear it in homespun tales and well-made music, and see it in intricately woven dances. ✂ That spirit is joyously embodied at the John C. Campbell Folk School in Brasstown. For eight decades, Saturday night dances have brought together

Studio of the late Fred Smith, renowned Woodcarver.

The Craft of Community

students and local citizens on the old oak dance floor of the school community room. Here, to the sounds of guitar, banjo and fiddle, enduring friendships begin with the simple call to "change partners." ⊙✗ Fellowship, in perhaps a slightly less exhuberant form, is also found every day in the literally hundreds of classes the school offers. Depending on your interest, and the amount of time you have to devote, you can learn to spin yarn, cane a chair, throw a pot, forge a knife, weave a basket, or carve a walking stick. ⊙✗ In the classrooms, and in the many different studios you will visit along the way, talented potters, wood carvers, weavers and blacksmiths reveal the "craft" of their work. In return, students and visitors offer their interest and enthusiasm. This, then, is the true communion of craft; for it is in this sharing between each other, that we find that we are all both givers and receivers.

The Lake Country

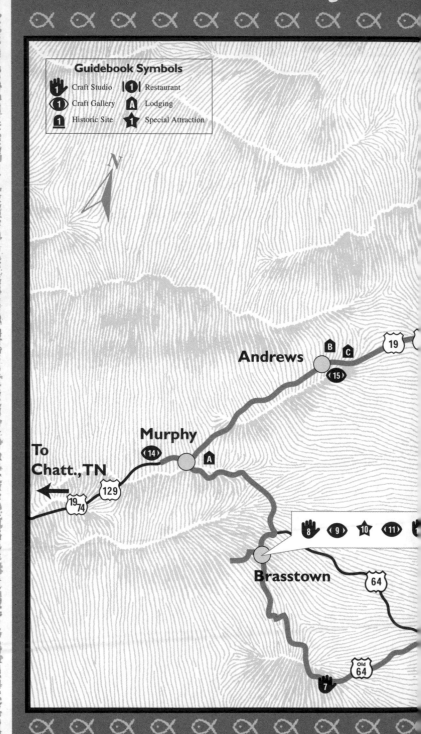

Guidebook Symbols

- Craft Studio
- Craft Gallery
- Historic Site
- Restaurant
- Lodging
- Special Attraction

N

Andrews

B C

19

15

Murphy

14

A

To
Chatt., TN

129

19 74

8 9 10 11

Brasstown

64

Old
64

7

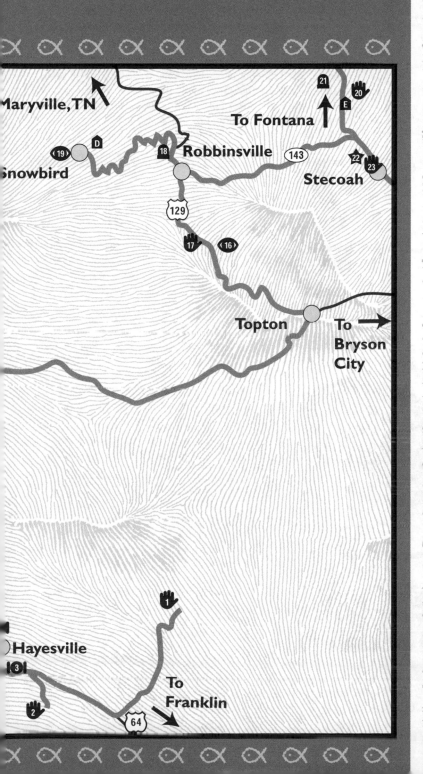

Lake Country represents the westernmost loop in the Craft Heritage Trail system and is most readily accessible for travelers coming up from the south, from Atlanta and Athens, for example, via US 441. If coming from the east, pick it up at the end of the Cascades Trail in Franklin.

Still waters run deep. The 165 miles of the Lake Country travel through some remote regions, but it is this very quality of native, frontier beauty that gives you the feeling you're blazing a trail instead of merely following one. And like all explorers of uncharted regions, the more time you take, the more you'll discover. To get totally submerged in all of it, give yourself a long weekend.

HAYESVILLE AREA

Robert St. Pierre's wood sculptural vase.

From Hayesville intersection of NC 69 and US 64 Bypass travel E on US 64 for 2.1 mi. Turn L on Cold Branch Rd. Travel 4.8 mi. Turn R on Tusquittee Rd. St. Pierre's Wood Pottery is .4 mi on L.

 St. Pierre's Wood Pottery 33 COMPASS MEADOWS DR – Robert St. Pierre casts his eye over the various stacks of hardwood in his studio and says, "every piece of wood in here has something to offer." Walk a few steps into his gallery and find out just how much. See how he uses spalted wood to create an art that's now in permanent collections throughout the world. Wooden vessels-bowls, lamps, vases, urns and boxes-not turned, but built up, layer upon layer and finely finished. Open year-round Mon–Sun 11am–5pm except Thanksgiving and Christmas. (828) 389-6639. www.stpierrewoodpottery.com

David Goldhagen's glasswork.

Return to Hwy 64 and turn R back toward Hayesville. Travel .7 mi and turn L on Hinton Center Rd. Travel 1.9 mi and Goldhagen Studio will be on R.

 Goldhagen Art Glass Studio 7 GOLDHAGEN STUDIO DR – A lofted gallery space above David Goldhagen's glass studio on Lake Chatuga offers a wren's eye view of a fascinating process—unique and massive sculptural or highly intricate–emerging from the end of a five-foot blowpipe. David rolls, pulls and stretches molten glass into ethereal shapes that appear fluid even after they harden. Open year-round Mon–Fri 9:30am–2pm & 2:30pm–5:30pm. (828) 389-8847.

The Road Goes On Forever

Side trips, tidbits, adventures, and treasure hunts

Return to Hwy 64, turn L. Travel 1.3 mi back to the intersection with Hwy 69. Turn R on Hwy 69. Travel .2 mi to Ice Cream Parlor on R.

|3| Hayesville's Best Lil' Corner Ice Cream Parlor 4 YELLOW JACKET DR – Enjoy an old-fashioned soda in this old-fashioned general store building. Ask about music happenings as the stars begin to gather. Open May–Nov Tue–Fri 11:30am–9pm & Sat 1pm–11pm. (828)389-0164.

Turn R on Hwy 69. Travel .4 mi. Museum is on L.

4 Clay County Historical and Arts Council Museum HWY 69– An excellent example of how jails benefit society–especially if the local Arts Council rescues the building so it can display artifacts from an ancient Indian river village. Open June–Aug Tue–Sat 10am–4pm. (828)389-6760.

Mosey up to the ice cream bar.

Continue .1 mi on Hwy 69 to Hayesville Town Square and park on square. The following sites are located on the square within walking distance of each other.

|5| Tiger's/Chinquapins 42 HERBERT ST – This particular soda fountain has been serving up treats since 1945 while the older part of the store has been continuously operating since the late 1800's. Order up a hand-mixed shake or soda and ask Rob about the town. You're in for another treat. Open year-round Mon–Sat 9am–6pm. (828)389-1342.

6 Phillips and Lloyd Book Shop 66 CHURCH ST – A fine selection of books and crafts with a regional bent. Open year-round Tue–Fri 11am–5:30pm & Sat 9:30am–1:30pm. (828)389-1492.

Tiger's/Chinquapins.

Guidebook Symbols

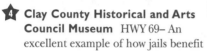

Craft Studio		Restaurant	
Craft Gallery		Lodging	
Historic Site		Special Attraction	

Continue around Hayesville Town Square and make R turn on Hwy 64 Business. Travel 1.3 mi and turn R on Hwy 64.

Totems at Smoke in the Mountains.

BRASSTOWN AREA

Going W on Hwy 64 out of Hayesville, make immediate L on Old Hwy 64 toward Warne. Travel 4.8 mi to Young Harris Rd and turn L. Travel .3 mi and turn R on West Rd. Travel .4 mi and turn R on West Gum Log Rd. Travel 1.0 mi and turn R into drive. Studio is 100 yards to L of drive.

7 Smoke in the Mountains 504 WEST GUM LOG RD – Discover how 2 potters (Kim and Rob Winthrow) X scrupulous high standards + delightful senses of humor = 2 magnificent totem poles! Functional bowls, mugs and vessels marked with their trademark stamp bring smiles with every use. Open year-round Thu–Sun 10am–5pm. (828)389-3971.

Return to Old Hwy 64 and turn L. Travel 5.4 mi. Sign to gallery is on L. Follow signs up drive to studio and gallery.

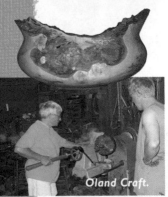

8 Oland Craft, Creative Wood Turning 10025 OLD HWY 64 W – A master at work—often instructing apprentices—in the age-old art of shaping wood. See what Lissa Oland's turned out at her studio in the midst of a forest wonderland. Open daily year-round 9am–5pm. (828)837-2273. www.olandcraft.com

Oland Craft.

Return to Old Hwy 64 and turn L. Gallery is immediately on L.

A sampling of work at the Brasstown Collective.

9 Brasstown Creek Artists Collective 10079 OLD HWY 64 W – Billie Shelburn, resident painter at John C. Campbell Folk School, transformed an ordinary building into a spacious, light-filled gallery on the banks of the Brasstown Creek. Her painterly eye and her mystical whimsy are reflected in her own work as well as that of compatriots she has assembled in the gallery. Open Feb–Dec Wed–Sat 11am–5pm & Sun 1pm–5pm. Closed in Jan, but call for appointment. (828)835-8200.

The Road Goes On Forever

Side trips, tidbits, adventures, and treasure hunts

Turn L on Old Hwy 64 and travel .9 mi. Turn L on Brasstown Rd and travel .2 mi. Turn L into craft shop.

10 John C. Campbell Folk School Craft Shop
7 FOLK SCHOOL RD – Lessons in craft and community are at the heart of the institution, founded in 1925. Renowned instructors teach a multitude of disciplines on a charmed, 380-acre campus. The work of over 300 craftspeople, including pieces made by the famous Brasstown carvers, is featured in an expansive new craft shop. Upstairs, in the school dining room, you'll marvel at a permanent collection of Doris Ulmann photographs from the early 1930s and selected works from the school's impressive folklore archives. (*See Heritage section on page 204-205*) Open year-round Mon–Sat 8am–5pm & Fri until 7:30pm. Sun 1pm–5pm. (828)837-2775. www.folkschool.org

Yesterday and today at the John C. Campbell Folk School.

Turn L back on Brasstown Rd and travel .6 mi to studio on R.

11 Laurel Mountain Studio 3757 BRASSTOWN RD – Here's an idea: set up an easel in a room surrounded by windows that frame scenes of constantly changing beauty. You can also buy a painting that's already on canvas. Open year-round Mon–Sat 10am–5pm. (828)837-8706.

Metcalfe Roush Forge and Design.

Turn L back on Brasstown Rd and travel .5 mi. Turn R on Folk School Rd and travel .4 mi to Waldroup Rd. Take immediate hard R into complex. The studio building is in a long shed to L.

12 Metcalfe Roush Forge and Design 18 WALDROUP RD – Artists-blacksmiths Lynda Metcalfe and Elmer Roush celebrated their wedding day by forging rings. They continue to celebrate being together by producing a range of high-quality home accessories and custom work that includes furniture, hand railings, candle holders, ladles, latches, and fine tools,

Silk as defined by Douglas Atchley at Birdfoot Studio.

all hand-forged. Open year-round Mon-Fri 9am –12noon & 2pm–5pm except during shows. (828)835-7313. www.metcaferoush.com

Return to intersection of Folk School Rd, Waldroup Rd and Mason Rd. Turn R on Mason Rd. Travel .3 mi. Birdfoot Ridge Studio is on L.

13 ⏚ Birdfoot Ridge Studio 157 MASON RD – Potter Lee Davis keeps the clay and the one-liners flying in the space he shares with Douglas Atchley, who prefers to let his stunning painted-silk clothing do the talking. While Lee disarms you with his wit, don't overlook his work, which includes ginko leaf motif dinnerware and inventive fountains/oil lamps combining "Zen and Busbee Berkley." Open year-round Mon–Sun 8am–12noon & 1pm–7pm. (828)837-7430.

Return to Brasstown Rd, turn R and return to Old Hwy 64 and turn L. Travel 2.0 mi and turn L on Hwy 64. Travel 4.7 mi to junction with Hwy 19/74. Turn L on Hwy 19/74/129.

MURPHY

From intersection of Hwy 64 and Hwy 19/74/129 turn L (as stated above) and travel 2.0 mi. Shop is a log cabin on R.

14 Appalachian Heritage Crafters 2016 HWY 64 W – A log cabin on a busy road crammed full of traditional Appalachian crafts (wood-carvings, crocheted mats and scarves, jellies and jams, handcrafted tables and chests) lovingly created by dozens of local artisans. Open Mar–Dec Mon–Sat 10am–6pm & Sun 1pm–5pm. (828)835-3500. www.ahccrafts.com

Work by potter Lee Davis.

Murphy B&B's

A Park Place B&B 54 HILL ST – Beautiful antiques, silver, crystal and lace adorn this stunning turn-of-the-century home, but there's nothing stuffy at all about friendly hosts Neal and Ricki Wocell. (828)837-8842. www.bbonline.com/nc/parkplace

Continue down 19/129/64/74 until you can turn around and go the other direction. Travel approximately 16 mi to Andrews.

APPALACHIAN HERITAGE CRAFTERS

A front porch welcome.

The Road Goes On Forever

Side trips, tidbits, adventures, and treasure hunts

Hold hands with a couple of friends and see if your arms can encircle one of the tulip poplars in the Joyce Kilmer Memorial Forest, a 3,800-acre wilderness area, full of trails and gargantuan trees (more than 100 species).

ANDREWS

Kingly rooms at Park Place B&B.

Traveling to Andrews from Murphy, turn R on Business 19/Main St and travel 1.1 mi. Gallery on R.

(15) Andrews Valley Artist's Gallery 1158 MAIN ST #B AT THE CORNER OF OAK AND MAIN – Regional painters featured in this gem of a gallery have a lot to say about the soft, inexorable charms of Andrews Valley and the greater Appalachians. Odds are you'll see more than one piece that speaks to you. Open year-round Wed–Sat 10:30am–5:30pm. Sun–Tues by appoinment. (828)321-9553. www.avartistsgallery.com

From Gallery, continue R on Main St for 1.8 mi. Rejoin Hwy 19/129/74, turning R onto it.

Andrews B&B's

B The Walker Inn of Old Valleytown 385 JUNALUSKA ST – This fine old colonial-style inn is on the National Register and has been graciously welcoming visitors since before the Civil War. Step across the threshold and into a world of bubble-glass window panes, heirlooms, and gatherings around the parlor's grand piano. Five guest rooms. Open Apr–Nov. (828)321-5019.

C Hawkesdene House B&B Inn and Cottages 381 PHILLIPS CREEK RD – The new hosts, David and Lesley Mastifino continue the English country charm and hospitality made legendary by the Sargents in this attractive B&B adjoining the Nantahala National Forest. Adding to the fairyland atmosphere are two llamas, Hawke and Dene, who will carry your lunch on trail hikes to Hidden Falls and other enchanted spots in the forest. Four guest rooms and five small cottages. Open daily year-round 9am–9pm. (800)447-9549. www.hawkesdene.com

A welcome at Hawksdene.

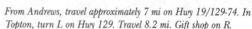

A growl of a time at Country Thyme Gifts.

ROBBINSVILLE

From Andrews, travel approximately 7 mi on Hwy 19/129-74. In Topton, turn L on Hwy 129. Travel 8.2 mi. Gift shop on R.

(16) Country Thyme Gifts 3253 TALLULAH RD – Just the place to find handcrafted gifts for your home or that of a freind. Delightful ceramic creatures, fragrant candles, cozy kitchen aprons and a general merriment of country crafts. Open Mar–Dec Tue–Sat 9:30am–5pm. Jan–Feb Tue & Thu–Fri 9:30am–4:30pm. (828)479-2549.

Turn R on Tallulah Rd (Hwy 129) and travel 1.0 mi. Turn L on Mill Creek Rd and follow signs to pottery (1/2 mi, 2 R turns.)

(17) Mill Creek Pottery 57 W MILL CREEK RD – Over the creek and through the woods, not to grandmother's house, but to Ray Kaylor and M.L.Bagwell's pottery and gallery. Another grand example of WNC's talented clay duos. It's all about creating pottery "to decorate your home and soothe your spirit," as they so nicely describe it. Open Apr–Dec Mon–Sat 11am–6pm. Jan–Mar Mon–Sat 12noon–6pm. (828)479-9449. www.millcreekpottery.com

Return to Hwy 129 and turn L. Travel 3.2 mi to Robbinsville. Turn L on E. Main St. Travel .4 mi and turn L on S. Main St. Junaluska Memorial is .5 mi on L.

Mill Creek Pottery's warm welcome.

The Road Goes On Forever

Side trips, tidbits, adventures, and treasure hunts

Junaluska Memorial S MAIN ST –A seven-sided memorial surrounding Junaluska's grave honors his life and contributions to the seven Cherokee clans. Open daily year-round. www.junaluska.com

If not traveling Snowbird Loop, return to Hwy 129 and the intersection with Hwy 143. Travel E on Hwy 143 to Stecoah, Hwy 28.

SNOWBIRD LOOP

Continue down Main St. 0.1 mi and turn L on Snowbird/Hwy 143 Business. Travel 5 mi and Snowbird will split L from Hwy 143. Continue on Snowbird 1.9 mi and turn L on Cornsilk Branch Rd. Travel .5 mi and the Trading Post is on R.

(19) Snowbird Indian Trading Post 524 CORNSILK BRANCH RD - SNOWBIRD COMMUNITY – The museum-quality work more than justifies the travel required. The masks, jewelry and other ceremonial objects leave no doubt as to their provenance. A sense of having been in the presence of the holy will follow you. Open Apr–Oct Mon–Tue & Thu–Sat 10am–5pm or by appointment. (828)479-8635. www.snowbirdindian.com

In the lair of Snowbird Indian Trading Post .

Return to Snowbird Rd and turn R, staying on Snowbird Rd at Santeelah/Snowbird intersection. Travel 2.1 mi on Snowbird (143) and turn L on Hwy 143/Massey Rd. Stay on Hwy 143 for 14 mi to intersection with Hwy 28 N.

D Snowbird Mountain Lodge 4633 SANTEELAH RD – Nestled on almost 100 acres of pristine mountaintop, this lodge boasts interior paneling, beams and furniture of maple, wild cherry, butternut, and chestnut crafted by local artisans. Open Mar 15–Dec 15 Mon–Sun 24 hours. Dec 16–Mar 14 Tue–Thu 9am–3pm. (828)479-3433. www.snowbirdlodge.com

View from the porch of the Snowbird Lodge.

Guidebook Symbols

Craft Studio | Restaurant
Craft Gallery | Lodging
Historic Site | Special Attraction

The Yellow Branch Pottery and Cheese.

OFF HWY 28 / FONTANA

At intersection of Hwy 143 and Hwy 28N, turn L and travel 3.9 mi and turn R on Old Yellow Branch Rd. Travel 1 mi and turn R on Yellow Branch Circle.

 20 **Yellow Branch Pottery and Cheese** 136 YELLOW BRANCH CIRCLE – You can sample Karen's own "Yellow Branch" handmade cheeses from one of her turned dishes. Or you can simply enjoy the beauty of her unique glazes in the joyous serenity of a mountain cove. Her butterfly habitat adds an ethereal touch in her surrounding gardens. Open Apr–Oct Tue–Sat 2pm–5pm. Nov–Mar by appointment only. (828)479-6710. www.yellowbranch.com

Turn back toward Hwy 28. (Possum Hollow Rd is on R.)

E **Mountain Hollow B&B** 24 POSSUM HOLLOW RD – A secluded mountain inn situated on 35 wooded acres. This may be one of the few B&B's that offers bird watching right from its porch. Trekking for such experiences is optional. Open daily year-round Mon–Sun 8am–5pm. (828)479-3608. www.mountainhollowbb.com

FONTANA SIDE TRIP

From intersection of Old Yellow Branch Rd and Hwy 28N, turn R and travel approximately 10 mi.

21 **Fontana Village** HWY 28N – Nestled between the Great Smoky Mountains and the Nantahala Mountains, you'll find a world unto itself at this resort village. Open year-round. (828)498-2070 or (800)849-2258. www.fontanavillage.com

Fontana Dam from the top.

BACK ON THE TRAIL

From intersection of Old Yellow Branch Rd and Hwy 28N, turn L on Hwy 28 traveling south for 3.6 mi back to intersection with Hwy 143. Continue on Hwy 28 for .9 mi past this intersection and turn R on Stecoach Rd. Travel .2 mi, crossing Cody Branch Rd onto School House Rd. Center is .1 mi on L.

The Road Goes On Forever
Side trips, tidbits, adventures, and treasure hunts

At a dizzying 480 feet, Fontana Dam is the tallest dam in the eastern United States. It took 6,000 people to build the dam. It was completed in 1945. The village created for the workers ultimately became the resort of Fontana Village.

Stecoah Valley Arts, Crafts and Educational Center Inc. 121 SCHOOLHOUSE RD – A former rock schoolhouse has been reborn of late into a kind of community center holding a library, visitor's center, and weaving cooperative. Also houses a shop carrying local crafts and studios of some note. Open June–Oct Mon–Fri 10am–5pm & Sat 10am–4pm. Nov–May Mon–Fri 10am–5pm. (828)479-3364. www.visitSVCenter.com

Think locally. Buy candles globally— at Bee Global.

Bee Global 121 SCHOOLHOUSE RD INSIDE STECOAH VALLEY CENTER – Something totally unique and beguiling: beeswax lanterns illuminated from within by a replaceable votive candle. Ferns, dogwood, Japanese maple, columbine, ground pine and other native flora are captured just below the surface of the globes, so that once lit, they reflect the patterns of nature. Open Jun–Oct Mon–Fri 10am–5pm & Sat 10am–4pm. Nov–May Mon–Fri 10am–5pm. (828)479-8284. www.beeglow.com

Return to Hwy 28 and travel 11 mi to rejoin Hwy 19/28/74. Bryson City is only 8 mi away from this point.

STECOAH VALLEY ARTS, CRAFTS AND EDUCATION CENTER
Stone schoolhouses stand as implacable reminders of the long reach of education throughout the mountains. For those who live nearby, the buildings are part of each community's heritage. More often than not, people who care are now doing something to bring them back to life for the future generations to enjoy. In Stecoah, between Bryson City and Fontana Dam, a former rock schoolhouse has been reborn into a kind of community center holding a library, a visitors' center, and a shop carrying local crafts. Open year-round Mon-Sat 10am–4pm. (828)479-3364.

Guidebook Symbols

Craft Studio | Restaurant
Craft Gallery | Lodging
Historic Site | Special Attraction

Index

Index

Clay

fiber

Galleries

Glass

Metal

Mountain Cities

String of Pearls

Cascades

Shadow of the Smokies

The Lake Country

About HandMade in America

The seeds of HandMade in America were sown in 1993 when a handful of Western North Carolinians, struggling to find fresh approaches to economic development and renewal in their mountains, realized that the answer didn't necessarily lie in newly recruited

industry, but could potentially be found in the invisible industry of craftspeople already working steadily and exceptionally in shops, classrooms, studios, and galleries tucked away on small town main streets and back roads throughout the Blue Ridge Mountains.

In December of 1993, HandMade in America received a three-year organizational development grant from the Pew Partnership for Civic Change. Over 360 citizens participated in a regional planning process to help determine how HandMade could establish Western North Carolina as the center of handmade objects in the nation.

We welcome the support and involvement of those in the public, private, and nonprofit sectors who share our commitment to that inspired joining of art and function we call "handcraft." Building on this support, HandMade has initiated programs

in education, community and economic development for thousands of citizens in our region. Demonstrable results include a 10-15% increase in income for many of our craftspeople, and over $11 million in investment in several of the region's smallest towns.

Soap Making

Our Mission is to celebrate the hand and the handmade, to nurture the creation of traditional and contemporary craft, to

revere and protect our resources, and to preserve and enrich the
spiritual, cultural, and community life of our region.

Why HandMade, Why Here?

Every region and every community has its unique gifts and
challenges. In Western North Carolina, one of the gifts is our
extraordinary, rich heritage of handcraft.

As we explored how to
bolster our economy and
preserve that heritage, we
considered our geography
and how our land is used.

**Western
North Carolina**

In 1995 HandMade in America, in association with researchers at
the John A. Walker College of Business at Appalachian State
University, conducted a survey to measure the economic
contribution of crafts in 22 counties in Western North Carolina.
This survey, <u>The Economic Impact of Crafts</u> revealed that crafts
contributed $122 million annually to the region's economy.
That figure is four times the revenue generated from burley
tobacco, one of the region's largest cash crop. The survey also
revealed some of the challenges and needs of the craft
community, including access to capital and marketing and
business education services.

The Western North Carolina region is home to over 4,000 artisans
whose work contributes over $122 million to the local economy.

Guiding Principles

• All work of HandMade in America is inclusive. Everyone
is welcome to participate from the first-time hobbyist to the
full-time, one-of-a-kind design professional craftsmen, and/or
any interested citizen of the region.

• All projects are done in partnership with other organizations
and institutions - all funding is written jointly or in the
partner's name.

• HandMade is regional. All communities come equally to the table in resources. Meetings are held throughout the region. Board members represent the region.

• HandMade is sustainable community development. No outside consultants or businesses are used. The people of the region serve as their own best resource. HandMade is focused on long-term solutions, hence a twenty year strategic plan.

• All HandMade projects are community-based. Each community defines its needs, resources and how it fits into the strategic plan.

• HandMade is self-sustaining. All projects must fit into the operation of an ongoing institution, or be financially self-sustaining.

Our Twenty Year Goals

• To develop community strategies that will collectively enhance Western North Carolina's role nationally and internationally within the handmade field.

• To establish an academic base to promote crafts throughout all levels of education as object, subject and process.

• To develop a communication plan that establishes Western North Carolina's role as the center for HandMade in America.

• To implement environmentally sustainable economic strategies for Western North Carolina that emphasize the handmade industry.

• To implement strategies that will enhance opportunities for handmade object makers within Western North Carolina.

• To actively encourage the public, private and nonprofit sectors to develop independent and interdependent vehicles that build the handmade industry.

Chair from recycled materials.

HandMade in America's Small Town Revitalization

Among the many joyful discoveries awaiting you along western North Carolina's Craft Heritage Trails are the region's creative folks of every stripe. Storytellers, musicians, painters, photographers, farmers, sculptors, gardeners, educators, writers, potters, weavers, doll-makers, quilters, basketmakers, pie-bakers...we've got 'em all, and then some, from the mountaintops to the valleys and on every backroad and main street.

And since 1996, HandMade has worked with the region's smallest communities to celebrate another form of ingenuity and artistry in our mountains...that of creative citizenship. HandMade launched the Small Towns Revitalization Program at the request of volunteers in communities along the Craft Heritage Trails who wanted to improve, restore and enhance their downtowns and public spaces and create new opportunities for economic development and civic engagement.

A textured program based on mentoring, technical assistance, resource development, leadership training and self-help, the Small Towns Program has served a dozen communities in the region and volunteers have contributed hundreds of thousands of volunteer hours to the creation of parks, greenways, creekwalks, festivals and arts events, public art installations and historic preservation projects.

But above all, the partnership between HandMade and its Small Towns is about valuing, respecting, and celebrating the qualities that give each community its own personality. They are, each, works of art in progress.

Communities currently participating in the program are: Andrews, Bakersville, Bryson City, Chimney Rock, Crossnore, Hayesville/Clay County, Hot Springs, Mars Hill, Marshall, Todd, West Jefferson. Stop a while in each and be inspired!

The EnergyXchange

Jon Ellenbogen, a long-time potter and board member of HandMade in America who lives and works in the Penland community, remembers how he used to haul trash to the six-acre landfill shared by Mitchell and Yancey County. "I'd almost always get stuck," he says, "and I'd have to get one of the bulldozers to pull me out."

Nowadays, it's likely that a visitor to this same site will be traveling with an entirely different agenda-to see the latest work of an incubator community of artists, aided in large part by recycled methane gases from the old landfill.

These gases, in a project called *EnergyXchange,* are redirected to power the kilns and ovens of a small group of on-site ceramic and glass artists who require lots of energy. In addition, recycled methane is also used to heat greenhouses dedicated to growing over-harvested, native ornamentals like flame azalea and galax. These greenhouse seedlings are then resold to local growers.

This richly collaborative project, designed in partnership with the Blue Ridge Resource Conservation and Development Council, Mayland Community College, Mitchell and Yancey Counties, and HandMade in America, nurtures both the economy, the livelihood of artists and the environment.

"The EPA helped our exploratory group understand what we were looking at here," says project manager Terry Woodruff. "The greenhouse gas we will capture and use over the next ten years is equivalent to removing 21,002 cars from North Carolina highways."

For former Penland student and resident glass blower John Geci, maker of strikingly luminous spiral bowls and vases, EnergyXchange has been a godsend, saving him about $700 a month in furnace costs.

For local high school students and college interns, an off-shoot of EnergyXchange called *Project Branch Out* has provided priceless hands-on learning experiences in gardening and agriculture.

And for Jon Ellenbogen, EnergyXchange supporter and board member, who now drives to the old landfill site in a merrier frame of mind, this project represents energy re-use in its best expression and stands as a model for making something extraordinary out of some 900 small landfills around the nation.

HandMade Holidays

Throw a pot. Milk a goat. Cut your own Christmas Tree.
Anytime of year, a HandMade Holiday might be just the thing
to reconnect with what is important – art, nature, your
family, yourself.

Our special interest tours, getaways and learning weekends were
created to offer you a new level of engagement in our North
Carolina Mountains. Private studio tours, quilting parties,
organic farming classes, mountain walkabouts, garden-to-table
cooking weekends....

Sure, you've visit-
ed our mountains,
but you've never
taken a
HandMade
Holiday...

KEEP
WHAT YOU
CATCH

Farms, Gardens & Countryside Trails of Western North Carolina guidebook

HandMade in America's guide to the best agriculture throughout Western North Carolina.

Tuck this book under your arm and head for the mountains.

With over 350 pages, the full-color book offers over 500 listings of farms, gardens, historic inns and restaurants of note throughout the 22-county area of Western North Carolina. Embroidered with colorful tales, fun sidetrips, route maps and exquisite photographs, the guidebook beckons you to the mountain roads and the pleasures of discovery that await you at every turn.

Travel along one or just part of the seven driving tours that stretch out from the Blue Ridge Parkway. You'll discover handmade treasures deep in the narrows of mountain coves, across rippling streams, and in storefronts on postcard streets.

Adventures at your fingertips

In the Farms, Gardens and Countryside Trails of Western North Carolina guidebook, everything you need is included: maps with each site indicated and numbered, places to stay, galleries to shop in, restaurants and cafes where you can stop and sit a spell, and how to find gardeners and farmers in town or out in the country. Each listing has a full description and includes phone numbers if you need special directions.

There are seven regional tours from which to choose and many trails to follow within each of them: Quilt Top Ramble, Jewels & Gems Meander, Arbors & Orchards, The Ribbon Garden, Whistlestop Tour, Foothill Forays, Water Ways Trail. Each trail takes its own path and has its own special heritage.

To Order...

To order your guidebook today call 1-800-331-4154, visit our website at www.handmadeinamerica.org or, fill out the order form on the next page and mail the form and payment directly to HandMade in America, P.O. Box 2089, Asheville, NC 28802. Checks, money orders, and major credit cards accepted.

farms, Gardens & Countryside Trails of Western North Carolina

Cost is $19.95 per book. NC residents, please add 7% sales tax per book. Shipping and handling fees are $4.50 for one book per address and $2 per additional book to the same address.

You can also order additional copies of this guidebook.

The Craft Heritage Trails of Western North Carolina

Cost is $19.95 per book. NC residents, please add 7% sales tax per book. Shipping and handling fees are $4.50 for one book per address and $2 per additional book to the same address.

Please Send Me More...

Name *(please print)*
_____

Address
_____

City   State   Zip
_____

Shipping address if different from above:

_____

Name
_____

Address
_____

City   State   Zip
_____

	Qty	Total
Farms, Gardens & Countryside Trails of Western North Carolina $19.95	_____	_____
The Craft Heritage Trails of Western North Carolina $19.95	_____	_____
Set, includes both books $35.00	_____	_____
Shipping and handling *($4.50 for one, $6.50 for set, add $2.00 for each additional)*		_____
NC residents add 7% sales tax		_____
Total		_____

Please charge my credit card
_____ MC _____ VISA _____ AMEX

_____

Card number
_____

Expiration date   Signature

Credit & Thanks

Project Coordinator
Betty Hurst

Authors
Jay Fields
Betty Hurst

Design
Scott Smith
1250 Design
Asheville, NC

Index
Donna Abranches
Erin Elder

Map Design
Scott Smith
Orrin Lundgren

Photography
Courtesy of artists
and HandMade staff

Printing
Tathwell Printing

Cover Photos
Basket by Billie Ruth Sudduth
Pottery by Cat Jarosz
Barn by Don Stevenson

A Very Special Thanks
To all the helpful people we
met on the trail and to Donna
Abranches, Becky Anderson,
Lynn Bender, Norma Bradley,
Pat Cabe, Erin Elder, Laurie
Huttunen, Carol Kline, Jan
Love, Polly Smith, and to
those folks who brought you
the first two editions, especial-
ly Jay Fields, Brad Campbell,
Laura Herrman, Robin Daniel
and Mark Wilson.

Notes

Notes

Notes

Notes

Notes

Notes

Notes

Notes

Notes